Sabine Sörgel
Dancing Postcolonialism

TanzScripte | edited by Gabriele Brandstetter and Gabriele Klein | Volume 6

Sabine Sörgel (Dr. phil.) teaches the history and theory of theatre and dance at Johannes Gutenberg-University Mainz. Her current research includes cross-cultural corporealities, contemporary performance and postcolonial theory.

Sabine Sörgel
Dancing Postcolonialism
The National Dance Theatre Company of Jamaica

[transcript]

Die vorliegende Arbeit wurde vom Fachbereich 05 Philosophie und Philologie der Johannes Gutenberg-Universität Mainz im Jahr 2005 als Dissertation zur Erlangung des akademischen Grades eines Doktors der Philosophie (Dr. phil.) angenommen.

Bibliographic information published by Die Deutsche Bibliothek
Die Deutsche Bibliothek lists this publication in the
Deutsche Nationalbibliografie; detailed bibliographic data
are available on the Internet at http://dnb.ddb.de

© 2007 transcript Verlag, Bielefeld

All rights reserved. No part of this book may be reprinted or reproduced or utilized in any form or by any electronic, mechanical, or other means, now known or hereafter invented, including photocopying and recording, or in any information storage or retrieval system, without permission in writing from the publisher.

Layout by: Kordula Röckenhaus, Bielefeld
Cover illustration: Rex Nettleford, NDTC's »moving spirit«, co-founder, principal choreographer, and current Artistic Director. Here seen in lead role of »Myal«.
Credits: Photographs: cover illustration and pages 100, 102, 103, 110, 112, 119, 131, 175, 176, 177 courtesy and copyright by Maria LaYacona and NDTC archives; page 140 courtesy and copyright by Denis Valentine and NDTC archives; page 194 courtesy and coypright by W. Sills and NDTC archives. All video stills: courtesy and copyright by NDTC archives.
Typeset by: Sabine Sörgel
Printed by: Majuskel Medienproduktion GmbH, Wetzlar
ISBN 978-3-89942-642-7

Table of Contents

Acknowledgements	7
Intro: Tracking the Cross-Cultural Field – The Journey to Jamaican Dance	9
On Creolization – Theorizing Caribbean Identity	23
The Self/Other Dynamic in Colonialist Discourse	23
Hybrid Cultures – Creolist Metaphors	28
Nationalist Rhetoric	35
The Politics of Representation	39
INTERLUDE I: DANCE AND POSTCOLONIAL THEORY	41
Dance and Postcolonial Nationalism – Embodying Emancipation	43
Towards a Creolist Aesthetic – African Caribbean Identity and Dance	43
Early African Jamaican Religious and Recreational Dances	47
Pioneers of Caribbean Dance Theatre	58
Beryl McBurnie (1914-2000)	58
Ivy Baxter (1923-1993)	67
From Sacred to Secular: The Institutionalization of Jamaican Dance Theatre	75
Re-inventing African Carribean Ritual through Modern Dance	75
Jamaica Festival	81
Jamaican Cultural Development Commission (JCDC)	84
The National Dance Theatre Company (NDTC) of Jamaica	86
The Jamaica School of Dance	91
INTERLUDE II: DANCE AND THE NEW JAMAICA	92

**Jamaica's National Dance Theatre Company –
A Postcolonial Reading of the Repertoire** 95
Dancing Cultural Roots: Kinaesthetic Memory and the Discovery
of Self 95
    Choreographing Independence 98
        African Scenario 98
        Plantation Revelry 109
    The Folk Repertoire 115
        Pocomania 116
        Kumina 125
        Gerrehbenta 133
        Bruckins 141
    INTERLUDE III: DANCE AND SELF-DISCOVERY 144
In Celebration of Diversity – The NDTC's Caribbean
Dance Vocabulary 146
    Rex Nettleford's Aesthetic of Caribbean Dance Theatre 156
        Ritual of the Sunrise 156
        Cave's End 164
    Eduardo Rivero: The NDTC's Cuban Connection 172
        Sulkari 172
        Congo Layé 179
    The Caribbean Modern Interpretations of Clive Thompson 181
        Of Sympathy and Love 181
    INTERLUDE IV: DANCE AND CULTURAL DIVERSITY 185
Next Generation's Re-Inventions: Jamaican Dance Theatre
Goes Global 187
    Arlene Richards: *Cocoon, Renewal of the Spirit* 188
    Arsenio Andrade: *Epilogo* 197
    Marlon Simms: *Millennial Beings, '100 Park Lanes' Redemption* 201
    Christopher Walker: *Fragile* 204
    INTERLUDE V: DANCE BEYOND THE COLOR LINE 207

Coda: After the Journey – The Remains of the Dance... 209

Bibliography 213
Books and Journals 213
Periodicals 225
Lectures and Audio Sources 227
CD-ROM and Videography 228
Miscellany 228
Interviews 229

Acknowledgements

This book has been assisted by many individuals and profited from numerable influences, direct and indirect. In acknowledging my gratitude I wish to thank everyone who has been supportive of this study in providing critical assistance, personal encouragement, institutional support, and creative inspiration. First of all, I would like to thank Prof. Dr. Christopher Balme, whose insightful comment this manuscript has benefited from throughout the research process. Over the years he has been an ever inspiring mentor, whose considerate critique has been challenging and highly rewarding. More generally, I might have never chosen to turn my scholarly interest towards the Caribbean, if it had not been for his thought provoking graduate seminar on postcolonial theatre.

Many thanks go to the National Dance Theatre Company of Jamaica (NDTC), especially Prof. Rex Nettleford, who, as the NDTC's artistic director, prime choreographer, and expert scholar, first sparked off the idea for this research project. Among the many NDTC members, dancers and choreographers, whose knowledgeable comments and boundless creativity have shaped this work, I wish to particularly thank Joyce Campbell, Clive Thompson, Arlene Richards, and Chris Walker.

Also, I would like to thank the faculty of the Jamaica School of Dance at Edna Manley College of the Performing Arts in Kingston as well as the Cultural Studies Group at the University of the West Indies, Mona Campus. I especially thank Alaine Grant and Cheryl Ryman who have shared valuable information and research material with me as well as Alma Mock Yen and Monica Lawrence. Further thanks go to Mervyn Morris who first showed me around Kingston and helped me find my way in more than just the literal sense. Several librarians and archives contributed time and effort to my research queries. I thank the staff of the West Indies Collection of the Main Library at the University of the West Indies, Mona Campus and at Jamaica's National Library in Kingston. A special mention goes to Mr. Blake at the CARIMAC Centre for opening extra hours at the NDTC video archive.

My doctoral research, which forms the basis of this book, was funded and intellectually stimulated by a generous dissertation grant from the Studienstiftung des deutschen Volkes (German National Academic Foundation). Additional support in the like vein came from the International PhD Program in Performance and Media Studies at Johannes Gutenberg-University Mainz. I thank Prof. Dr. Alfred Hornung, Prof. Dr. Kati Röttger, the program co-ordinators and faculty as well as my fellow colleagues and friends for their thorough reviews, in-seminar discussions and helpful critique of this project. In the final stages before publication Prof. Dr. Gabriele Brandstetter and Prof. Dr. Gabriele Klein gave their generous support to include this study in their edited series TanzScripte, which I am highly appreciative of. I am also grateful to the 2005 funding of the "Forschungsförderpreis der Freunde der Universität Mainz e.V." to aid the publication of this book. A very special thank you goes to NDTC photographer Maria LaYacona for the permission to reprint her most beautiful photographs, in particular the one which is used as cover illustration for this book.

Finally, I wish to thank my parents and family, who have been a constant source of loving encouragement and support of all of my scholarly and personal projects.

Intro: Tracking the Cross-Cultural Field – The Journey to Jamaican Dance

Cultures are most fully expressed in and made conscious of themselves in their ritual and theatrical performances. [...] A performance is a dialectic of "flow," that is, spontaneous movement in which action and awareness are one, and "reflexivity," in which the central meanings, values and goals of a culture are seen "in action," as they shape and explain behavior. A performance is declarative of our shared humanity, yet it utters the uniqueness of particular cultures. We will know one another better by entering one another's performances and learning their grammars and vocabularies.

(VictorTurner)

London, 21st Sept. 2001

The first time I see the National Dance Theatre Company of Jamaica perform is on a research trip to London. Newspaper clippings, photographs, poetry, and drama as well as some postcolonial discourse inform much of my understanding of the Caribbean at this point. I might have a vague notion of the geography from looking at maps, but entering Queen Elizabeth Hall at the Southbank Center – only a foot-walk away from "Shakespeare's Globe" – the Caribbean is all of a sudden astonishingly real. While multi-cultural London I find myself quite familiar with, the cross-culture in here moves to a rather different vibe. Performative gestures, a different tone of voice and music to the language, which I cannot yet place, but do quite enjoy. The atmosphere in the lobby is already part of my journey into Jamaica's dance. As I watch people move, my body, too, takes in of their energy, and what I have read about comes fantastically into being. I'm engulfed by the presentness of situation, as I discern the group of dancers on the other side of the room. Sort of desperately I wish to walk over. But they are safe-guarded away from me and I also would have felt far too embarrassed to step up and converse with them. Standing in that crowd, I have entered my own dream-world, which is a fiction of discursive fragments, suddenly blurred with what feels somewhat more real, as it appears directly in front of me. And then, the next thing I even more vaguely recall is not even much, as I struggle to find the words for the sort of sensation that still feels very dear to me. For what remained of their dance, is only an imprint of color, its beauty, and maze – fantastic imaginary of an unknown vigor and elegance ...[1]

Pondering upon the meaning of "crossing" in the context of my journal/ey towards an academic understanding of Jamaican dance theatre, I have come to realize that it is actually far easier today to cross the borders of countries than that of their cultural communities and practices. While I can easily hop on an airplane and fly from Germany to London or Jamaica, what I see first hand is seldom what I get.[2] Enticed by the exotics of a faraway place – Jamaica, for example – I remain a

---

1 Entry from my personal research journal.
2 James Clifford pointedly addressed the twentieth century's ethnographic-crisis of authority. Compare James Clifford, *The Predicament of Culture. Twentieth-Century Ethnography, Literature, and Art* (Cambridge, Massachusetts: Harvard UP, 1988). See also Clifford's more recent *Routes. Travel and Translation in the Late Twentieth Century* (Cambridge, Massachusetts: Harvard UP, 1997), where he proposes the notion of "travel" and "translation" as alternative paradigms to the hegemonic claims of traditional ethnographic field work.

tourist wherever I go. Walking in the shadow of those who went before me, I cannot escape the "classic quest – exoticist, anthropological, orientalist," whichever way I venture (Clifford 1997: 5). Traveling to Jamaica, I become an exotic 'whitey,' all too aware of her European ancestry and its troublesome burden, which though no longer that of presumptuous 'civilization,' is still one of colonialist guilt and economic privilege. Yet, against all odds, why would I choose not to write about Jamaican dance theatre, if that is actually what I find myself most interested in? So, this researcher enthusiastically packed her suitcase to set out in Victor Turner's best sense, precisely to get to "know one another better by entering one another's performances" (Schechner 1990: 1). Yet, as I traveled along, the journey itself turned into an ever more curious performance that appeared after all at least as fascinating as Jamaican dance theatre itself. For example, I remember how estranged I found 'duty free' London Heathrow on my first return: the cleanliness of the airport's glass lounge glitter – something I had formerly not really paid attention to. Suddenly, my own role transformations, their unexpected twists and turns, became as much part of the present analysis as the dance itself which ultimately cannot be separated from each other to begin with.

Contemporary performance studies, in the wake of Richard Schechner's and Victor Turner's pioneering collaboration between theatre studies and anthropology since the mid-1960s, examine precisely such limits of life and theatre within the intercultural context. Performance studies' interdisciplinary approach appeared therefore particularly rewarding for this research project, as the discipline addresses the increasingly complex "questions of embodiment, action, behavior and agency" in the global context (Schechner 2002: 2). Starting from Turner's intercultural studies of theatre and ritual, performance studies have bridged the discursive divide between so-called cultural as opposed to more traditionally speaking theatrical performances. According to Schechner, studying performances involves analyzing as much as doing performance. "Performing fieldwork," hence proposes an alternative theatre-anthropological paradigm to locate Otherness within oneself, rather than to confine it to an outside object of inquiry (Schechner 2002: 2). Acknowledging that there can never be a neutral much less objective perspective, performance studies finally investigate the interrelated politics of research's analytic propositions in order to critically interrogate their hegemonic foundations.

While such meta-critical awareness of analytic bias has certainly become indispensable, it may, however, set up its own discursive entrapment, as I have come to experience. In fact, constant questioning can lead to some degree of intellectual paralysis, especially, when working in the so-called cross-cultural field of ever more difficult class, gender, and "race" divides.[3] Thus, throughout this project's journey, the research process was haunted by several interrogative suspicions and torn between their manifold implications. When in Jamaica, for example, I found myself representing quite unwillingly the colonizer/tourist self, whereas people in Germany would suspect me of pursuing the age-old exotic/erotic desire enticed by the presumed pleasure of spending quality time in tropical environs. Certainly, there were many more dubious roles and research-performances to be played: amateur dancer, scholarly critic, interviewer, observer and participant. The dull old stereotypes abounded on both sides and posed several crossings that research obviously still has to face. Dance research has since become much more of a methodologically experimenting quest than expected: in-between disciplines, I found myself analyzing and performing in rather distinct cultural and theatrical spaces, and yet discovering that somehow all of them were hardly separate, but curiously intertwined. In this respect, methodology and style of this scholarly investigation will vary throughout the three larger sections in order to reflect at least to some extent this discursive cross-disciplinary mediation between performance studies, postcolonial theory, and dance historiography and analysis.

Historically, Jamaican dance theatre emerged as a highly complex art form, which blends ritual-based African Caribbean folk dance movement with German expressionist and U.S. modern dance techniques. Consequently, Jamaican dance theatre has evolved as a cultural hybrid with social, political, and aesthetic implications. Certainly, Jamaica's performative hybridity does not only apply to dance theatre, but presents rather another variant of the Caribbean islands' exuberant cultural creolization processes (see Shepherd/Richards 2002). Moreover, the region's confusing texture of modernity and ancestral tradi-

---

3 Despite the recent deconstruction of "race," academic discourse and political correctness in their attempt to do away with the concept, have too often overlooked the political impact of contemporary raci(ali)sm still at work. However historically constructed "race" appears, its historicity proves unfortunately still real enough to be critically acknowledged for (Gilroy 2000: 286-287; Mills 1998: 14).

tions makes it difficult to place Caribbean culture within either one of the two paradigms (Mintz 1974: 37-38). The Caribbean's alleged sameness is oftentimes misleading, because it may allow for an easy surface consumption at the cost of missing the better half of it.[4] In order to acknowledge Jamaican dance theatre's complexity, one therefore needs to investigate as much of the region's socio-political history as well as the evolution of Jamaican dance forms in terms of their aesthetic transformation and theatrical meaning from ritual setting onto the theatre stage. Emerging from dance traditions under plantation slavery, Jamaican folk dances inform not only the recreational dance sphere, but have also significantly shaped the artistic dance theatre vocabulary. Conventional distinctions between popular and high art performances do consequently not apply, since both forms have mutually inspired and enriched each other.

Due to the Caribbean's history of colonization, Jamaican dance theatre thus falls into the broader category of what Jacqueline Lo and Helen Gilbert have termed "cross-cultural theatre" (see Lo/Gilbert 2002). According to their definition, cross-cultural theatre is "characterized by the conjunction of specific cultural resources at the level of narrative content, performance aesthetics, production processes, and/or reception by an interpretive community" (Lo/Gilbert 2002: 31). This umbrella definition for the wide range of theatrical practices to be encountered in the global arts market of today is further divided into subbranches, of which "postcolonial theatre" engages in "both a historical and discursive relation to imperialism, whether that phenomenon is treated critically or ambivalently" (Lo/Gilbert 2002: 35). As such it is often also cross-cultural, since it involves processes of inter-/intra-cultural negotiation in terms of dramaturgy, aesthetics, and interpretation according to oftentimes varying audiences. Caribbean postcolonial theatre performances fit into this model, since they not only present cross-cultural aesthetics, but have also continuously been involved in the emancipation and decolonization struggles of the region's multicultural populations (see Balme 1999; Gilbert/Tompkins 1996). Whether one thinks of the renowned Trinidad Carnival, Bob Marley's Reggae or contemporary Dancehall, the performative aspects of Caribbean popular culture have been widely discussed (see Hill 1972; Mason

---

4 Awam Amkpa in his study of Nigerian and English postcolonial theatre has referred to this phenomenon as "overlapping modernities," i.e. postcolonial identity formation conceived as the "site of perpetual hybridity and translations of subjectivity" (2004: 1-18).

1998; Cooper 2004). However, as Caribbean dance theatre somehow falls in-between the performative popular and traditional modern dance theatre conventions, it appears to have been slightly neglected by recent academic discourse.

Yet, Gilbert and Tompkins have stressed that an analysis of dance and dance theatre in the postcolonial context appears most urgent, for dance's embodied body politics (1996: 237-242). According to their analysis, the postcolonial body emerges as "locus of struggle," which speaks its "own forms of corporeality" as opposed to the Western practice of logo centric expression (1996: 242). More generally, the dancing body not only functions as one of the most charged sites of theatrical representation, but it can also be regarded as a marker of cultural identity (Albright 1997: xxvi). Dance theatre thus oscillates between representational and embodied performances of cultural self-definition. Moreover, dance theatre also speaks of cultural sameness within difference, since each dance presents an individual and simultaneously shared history.[5] The controversial question of an alleged universality of dance movement is thus raised against the apparent individuality of movement created by different enculturation processes. While everybody does indeed move, the particular style and significance of such movement may vary considerably.[6] As opposed to the much contested and yet still prevalent Cartesian separation of body and mind in Western discourse, an understanding of cultural expression as primarily embodied interrelates both entities in the conceptualization of self-identity.

In comparison to lay people, trained dancers, athletes and actors achieve heightened body awareness as they constantly mediate between an experiential consciousness of the interconnectedness of body movement and self-enactment. As J. L. Lewis argues, the artist's body finds itself in continuous moments of "ecstatic action," i.e. "using the body as an instrument for action on and in the world" (1995: 225).

---

5 Balme points out that dance plays a significant part in most syncretic theatre forms, for indigenous dance traditions may simultaneously function as an "almost universal form of performative expression" as well as "an index of historical and cultural authenticity" (1999: 202-213).

6 J. Lowell Lewis has thus argued that "bodies are culturally co-constructed" in so far as "people name, divide, understand, and imagine bodies differently in different societies," thus arguing "that there are real constraints as to the possible ways bodies can be enculturated; in fact, the similarities between cultural systems in this regard are just as striking as the differences, if not more so" (1995: 225).

Dance thus performs identity in an "intermediate mode" by constantly "monitoring" between self/body, i.e. awareness/practice (1995: 229-230).[7] Focusing on embodiment rather than representation, phenomenological dance analysis therefore seeks to liberate the body from the constraints of ideological objectification. By evidencing that in fact our bodies constantly mediate between the objective and the pre-objective, Thomas J. Csordas stresses that it is rather through "perceptual processes" than essentialist givens that we "end in objectification" of our body/selves (1994: 7). Phenomenology therefore posits our bodies not as the object, but rather "the source of subjectivity, and mind [vice versa] as the locus of objectification" (Csordas 1994: 8-9). As opposed to the Cartesian immanent claim of 'I think, therefore I am,' phenomenology refers to enacted "interpersonal engagement" as the source of self-knowledge (Csordas 1994: 10). However, simply identifying bodily practice as non-representational does not suffice. Csordas consequently suggests to methodologically juxtapose semiotics and phenomenology as "dialectical partners" rather than exclusive concepts (1994: 12).

Such a partnering of approach is particularly crucial for a discussion of dance theatre, because dance theatre presents both the actively empowering activity of embodied self-knowledge as well as the more passive conveyance of a representational stage image.[8] Especially, since much of the NDTC (National Dance Theatre Company of Jamaica) vocabulary derives from an African Caribbean ritualistic source, the experiential element of empowerment appears stronger in Jamaican dance theatre than, for example, in more visual-based forms of theatrical dancing, such as classical ballet.[9] Religion as an expression of the Caribbean's cosmological world view is essential to an understanding of the region's dance theatre in this context. Caribbean dance cannot be separated from its religious roots, since much of the NDTC's distinct modern dance style derives directly from African Caribbean religions

---

7 Similarly, Richard Schechner has argued for "imitation as a way of acquiring performance knowledge" in the sense that expert performers apprehend "the body on its own terms, as movement, gesture, tone of voice" (2002: 198).
8 In his phenomenological study of theatre Bert O. States pursues a similar argument, where he critiques semiotics as a "useful, if incomplete discipline" in regard of performance analysis (1998: 6-8).
9 For a phenomenological analysis of different dance cultures compare Bull 1997: 269-287.

and their embodiment of ancestral spirits in dance performance.[10] Rex Nettleford, artistic director of the NDTC, has therefore argued "that viewers of African dance need to understand Africa's cultural heritage if they are to understand and critically appreciate in any depth the true meaning and aesthetic authority of what is being seen" (1996: xiv). Considering the prevalence of Western epistemic hegemony, he furthermore urges a re-assessment of the aesthetic value and meaning of these dance forms, of which many must still be fully acknowledged of, particularly in the New World African diaspora. As Nettleford points out:

The acknowledgement of such logic and consistency in African dance still presents difficulties to many in the diaspora where the creolization process, through the cross-fertilization of cultures, defines the existence of all inhabitants and pushes a great number of the cross-fertilized beings and their cultural expressions to stations of confusion as to what, of the ingredients in the plurality are proper and what not, what are superior and what are inferior, what are aesthetically acceptable, and what forbidden and so on. Needless to say, in the world of colonizer-colonized the dance and all other artistic expressions of the overlord take precedence over those of the subjugated which have been frozen at the base of some rigid and arbitrary cultural pyramid (1996: xv).

Hence, the present study not only suggests to question such cultural pyramids per se, but also to propose an alternative analytic paradigm of critical assessment.

Facing these rather complex discursive challenges, an accounting for the Caribbean's kinaesthetic performativity in dance theatre will hence be pursued via the interdisciplinary approach suggested above. As Jane C. Desmond has explained: "dancing bodies are performative in every sense of the word, [since they] enact a conception of self and social community mediated by the particular historical aesthetic dimensions of the dance forms and their precise conditions of reception" (1997: 16). Only by looking through the multi-faceted perspective of juxtaposing a socio-historical with a dance aesthetic reading, can Caribbean dance more adequately be circumscribed. As also Cynthia J. Novack asserts, dance as a "complicated, multivocalic" cultural prac-

---

10 For further entries primarily on dance anthropological research of Caribbean dance forms compare Adamczyk 1989: 61-63; 88-89. See also Emery 1989: 61-63; 88-89.

tice becomes performatively speaking particularly significant, because the "same dance form may generate different meanings as its setting, participants, and institutional frameworks change" (1995: 181). Yet, to complicate matters further, dance not only alternates its meaning depending on the representational frame, but also presents alternation in terms of its constant disappearance as Peggy Phelan has pointed out (1995: 204-205). An apprehension of dance theatre can therefore only be assumed by a writing, which resists closure as it merely "traces the motivations, technologies, and discursive possibilities" of the dance at hand. Consequently, dance writing becomes necessarily a "mediating discourse," which in the case of Caribbean dance theatre not only translates between movements and language, i.e. the kinaesthetic and the written, but also has to examine a complex web of different cultural (con)texts. However, incomplete, contested and reviled as such descriptive and analytic discourse will undoubtedly stand; the study insists that – considering dance theatre's impact and importance in the Caribbean – such research remains an absolute necessity to further intercultural communication.

To summarize these preliminary remarks then, the book begins its cross-cultural journey from the author's first observations of the NDTC's 2001 UK Tour to investigate, which elements exactly distinguished Jamaican dance theatre from other modern dance companies throughout the world. Source data is based on historical, as well as sociological, religious, political, aesthetic and dance related information as they enable more comprehensive analysis and interpretation of the NDTC's dance vocabulary and repertoire. However, as has already been stated, such literary-based reading about dance will hardly suffice, for as one of the arts' most ephemeral genres, dance can only if ever be traced in direct performance.[11] Therefore, the present analysis of NDTC choreography seeks to methodologically balance the discursive and experiential impact of Jamaican dance theatre by providing 1.)

---

11 For an introduction to dance analysis compare Susan Leigh Foster, *Reading Dancing. Bodies and Subjects in Contemporary American Dance* (Berkeley: University of California Press, 1986) and Janet Adshead, *Dance Analysis* (London: Dance Books, 1988), Janet Adsheard-Landsdale and June Layson, eds., *Dance History: An Introduction* (London: Routledge, 1994), and Sondra Horton Fraleigh, *Researching Dance* (1999). See also Judith Lynne Hanna, *To Dance is Human: A Theory of Nonverbal Communication* (Chicago: Chicago University Press, 1987) for an ethnographic approach to dance and movement analysis.

a postcolonial theory frame, 2.) the historical background, as well as 3.) a close reading of selected examples of the NDTC repertoire.[12]

Hence, the book proposes an in-depth study of Jamaican dance theatre in terms of its Caribbean cultural aesthetics, socio-political impact, and significance in the postcolonial theoretical context. Since dance criticism has only recently started to investigate the complex socio-cultural implications of certain dance vocabularies, I suggest that Jamaican dance theatre actually performs subversively from within western modern dance rather than presenting a mere adaptation of it. Whereas "colonial mimicry" has traditionally been defined as "a performance of everyday life in which colonized persons adopt in part or wholesale the culture of their colonizers", more recent critical reassessment by postcolonial theory has pointed to the inherent ambivalence of these performances (Schechner 2002: 233). In the wake of Homi K. Bhabha's seminal analysis therefore, so-called 'colonials' may perform under the guise of apparent likeness, however, as they do so, their imitative performances accomplish quite revolutionary performative effects. As Bhabha defines:

> Mimicry is, thus the sign of a double articulation; a complex strategy of reform, regulation and discipline, which 'appropriates' the Other as it visualizes power. Mimicry is also the sign of the inappropriate, however, a difference or recalcitrance which coheres the dominant strategic function of colonial power, intensifies surveillance, and poses an immanent threat to both 'normalized' knowledges and disciplinary powers (1994: 86).

Presenting "at once resemblance and menace," colonial mimicry may therefore evolve as the site of an anti-essentialist articulation of identity, which dismantles colonialist racism as much as it defies pre-

---

[12] Selections in terms of the NDTC repertoire have naturally been privileging those works, which I have seen in live-performance in London 2001, as well as in Kingston in January 2003, and during the NDTC's 41st dance season from June to August that same year. However, by accessing the NDTC's Kingston archive, I was also able to include video-taped performances of the NDTC's earlier works in order to historically contextualize the company's artistic development. That such a selection can of course hardly acknowledge in full for a repertoire, which encompasses close to 200 choreographies over a time-span of forty years, is self-understood. Focusing on the artistic director Rex Nettleford's work as well as the company's major contemporary choreographers though, certain aesthetic and thematic tendencies and trends can still be ascertained.

colonialist nostalgia for an imaginary homeland. Postcolonialism, consequently, addresses precisely these ambivalent metonymic presences, which strategically perform coherence – whether that be in terms of a subject, nation or state – to access political agency and start off their performers' emancipatory projects (McLeod 2000: 74-75; see also Rajchman 1995).

The first chapter of this book will thus introduce and to some extent reiterate the problematic discourse on Caribbean identity as it has been theorized under the politico-aesthetic creolization paradigm. While Caribbean creolization shares discursive overlap with postcolonial discourse on hybridity, this chapter, however, proposes to rather reassess creolization discourse than to abandon it in favor of a somewhat generalized notion of cultural hybridity.[13] For despite of its ongoing contestment, creolization discourse has historically emerged and survived in the Caribbean, where its contradictory rhetoric has continuously expressed and to some extent also mirrored the political struggle of the islands' diverse populations for postcolonial self-definition. In this respect, creolization discourse oscillates precisely between degrees of cultural imitation and reinvention, which will become useful for my later discussion of Caribbean dance theatre aesthetics and their postcolonial political dynamic in terms of identity formation and nation-building.

The second chapter confronts these discursive debates with the socio-historical background of Jamaica's emancipation and independence movement. Creolization, Afrocentrism and Marronage have been the ongoing rhetorical paradigms of Jamaica's quest for national independence. Yet, while the degree of Creole integration as opposed to an Africanist-oriented resistance will vary, all of these have traditionally built their foundational claim on embodied folk cultural and religious practices, which have survived the hardships of the Middle Passage,

---

13 Hybridity discourse has been frequently attacked for its derogative association with 19th century biopolitics of social Darwinism and its racist concerns over 'racial purity' and miscegenation. Despite this contested etymological legacy though, hybridity discourse has become a trope of postcolonial theory to articulate an oftentimes conflated notion of cross-cultural synthesis, which lacks historicity and a theorizing of the exact institutional frameworks through which such discourse and its propagated 'hybrid identities' actually come into being (see Brah/Coombes 2000). I therefore consider and somehow reintroduce 'creolization' discourse as the more historicized – if no less contested – concept to articulate anti-essentialist identity discourse and postcolonial national affiliation in the Caribbean.

slavery and plantation economy. Dance as the Caribbean's "weapon of self-defence" (Rex Nettleford) and "cultural guerilla resistance" (Sylvia Wynter) has hence played a not to be underestimated political function throughout the region's ongoing decolonization struggle. As Rex Nettleford proclaims:

Reaching beyond mere survival, the dance in Jamaica long ago refused to get stuck in genres of light-hearted entertainment despite the ring games, lancers, schottische, and quadrille suitably adapted from the court and country dance of Europe. Instead the dance preserved its force through integrated links with religion in the worship of forbidden but persistent gods, divination rituals, and the configurations of a nether world beyond the master's laws (1995: 99).

This section therefore traces the politico-aesthetic creolization process of Jamaican dance theatre's ongoing abstraction from African Jamaican folk ritualistic roots in order to first contextualize and then highlight Jamaican dance theatre's genesis of a unique modern dance vocabulary.

Far from mere imitation of a Western modern dance idiom, Jamaican dance theatre pioneers of the pre-Independence years have – as will be shown – developed highly original dance works, which were and continue to be deeply rooted in the region's folk and religious dance practices. In fact, Caribbean dance pioneers Beryl McBurnie (Trinidad) and Ivy Baxter (Jamaica) developed a creolist aesthetic from African Caribbean dance religions, which appears highly deceptive in its metonymic resemblance to U.S. modern and also German expressionist dance. Caribbean dance theatre thus emerged from an autochthonous source, which was later on incorporated into Jamaica's postcolonial education system, the annual arts festival, and the foundation of the National Dance Theatre Company. This section surveys the nationalist-emancipatory dance agenda behind and at the heart of the New Jamaica's claim to postcolonial nationalism, folk cultural affiliation and legitimacy.

Part three finally, provides a close reading and aesthetic analysis of selected examples of the Jamaica National Dance Theatre Company's repertoire in performance and on video. Analysis will focus on the NDTC's evolving tradition, Caribbean dance theatre vocabulary and modern innovative explorations. Supporting my previous theoretical and historical argument, these analyses of the repertoire build on the NDTC's claim to postcolonial nationhood. My reading thus seeks to introduce a new dance analytical paradigm in order to more adequately address Jamaican dance theatre's cross-cultural complexity. Introducing a praxis-informed – at times rather poetic-translational than dance notational – approach, I juxtapose semiotics with phenomenological accounts, as well as several excerpts from interviews with National Dance Theatre Company members and affiliated choreographers.

On Creolization –
Theorizing Caribbean Identity

The Self/Other Dynamic in Colonialist Discourse

Ever since Columbus first set foot on the Caribbean islands in 1492, the collision of different cultural attitudes and practices has marked the development of the emergent New World societies and their complex processes of identity formation. As Tzvetan Todorov in his seminal work on the discovery of America has argued, the New World "conquest" marked the "beginning of the modern era," when Christian missionary doctrine and its discourse of conquest appropriated alterity in the name of 'Colonial Other,' i.e. according to its own strategic needs and discursive modalities (1984: 5). Columbus' conquering spirit was thus guided by what Todorov calls a "finalist strategy," i.e. the belief in biblical revelation, rather than empiricist doubt (1984: 17-23). Colonialism's authoritative argument did not allow for experience to find its own explanations, but conceived of Columbus' 'discovery' of America as the fulfillment of divine will and prophecy. While the early conquest was still bound to this medieval-oriented mindset, Spain's quest for gold and other resources articulated a pre-capitalist attitude, which was clearly oriented towards a modernist paradigm (Todorov 1984: 42). Accordingly, Columbus' perception of the Amerindians negotiated between a Christian universalist acknowledgement of their humanity on the one hand, and a capitalist exploitative denial of it on the other. Amerindian alterity was thus construed from an egocentric perspective as in-between (as)similar and different, prone to assimilation as much as exploitation and slave labor. As Todorov describes, this attitude denied "the existence of a human substance truly other, something capable of being not merely an imperfect state of oneself" (1984: 42-43). This ego-centered constitution of ambiguous alterity became paradigmatic for the subject formation in the colonial contact zone, where the Self/Other dynamic resulted in a mutual failure of recognition. While difference and otherness were discovered, they were not accepted on their own terms.

The colonial Other's contradictory image appeared similarly ambiguous on behalf of the colonization of the African continent. While the first conquerors in the 15th century appeared more interested in trade and geography than ethnic categorization, African phenotypical and cultural difference, however, were soon categorized by the imperialist rhetoric as 'heathenish savages,' allegedly in need of Christian 'civilization.'[1] In fact, the pejorative connotation of 'blackness' dated back to Graeco-Roman antiquity and became epitomized during medieval and Renaissance Christianity in Europe, as Mervyn Alleyne in his recent study *The Construction and Representation of Race and Ethnicity in the Caribbean and the World* (2002) has pointed out. Colonialism thus reinforced that pre-classical black/white dichotomy in terms of a psycho-sociological argument by superimposing a metaphorical reading of darkness versus light, wilderness vs. civilization, etc. Through such allegorical transformation, phenotype became symbolically charged and ultimately foundational for the white Western claim to cultural hegemony (Alleyne 2002: 52).

According to this brutal reasoning, Africans were captured, enslaved and shipped to the Caribbean in exchange for exclusive tropical goods, which at the end of the gruesome journey filled the plates and coffee cups of imperial Europe.[2] Following the Portuguese slave trad-

---

[1] From the sixteenth century onwards, Western colonial expansion had been claiming power in the name of putative 'civilization' or a "civilizing mission" in order to justify the oppression and enslavement of colonized peoples. Colonial administration, missionary work and education system thus sought to superimpose their Eurocentric value system in order to supersede and erode indigenous cultural practices (Bolaffi et al. 2003: 38).

[2] According to recent estimates approximately 12 million Africans count victim to the transatlantic slave trade between 1450 and 1870 (Guérivière 2004: 31-32). Wole Soyinka in his call for reparations and „full cognition of the African world as an equal sector of a universal humanity" has pointed out that „the Atlantic slave trade remains an inescapable critique

ing presence on the African coastline since 1500, John Hawkins was the first English slave trader, who in 1562 captured 300 African slaves in Sierra Leone and sold them to Hispaniola. His example was soon to be followed by other European countries, all of them keen on introducing African slave labor to their expanding colonies in the Americas. These first looting encounters furthered the colonialist image of 'savage Africans,' who of course violently resisted their enslavement (Walvin 2001: 23-26). Even though slavery had been an ongoing cultural practice of Trans-Sahara trading before the arrival of the first Portuguese explorers on the African West Coast, slave trading rose to a formerly unknown level, when European goods were first exported in exchange for African captives (Guérivière 2004: 30). Thus, one might argue that when Columbus undertook his second voyage to the Caribbean in 1493, right there and then the world's first global trading had begun. Columbus, in fact, first introduced sugar cane to the islands' natural crops. By 1516, only a couple of years later, the first sugar was already grown in Santo Domingo and soon to be shipped back to Spain. With the rise of sugar prices in Europe, the demand for African slaves increased steadily and the 'business' was transformed into an early system of mass production by the English in the early 17th century.

The English colonizers conquered Barbados in 1625 and Jamaica should follow soon after, when taken over from the Spanish in 1655. From 1702 until 1808 an estimated 830,857 Africans had been shipped to Jamaica to produce the wealth, pleasure and consumption of the British Empire in the commercial products of tobacco, tea, coffee and sugar (Walvin 2001: 6). Slavery and the exploitative plantation system – "combining the worst features of feudalism and capitalism without the virtues of neither" (Eric Williams) – thus created a distinct hierarchy of oppression and societal sectionalism, which were to endure long after Jamaica's emancipation from slavery in 1834/38.[3] Under the British 'black' as a phenotype designation finally became synonymous for the status of slave, a chattel, deprived of humanity and subjected to brutal exploitation. Hence, James Walvin has claimed that "the slave trade

---

of European humanism [...] that voided a continent, it is estimated, of some twenty million souls" (1999: 38-39).

3   Emancipation was officially granted in 1834, yet followed by four years of so-called 'apprenticeship,' which means that full freedom was actually only achieved by 1838. Eric Williams pointed out that slavery in the Caribbean had been less of a racialist than economic system (1964: 7).

was a system conceived, sustained and nurtured by interrelated systems of violence" (2001: 19).

With the rise of sugar production and plantation society in the 18th century, colonialist identity politics were increasingly defined by the ideological mix of social Darwinism and its racist rhetoric of biological determinism, which discursively cemented colonialist hierarchy in the Caribbean. Enslaved Africans were exploited as convenient slave labor commodity and – in order to disguise the inhumanity of that capitalist practice – Europe constructed a psychologically powerful and discursively convincing counter-image of African alterity to maintain its putative state of superior civilization, knowledge, and – likely the most important of the three – economic wealth (Alleyne 2002: 63). European ethnocentrism in combination with its military super-power hence levered to a great extent the Self/Other relation in the Caribbean and achieved "virtually complete control over significant symbols and values" (Alleyne 2002: 13; 25). Africans in the New World environment were consequently forced to adjust to a system of control that from their own epistemological background was inaccessible to them, because they were suddenly confronted with a racist scheme that debased 'blackness' and assigned Africans to the lowest social strata (Alleyne 2002: 84).

Furthermore, the trauma of the Middle Passage, of slavery and the internalization of colonialist racism resulted – according to Martiniquan psychiatrist Frantz Fanon – in a psycho-pathological personality complex. In his influential study *Black Skin, White Masks* (1952), Fanon has thus described the diaspora's psychological trauma in terms of a "black skin, white mask" dichotomy. In this work, he first addressed the paradoxical absence of an African cultural heritage in Caribbean identity discourse and analyzed the distorted self-image that this absence had created. His analysis of the culturally alienated French Antilles as "zone of nonbeing" and "existential threat to the Afro-Caribbean ego-genesis," has since become one of the key texts to outline the psycho-pathology of African Caribbean self-perception (Henry 1996: 231). Based on Hegelian dialectics and French existentialist thought, Fanon's theory of black alterity – similar to what Sartre described in "Anti-Semite and Jew" (1948) – argues that black Otherness suffers from cultural "over-determination" and is therefore denied access to free identity formation.

According to Hegelian dialectics, self-consciousness results from a primary relatedness of the I to an outside Other: "Ich ist der Inhalt der

Beziehung und das Beziehen selbst; es ist es selbst gegen ein Anderes, und greift zugleich über dies Andre über, das für es ebenso nur es selbst ist" (Hegel 1999: 132). The Other as desired object of self-consciousness and recognition is annihilated in the process of self formation, yet because of that conscious act of annihilation the Other also comes into being, i.e. as a Self ("daß dies Aufheben sei, muß dies Andere sein" (Hegel 1999: 138). As a result, Hegel points out that self-consciousness can only be realized through this doubling process of mutual recognition. He argues: „Die Bewegung ist also schlechthin die gedoppelte beider Selbstbewußtsein. Jedes sieht *das Andre* dasselbe tun, was *es* tut; jedes tut selbst, was es an das Andre fordert; und tut darum, was es tut, auch *nur* insofern, als das Andre dasselbe tut; das einseitige Tun wäre unnütz; weil, was geschehen soll, nur durch beide zustande kommen kann" (1999: 141). While Hegel's master slave dialectic is based on the unequal power binary that divides into an independent and a dependent consciousness, it is, however, through the slave's work for the master that such division will ultimately be subverted and self-consciousness be gained. Through the act of rebellion, the slave fights successfully for self-recognition (Hegel 1999: 142-146).[4]

Transferring this argument to colonialist discourse, David T. Goldberg has argued that the colonialist objectification of Otherness hence posed under a highly permeable guise (1996: 184). Representing the colonized as a subhuman species, colonialist hegemony was founded on a make-belief strategy which superimposed colonialist discourse on difference as Other, i.e. inferior and more importantly: free labor to uphold early capitalism. Following Hegel's dialectic, European selfhood thus asserted itself via the annihilating construct of African alterity. However, this could only succeed as long as the ones thus subdued were also made believe in that superimposed self-image. As Michael Pickering's analysis of the Self/Other dynamic has claimed: "Otherness exists to subjugate its objects and assign them to their natural place at the behest of those who thereby reconstitute themselves as subjects" (2001: 71). Far from 'natural,' however, the process of objectification is split. As Anthony Froude's 1888 depiction of a black boy, whom he had encountered on board his ship towards the West Indies, for example, illustrates, the perception of the Other in the colonial encounter appears inherently ambivalent:

---

4   Robert Stern has furthermore argued that precisely through working for the master, the slave will achieve a fuller self-consciousness for being made aware of controlling the objective world (2002: 85).

There was a small black boy among us, evidently of pure blood, for his hair was wool and his colour black as ink. His parents must have been well-to-do, for the boy had been in Europe to be educated. The officers on board and some of the ladies played with him as they would play with a monkey. He had little more sense than a monkey, perhaps less, and the gestures of him grinning behind gratings and pushing his long thin arms between the bars were curiously suggestive of the original from whom we are told now that all of us came (1969: 25).

Froude's racist reasoning here clearly contradicts its own discourse, when he assumes that the boy must have received education and ergo possesses higher intelligence. The example thus reveals Froude's imperial eye/I-constitution as an ambivalent mode of self-assertion, so regrettably common of his time. So while colonialism and its make-belief strategies sought to dominate alterity by rendering it inferior, the Other's mere presence continuously undermined colonialism's hegemonic claim.

Fortunately, therefore, self-recognition is no one-way street. In contact with the New World's Others the European Self was also altered. Considering the nature of slavery in Jamaican plantation society, Edward Kamau Brathwaite has thus commented that, in fact, slavery in the Caribbean was hardly abstract, but shaped colonials as much as colonized, when "white attitudes to slaves and to slavery, were [...] in a subtle, intimate manner, also white attitudes and sentiments about themselves" (1971: 178-179). The undeniable reciprocity of the colonial Self/Other dynamic and its process of mutually affecting the constitution of self consciousness consequently marked the beginning of the Caribbean's emerging anti-essentialist Creole identity – precisely, the point where the Other's resistance and fight for self-assertion historically set in.

Hybrid Cultures – Creolist Metaphors

While according to Fanon's dialectics black self-constitution appears trapped by the othering gaze of white supremacy, Homi K. Bhabha's poststructuralist reading has reassessed this argument and positioned Fanon's analysis as the theoretical "purveyor of the transgressive and transitional" (1986: xiii). Even though Bhabha's analysis has been critiqued for stretching Fanon's argument unduly, I would still defend his reading against the grain, for it approaches Fanon's underlying Hegelian dialectics in terms of their revolutionary potential. At least theoretically, this shatters the fixity of the divisional bind. Hence, regardless of whether this theoretical transgression can be achieved in reality or not, Bhabha's "performative politics" of cultural hybridity turn the gaze on the oppressor and enable a powerful starting point for postcolonial critique.[5]

By appropriating Fanon, Bhabha declares the Other's subservient state ultimately over. He claims:

The Black presence ruins the representative narrative of Western personhood: its past tethered to treacherous stereotypes of primitivism and degeneracy will not produce a history of civil progress, a space for the Socius; its present, dismembered and dislocated, will not contain the image of identity that is questioned in the dialectic of mind/body and resolved in the epistemology of 'appearance and reality'. The White man's eyes break up the Black man's body and in that act of epistemic violence its own frame of reference is transgressed, its field of vision disturbed (1986: xii).

---

5   Bhabha's hybridity discourse has been frequently attacked for its alleged evasiveness towards the political struggle. Shalini Puri, for example, considers his "separation of the material and symbolic" problematic, for Bhabha's "valorization of a formal deconstruction of narrative authority displaces any exploration of the continuing effects of power and inequality as well as any work to construct an opposition to that inequality" (2004: 19). Hybridity as a trope in postmodern academic discourse gained currency despite of its conceptual slipperiness, because it enabled the deconstruction of formerly totalitarian and essentialist thinking. As such, Puri argues, it remains largely a discourse of the privileged cosmopolitan centers and its academies in New York, London, and Toronto, with relatively little impact on the persistent inequality between the cultural agents thus described (2004: 22). Ultimately, Puri concludes that hybridity discourse remains seriously flawed, because of its problematic "tendency to present hybridity as the synthetic transcendence of tyrannical and reductive binary oppositions" (2004: 38). Rather than to further blind oneself to the factual injustices at hand, Puri hence suggests a critique of Cultural Studies' anti-essentialist stake, which according to her argument only serves to conveniently prevent one from the more complicated task of taking a distinct political stand. However, against her critique I assert that "synthetic transcendence" points to a utopian vision that postcolonial politics need to hypothesize in order for the political struggle to continue, i.e. precisely as the vision of an anti-essentialist, ideally color-blind, just and free world for everyone.

Identity can consequently only – if ever – be achieved the instant that it is already lost: i.e. in the relational encounter. Whatever I perceive of the Other will in the continuing process of never ending self-constitution alter my own self-image. Bhabha's recuperation of Fanon's 'critical edge' thus transgresses the racist stigma as he opens it for redemptive reassessment. As Bhabha's argument quite convincingly claims, this strategic subversion of the status quo sets out "not to unveil the fullness of Man, but to manipulate his representation" (1986: xxiii).

Bhabha's notion of "cultural hybridity" as the "interstitial passage between fixed identifications [...] that entertains difference without an assumed or imposed hierarchy" thus strives to dislocate the totalitarian assumptions underlying the binary opposition (Bhabha 1994: 4). As he points out, "the act of cultural enunciation – the *place of utterance* – is crossed by the différance of writing," thereby ensuring that "meaning is never simply mimetic and transparent" but rather remains ambivalent (1994: 36). The Derridean notion of *différance* in Bhabha's postcolonial theory thus "puts difference into play" as it deconstructs any claim to hegemonic knowledge and points to the underlying "system of thought, which makes binary logic possible" (McQuillan 2000: 18-19). While *différance* does not dissolve the binary, it strategically splits hegemonic discourse in order to subvert its oppressive meaning. Hybridity can therefore be thought of as "that which makes all identity possible just as it undoes the possibility of a pure identity" (McQuillan 2000: 22). As a result, "hybrid identity" is impossible as it, too, disappears as it appears and ultimately gives depressing proof of the recuperative effects of the binary logic.[6]

In this respect, postcolonial discourse on hybridity intersects to some extent with Caribbean discourse on creolization. Hence, it is no longer a secret that "non-Caribbean scholars have increasingly turned to the Caribbean for theoretical tools – such as the concept of creolisation – with which to decipher global culture" (Shepherd/Richards

---

6   McQuillan points out that deconstruction of racial identity is in fact never-ending, because of the "recuperative effects of metaphysics" (2000: 15). And yet, despite of constant frustration deconstruction needs to continue in an effort to unveil the underlying power play of identity politics worldwide. Similarly, Mills has argued for a "social ontology of a racial world," which despite of the constructedness of the concept of race, "need[s] to locate race, not merely the overtly raced nonwhites, particularly blacks, but the seemingly unraced whites, whose racial markers vanish into the apparent universality of the colorless normative" (Mills 1998: 12).

2002: xv). Tracing the etymological origin of the term *creole*, Carolyn Allen in her article "Creole: The Problem of Definition" lists the following possible derivations of the term which either was introduced by Portuguese conquerors and later taken up by the Spanish (meaning "to create" = Latin *criar*), or stemmed from African Kikoongo (= "outsider") source (2002: 49). One of the earliest available documents, however, suggests that "criollo" was, indeed, a term originally introduced by Africans with reference to their children born in the New World. As Garcilaso el Inca (Peru 1602) states:

Es nombre que inventaron los negros y así lo muestra la obra. Quiere decir entre los negros, nascido en Indias; inventáronlo para diferenciar los que van de acá [es decir, del Viejo Mundo, que incluye Africa], nascidos en Guinea, de los que nascen allá [América], porque se tienen por mas honrados y de mas calidad por haber nascido en su patria, que no sus hijos, porque nascieron en la ajena, y los padres se ofenden si les llaman criollos. Los espanoles, por la semejanza, han introducido este nombre en su lenguaje, para nombrar los nascidos allá (in: Shepherd/Richards 2002: 49).

While there is as of yet no concluding argument for whether "creole" referred indeed to a racial discourse of favoring either a 'whitening,' or respectively 'blackening' of the New World born generation in terms of colonialist racial policy, the more important point needs to be made for its claim of locality over foreignness to the New World environment.[7] In this respect, Creole identity was an indigenous creation, as it also distinguished descendants of the New World diaspora from the autochthonous Amerindian population of the time. Allen stresses the importance of that dual quality of Creole identity, because it asserted cultural difference as a relational rather than essential feature (Shepherd/Richards 2002: 50). Moreover, creolization not only involved Europeans and Africans, but also different African ethnicities, who came in fact from rather different ethnic backgrounds yet merged into one strategically effective community under the stress of racialized slavery (Lovejoy/Trotman 2002: 85). Creolization thus evolved as a

---

[7] The controversy here arises from the different employment of the term in Latin America and the Caribbean islands. While "criollo" in Latin America referred to the New World born descendants of the Spanish and their ideology of "criollismo," a whitening of their culture, "creole" on the islands rather referred to the cultural impact of the Africans. It is this conflated usage of the term that has made it problematic in the eyes of many Caribbean intellectuals (Shepherd/Richards 2002: 53-55).

theoretical discourse of an anti-essentialist postcolonial Caribbean identity.

In this context Edward Kamau Brathwaite's *The Development of Creole Society in Jamaica 1770-1820* (1971) and *Contradictory Omens: Cultural Diversity and Integration in the Caribbean* (1974) are considered two key texts for Creole identity discourse in the Anglophone Caribbean. His seminal analysis defines creolization for Jamaica as "a cultural process perceived as taking place within a continuum of space and time" (1974: 10).[8] His concept encompasses two aspects: 1. "ac/culturation" as "the yoking (by force and example, deriving from power/prestige) of one culture to another (in this case African to European) and 2. "inter/culturation" as the "unplanned, unstructured but osmotic relationship proceeding from this yoke" (Brathwaite 1974: 6). According to Brathwaite's analysis of plantation society, colonialism operated under three systems of control: 1. the mercantilist system that extracted raw material from the region and which caused the economic dependency that goes on to the present day, 2. the plantation system that created social inequality and racism, 3. the imperial government that was at the heart of a fragmented, Euro-centered elite, a Euro-oriented Creole upper class and a small Creole intellectual elite "lacking in vision and roots" (1974: 28-29). Hence, creolization in his definition does not create a synthesis of different cultural elements, but must rather be perceived as "cracked, fragmented, ambivalent, not certain of itself, subject to shifting lights and pressures," for it constantly faces new cultural input from East-Indian, Lebanese and Asian immigration as well as North American economical and cultural influence (Brathwaite 1974: 6).

Brathwaite's conception of Creole identity was at the time conceived in direct opposition to M.G. Smith's work on the plural society model for the West Indies (see Smith 1965). While Smith had stressed the region's sectionalism of color, culture and class, Brathwaite sought to overcome this division. Smith had argued that the slaves were for

---

8 Brathwaite's understanding of the term "creole" derives from its use in Jamaica, where the Spanish "criollo" referred to those who were "born in, native to, committed to the area of living, [...] used in relation to both white and black, free and slave" (1974: 10). Part of the controversy around creolist discourse of the Anglophone Caribbean has been raised for its racist assimilationist ideology in promoting Eurocentrism and marginalising the African influence. Brathwaite is not negligent of this fact, but refers to it specifically as "Euro-creole" (1974: 6). For further critique of the discourse compare Burton Sankeralli, "From Attempted Theory to Failed Praxis. A Look at Creolist Ideology" (unpubl. seminar paper 2002).

the most part excluded from British cultural and social life, because of the prevalent laissez-faire economic doctrine and racism of the colonial administration. Even after Emancipation and the 1865 Morant Bay Rebellion, Jamaican Creole society had failed to enfranchise and thereby integrate the majority of the former slave population.[9] As a result, up until 1938 the island was still ruled by the 1% white population in control of the monopoly on political and economic affairs (Smith 1965: 314). Smith's argument therefore concluded that Creole society had never achieved full integration and thus remained plural in a sectional sense, i.e. mainly divided into a white European versus black African "mixture of discordant and incompatible elements" (Smith 1965: 307). However, against such binary logic, creolist discourse in the wake of Brathwaite and the post-independence struggle for national reconciliation sought precisely to overcome this sectionalism by stressing the African Creole heritage in counterbalance to Eurocentric hegemony.

Post-independence theoretical (re)assessment of creolization in the wake of Brathwaite's pioneering analysis, hence, divides into two strands: the one which declares Creole culture as "entirely new", the other which rather regards it as a New World African continuum (see Mintz/Price 1992; Alleyne 1988). The controversy clearly marks the political struggle for recognition, which accuses the former view of a European-assimilationist bias, while the latter stresses an Afrocentric perspective. Celebratory visions of creolization, such as the French Caribbean notion of "créolité," are partly contested, because they seem to support a European-oriented assimilationist agenda (see Bernabé et al. 1989; Glissant 1989). Historically torn between a colonial Europe and colonized Africa, Caribbean society thus still struggles for a balancing representational politics to negotiate ethnic polarization with an ongoing effort towards integration (Shepherd/Richards 2002: xiv). As Nigel Bolland has furthermore pointed out, the interconnectedness of Creole discourse as a metaphor for political decolonization links Creole identity politics also directly to the question of postcolonial nation-building. Creolization in this context, he argues, primarily presents "the ideology of a particular social segment, namely a middle class intelligentsia, which seeks a leading role in an integrated, newly independent society" (Bolland 2002: 17-18).

---

9   The 1865 Morant Bay Rebellion was led by Paul Bogle and George William Gordon, two leaders of the Native Baptist Church. Their rebellion was a further step of the impoverished African Jamaican workers towards full civil rights and liberty (Sherlock/Bennett 1998: 246ff.).

Contradictory as the concept of creolization thus appears, Allen's critical assessment of the discourse subsumes the following seven principles, which I believe to outline the continuing issues of Caribbean identity politics as being:

1. A movement away from origin and the difficulty of reconstructing a path back to the source(s) suggested in the etymology of the term.
2. The inescapability of difference, recalling that Creole was introduced to mark the appearance of a simultaneously similar/dissimilar type.
3. With the historical experience of colonialism which gave rise to its use, the primacy of cross-cultural encounter and the location of Creoleness at an intersection, negotiating between identities and forces, and defined by its relations.
4. The consequence, however strongly resisted, of a modification of type involving rejection, adaptation, accommodation, imitation, invention.
5. The value of nativisation or indigenisation, marking the point of recognition of that new type as belonging to the locale.
6. Yet, the difficulty of fully accounting for this type which does not become a fixed form but continues in a dynamic process of interaction with new influences.
7. The multiplicity of Creole forms/types making context and point of view crucial to understanding (Allen 2002: 56-57).

Following the above chart, creolist discourse in the Caribbean has consequently emerged as a powerful discursive metaphor to announce the region's anti-essentialist in-betweenness to deconstruct Eurocentrism's hegemonic claim to colonial power. In line with Robert Baron's recent suggestion to adapt the metaphorical meaning of the term *Creole* from its culture specific origin in identity and language discourse to a broader conceptual framework, creolization may therefore lastly – probably precisely because of its inner controversy – acknowledge the cultural dynamics in an increasingly transcultural world (Baron 2003: 88; 90-92).

Considered as strategic metaphor, creolist discourse encompasses in fact a variety of political performances, which via language, dance, and music have traditionally informed many of the subversive and revolutionary anti-colonial struggles of the African Creole cultural complex. Speaking of creolist 'metaphors' in this context, I will suggest that the subversive power of creolist discourse is based precisely on its metaphoric ambivalence. As will be demonstrated in the following analysis of Caribbean dance theatre choreography, the identificatory moment of these performative gestures appears to rely largely on a shared iconicity derived from Africanist diasporic aesthetics in the New World, despite of the certainly also present European mnemonic trace. Throughout its historical development from New World emancipatory rhetoric towards the transnational reality of the new millennium then, creolization continues to delineate a powerful metaphor with which to address the political implications of the Caribbean quest for postcolonial nationalism.

Nationalist Rhetoric

We are sorely troubled in Jamaica over this question of identity. We are in doubt about the use of the phrase "Jamaican Culture" but it is used everywhere today, vague, in definition, being held doggedly by a people suffering from what, on the face of it, is the multiplicity of cultural choices (Dawes 1975: 34).

Nationalist rhetoric argued that the diverse mixtures on the islands did not preclude a common identity but could allow for the possibility of unification through a blended culture, the tertium quid. The politics of creolization was simultaneously engaged to articulate nationalism, pan-Caribbeanism, and pan-Africanism as black cultures became the new domain of struggle. The marginal majority, the disenfranchised black people, became the central referents in the national culture of the "common man," as the global processes of democratization and decolonization coincided with the emergence of black consciousness and working-class struggles (Nair 2000: 239).

Discourse on nationalism has been varied and at times highly conflated in its ideological output. While in the 19th century national identity formation came to have racist outgrowths, it became increasingly militant and fascist in its totalitarianism towards the middle of the twentieth century (see Hutchinson/Smith 1994). Inherent to nationalism's many conceptual definitions is a somewhat primordial sense of communal belonging, of a priori shared kinship and a presumed common/shared identity. Also, nationalism promotes an instrumentalist approach as its rhetoric mobilizes disenfranchised groups towards their emancipatory projects. In short, nationalism makes use of the past in order to subvert the present and bears the auspicious promise of a better world for all of 'us'. Just to whom this 'us' refers has often been the cause of sometimes heated debate other times gruesomely violent military confrontation and abysmal genocide.

In his influential *Nations and Nationalism* (1983), Ernest Gellner – next to Benedict Anderson's *Imagined Communities* (1983) and Eric Hobsbawm's *The Invention of Tradition* (1983) – was among the first historians to suggest a reading of nationalism as part of the process of modernity. By demystifying the supposed origin of nations and nationalist movements, Gellner's "modernist approach" relates emerging nationalist movements directly to their level of industrialization.[10] As economic well-being and advance increase, Gellner argues, industrialization calls for a culturally homogenous group of people, which by a standardized education is, at least theoretically, provided with egalitarian access to the market place. National culture becomes the legitimizing force for the existence of the nation as it unites a formerly diverse population under one common set of identifications. During this process of cultural unification dissenting groups have either the choice to assimilate to the national norm, or to form their own separatist nation. Either way though, in order to convince the people of their nationality, nationalism has to build on that oftentimes rather romanticized notion of a common cultural heritage and tradition. As the nation is invented, so to speak, identifications borrow from pre-existing low or folk cultures, to yet form another variant of high culture of its own. Gellner describes the process as such:

Nationalism usually conquers in the name of a putative folk culture. Its symbolism is drawn from the healthy, pristine, vigorous life of the peasants, of the Volk, the narod. There is a certain element of truth in the nationalist self-presentation when the narod or Volk is ruled by officials of another, an alien high culture, whose oppression must be resisted first by a cultural revival and reaffirmation, and eventually by a war of national liberation. If the nationalism prospers it eliminates the alien high culture, but it does not then replace it by the old local low culture; it revives, or invents, a local high (literate, specialist-transmitted) culture of its own, though admittedly one which will have some links with the earlier local folk styles and dialects (1983: 57).

---

10 Anthony D. Smith defines the "modernist approach" to nationalism as being "sociologically necessary" while "obviously logically contingent" (1999: 47).

Certainly, such "invention" of high culture, which is based on elements from the former low culture, was particularly evident in the emergence of postcolonial nationalism of the 1960s.

However, postcolonial nationalism should oftentimes rather be regarded as a culturally empowering corrective to the experience of dislocation and estrangement than as a reversed kind of imperialism in this context. Also referred to as "alternative modernity," postcolonial nationalism thus reclaims nationalist concepts in order to arrive at new modes of self-representation (Gunn et al. 1999: 4-5).[11] In this respect, postcolonial nationalism becomes decidedly *inter*nationalist in perspective (Bhabha 1994: 38-39). As Frantz Fanon's argument in *The Wretched of the Earth* (1961) makes clear, folk culture serves as a legitimizing tool to heighten a formerly denigrated pre-colonial past. However, as such it will always be bound to present a response to that denigration rather than to generate an authentic claim. It is thus through the nationalist "rhetoric of belonging" that postcolonial nationalism developed first of all into a strategic statement of resistance and decolonization (Pickering 2001: 101).[12] Cultural revolution, though, is ultimately brought about by a self-critical re-appropriation of the past, which Fanon has characterized as follows:

A national culture is not a folklore, nor an abstract populism that believes it can discover the people's true nature. It is not made up of the inert dregs of gratuitous actions, that is to say actions which are less and less attached to the everpresent reality of the people. A national culture is the whole body of efforts made by a people in the sphere of thought to describe, justify and praise the action through which that people has created itself and keeps itself in existence. A national culture in under-developed countries should therefore take its place at the very heart of the struggle for freedom which these countries are carrying on (1990: 188).

---

11 Similarly Bhabha speaks of "postcolonial contra-modernity" as being "contingent to modernity, discontinuous or in contention with it, resistant to its oppressive, assimilationist technologies" but also "deploy[ing] the cultural hybridity of their borderline conditions to 'translate', and therefore reinscribe, the social imaginary of both metropolis and modernity" (1994: 6).
12 Edward Said referred to this circumstance as "the tragedy of resistance," as "it must to a certain degree work to recover forms already established or at least influenced or infiltrated by the culture of empire" (Said 1994: 253).

As an integral instrument in the liberation struggle, postcolonial nationalism hence operates under two intertwined agendas: the one to assert an identity and demand recognition, the other to modernize and progress towards full participation in the global market-place and its politics (Geertz 1994: 30).[13] Furthermore, postcolonial politics operate on the ambivalence within nationalism itself, which – as Anthony D. Smith has pointed out – simultaneously operates on modern and pre-modern concepts (1999: 56). Especially the evocation of the latter serves as the foundational claim that lends the new nation "political definition and social depth," since "[t]hese memories, myths, symbols and traditions are not only alive in sections of the population, they are [also] ancestral and distinctive" (Smith 1999: 56).

Afrocentric discourse within the Caribbean national paradigm of creolization pays therefore tribute to precisely such "ancestral and distinctive" memory. Re-shaping the postcolonial nation as "African Jamaican," for example, speaks to such a unifying sensibility that exceeds Gellner's and particularly Anderson's model of more or less arbitrary composition, since Jamaica's African traditions are directly derived from the cultural heritage of the formerly disenfranchised. Not only are these living testimonies of survival and resistance, but they also convey an alternative frame for national identification. The postcolonial "return to ethno-history" is thus not only motivated by modernist progress, but also relies on its mass popular appeal which usually predates the modern development. As Smith concludes his argument:

> [...] we must look to the fund of ethnic myths, symbols and values, and to the corpus of ethno-historical traditions, to inspire a sense of cohesion among the very different groups and often conflicting classes in a modern industrial society. While the mass media, mass education and political socialisation may all help to spread the ideas and beliefs of citizenship and democracy, only ethnic history and national traditions can unite the body of individual citizens and furnish a sense of belonging for groups with often disparate interests. Despite the familiar problems of selecting and cultivating ethnic history and traditions, particularly in polyethnic states, the creation of nations with a minimum sense of cohesion requires some set of ethnic memories and tradi-

---

13 Similarly, Rustom Bharucha has argued for a positive reassessment of a pro-nationalist perspective in one's definition of the cultural as a "potentially liberating force [...] particularly in relation to those people's movements against globalization in Third World countries, which could be the only hope for challenging and redemocratizing the state" (2000: 4).

tions, and to have some resonance, they must be drawn from the ethnic past of the majority or dominant *ethnie* (1999: 57).

As a result, "imagining the people" as unified in their diversity prevails as a political necessity in the Caribbean context, despite the region's postmodern hybridity. As Shalini Puri has stressed, colonization "has made national sovereignty and regional self-determination hard to sustain" and therefore indispensable to uphold against deconstructive aims (2004: 12). Postcolonial nationalism and its invention of a shared communal identity are consequently directly linked to the public's institutionalized means of representation, i.e. the nation's cultural performances.

The Politics of Representation

Public representations have the power to select, arrange, and prioritise certain assumptions and ideas about different kinds of people, bringing some to the fore, dramatising and idealising or demonising them, while casting others into the social margins, so that they have little active public presence or only a narrow and negative public image (Pickering 2001: xiii).

We live of course in a world not only of commodities but also of representation, and representations – their production, circulation, history, and interpretation – are the very element of culture. In much recent theory the problem of representation is deemed to be central, yet rarely is it put in its full political context, a context that is primarily imperial (Said 1994: 66).

As the preceding historical and discursive overview has shown, to speak of a Caribbean identity is already somewhat paradoxical, as cultural oneness is defied by the region's ethnic diversity. It is therefore interesting to look at the history of the term 'Caribbean' in order to understand the troublesome discomfort surrounding the many representational labels that have been ascribed to the region. As Norman Girvan summarizes the Caribbean's genealogy in his essay "Reinterpreting the Caribbean," it was not before the end of the nineteenth century that the term was introduced, and only in the 1940s that it actually gained currency (2001: 6-7). The Spanish colonizers had referred to "los caribes" as those allegedly cannibalistic tribes they first encountered in the New World. Later on the term "Caribbean" was applied by the US forces, whenever they felt need to "intervene South." In both cases though, the designation appeared as a biased construct of imperialist power and only thereafter was it re-assessed and positively connoted by Caribbean intellectuals such as C.L.R. James, Eric Williams and Lloyd Best (Girvan 2001: 4). As a result, just who they are and where exactly they came from remained an obstacle for most of the Caribbean populations, who after only a century under colonial rule could trace their lineage(s) to all corners of the world.

Stuart Hall in "Negotiating Caribbean Identities" (2001) has furthermore remarked that the loss and mourning over origin must be linked to the question of representation, i.e. the question of who gets the say and who, on the other hand, is silenced in the rhetorical identity (re)invention process (26). In order to oppose the prevalent colonialist discourse, Caribbean intellectuals of the post-independence era therefore needed first of all to define a common set of identification models in order to effectively address the pressing political, cultural and economic exigencies. Among those identification "exercises" Stuart Hall lists the following three processes of cultural practice: 1. retention, 2. assimilation and 3. cultural revolution. Afrocentric discourse thus works as "strategic essentialism" of "black popular culture" as it paves revolutionary ground. However, Hall also makes clear that "blackness" as cultural signifier must necessarily be regarded as a "contradictory space," for it "can never be simplified or explained in terms of the simple binary oppositions that are still habitually used to map it out: high versus low; resistance versus incorporation; authentic versus inauthentic [...]" (1997: 128).

Similarly, Paul Gilroy in his seminal work *The Black Atlantic: Modernity and Double Consciousness* (1993) has referred to this strategic essentialism as a direct reaction to the African diaspora situation. According to his argument, the New World African diaspora's counter discourse drew self-consciously on pre-modern images and symbols – such as nationalism, universality, coherence of the subject, foundational ethnocentrism – to "gain an extra power in proportion to the brute facts of modern slavery" (1993: 56). Basing his argument on W.E.B. DuBois' notion of "double consciousness," Gilroy argues for the double significance of the black arts movement as it instigated the process of redefining modernity in the shadow of plantation society and slavery (1993: 56). While Gilroy's suggested "continuity of expressive culture" actually appears as an essentializing, pre-modern concept, he claims that its active re-imagination in the present creates, quite to the contrary, a distinctly modern interpretation of diaspora identity. As such

"Black Atlantic" identity evades binary coding as a "non-traditional tradition," which performatively fulfills the "mnemonic function" of upholding "social memory" against "the narrative of loss, exile, and journeying" (Gilroy 1993: 198).

However, even though such strategic representation seeks to avoid a fixed one to one relationship between signifier and signified, difference still remains culturally inscribed. The dilemma thus results in the question of how to deal with difference by neither dissolving nor fixing it. As Stuart Hall points out on behalf of assessing the "black subject" as culturally constructed, one needs to "re-theorize the concept of *difference*" as closer to Derrida's *différance*, i.e. a concept prone to constant deconstruction (1996: 447). Moreover – and at this point Hall appears to address what might be read as a prerequisite of Fanon's envisioned "new international humanism" – such "new ethnicity" would no longer be limited to signify the one nation or 'race,' but rather purport the "recognition that we all speak from a particular place, out of a particular history, out of a particular experience, a particular culture, without being contained by that position as 'ethnic artists' or film-makers" (Hall 1996: 447).

Interlude I: Dance and Postcolonial Theory

Whereas postmodern deconstruction and hybridity discourse aim towards the relational openness of an endless signification process in order to evade the notion of essentialist unity, Caribbean postcolonial politics seek to construct and maintain precisely such strategic unity for achieving certain political ends. Caribbean identity politics thus struggle towards postcolonial nationalism and operate along the rhetoric of strategic essentialisms in order to gain representative power. Yet, as Bruce Robbins points out, such a humanist stance does not necessarily have to contradict the postmodern anti-humanism and enlightenment critique, since "humanism in at least one of its established meanings" has always been part of the postcolonial field (2000: 557ff.). Calling for a "new humanist paradigm," Robbins, hence, advocates a political stance that renounces the theoretical affiliation of universalism with imperialism. Instead of easily abandoning the normative claim of ethical universals then, Robbins suggests to face the challenge of those "large abstractions," which in practice have actually more often been failed than fulfilled, when he quotes from Laclau, who elsewhere convincingly claimed:

If social struggles of new social actors show that the concrete practices of our society restrict the universalism or our political ideals to limited sectors of the population, it becomes possible to retain the universal dimension while widening the sphere of its application – which, in turn, will define the concrete contents of such universality. Through this process, universalism as a horizon is expanded at the same time as its necessary attachment to any particular content is broken. The opposite policy – that of rejecting universalism *in toto* as the particular content of the ethnia of the West – can only lead to a political blind alley (1995: 107).

In which respect exactly the fleeting art of dance can play an important part in this process will be the central focus of the following analysis of Jamaican dance theatre, its Creole aesthetics, and postcolonial identity politics.

Dance and Postcolonial Nationalism – Embodying Emancipation

Towards a Creolist Aesthetic – African Caribbean Identity and Dance

[...] post-colonial societies must accomplish two things if they are to re-establish self-confidence and re-embark upon the process of self-discovery that is expressed by the evolution of a people's culture. They must rediscover the validity of their own culture at the moment of the colonial intervention and retrace the steps that had led through history to that point. And they must establish within a frame of reality of the culture which colonialism imposed upon them so that this may loom neither larger nor smaller than it deserves and suffer from none of the distortions which can result from the ambivalence of a ruler subject situation (Manley 1974: 146).

The guiding principles for revitalizing the Jamaican nation and making the educational system a source of inspiration begin with the affirmation that Jamaica is predominantly a black nation whose ancestral motherland is West Africa. The only way to destroy the psychosocial controls instituted by European imperialism is to set the historical record straight. This is the self-liberation of which Garvey spoke. Once this has been accomplished, the nation will find a perennial source of strength in its past (Sherlock/Bennett 1998: 410).

In their 1998 history titled *The Story of the Jamaican People*, Sir Philip Sherlock and Hazel Bennett revise colonialist historiography as their original approach offers a first time interpretation by Jamaicans rather than former colonialists; and hardly surprising, their account differs remarkably from earlier investigations in that they make Africa a cultural reference point as significant as Great Britain, if not even more so. The final chapter "Culture and nationhood" is of particular relevance to the study of dance, since the authors refer to the important role of the arts in the process of Jamaican nation-building during the pre- and post-Independence era. Almost forty years after Jamaica's national independence in 1962, they argue that the outspoken Afrocentrism appears as a likely response to what Michael Manley had called for about twenty years earlier, when demanding the recovery of Africa as Jamaica's "own culture at the moment of the colonial intervention" (Nettleford 2003: 68). In comparison to other Caribbean islands that have been more hesitant to proclaim an Africanist identity, Jamaica's proud declaration of 'blackness' dates back to the island's turbulent history of slave revolt and subsistence. Jamaican Afrocentrism must therefore be perceived in the historical context of plantation economy and slavery, since black identity politics first of all aimed at a positive self-(re)evaluation.

While other Caribbean islands may have adopted more assimilatory identity discourses, Mervyn Alleyne has convincingly argued that African Jamaican identity politics have more than enough good reason to resist such self-deception. Following his argument, Jamaica's African focus is thus based on the continuity of the island's dominant Akan-Twi retention, which went into the living testimony of Jamaica's African Creole religions Myalism, Pukumina and Revival (Alleyne 2002: 199; 201). In addition, Jamaican history has also witnessed a quite unusual consistency of continuous slave rebellion for the region as a consequence of white planter absenteeism and the brutality of the plantation attorneys and overseers in charge. At the same time though, Jamaican slave resistance occasioned what Alleyne calls a "symbiotic relationship between ethnicity, preservation of African culture, and resistance, one manifestation of which was the desire to maintain a physical distance from the white population" (2002: 202). Hence, Jamaica's Maroon heritage is of particular importance in this context.

As early as 1655, when the British troupes defeated the Spanish, various slaves fled into the mountain areas. The majority of these first runaway slaves (= "Maroons") were of Akan (Ashanti) origin, an ethnic group renowned for their rebellious warriors. Ashanti thus assembled with the island's remaining Arawak Indians to form an independent community. In strategic alliance, both groups managed to safe-guard and maintain many of their former cultural traditions.[1] The Maroon's 1738/39 peace treaty with Great Britain had first granted freedom to their community so that, historically, the Maroons were the first African Jamaicans to obtain independence. In comparison to the African slaves on the plantations, Maroons were therefore able to live and recreate their own cultural practices, comparatively free from the European influence. Noted especially for its powerful Myal-Men, who were successfully practicing herbal medicine and healing ritual, "Maroon society [...] was able to act as a catalyst and give form to the resurgence of African identity and consciousness during and especially after slavery," as Cheryl Ryman has pointed out (1980: 5). So while ethnic division between different African groups existed and led to rivalries and disputes, the common fate of slavery forced their alliance in revolt (Barnett 1979: 22).

Among the basic cultural commonalties between these different West African traditions, Sheila Barnett lists ancestor worship, possession, adoration of the earth as universal force and community base, secret societies, yam festivals, impersonation of the spirit world through masquerade and festival, the use of song, drums and dancing in ritual as well as the belief in shamanism (1979: 22-24).[2] Religion, dance and music have thus from the very beginning of the colonial contact been integral to the process of African Jamaican identity formation. Since traditional dances survived mostly within former and still existing Maroon communities, it is hardly surprising that up until today, the African Jamaican folk retention remains strongest in their outreach area, namely, in the parishes of Portland, St. Thomas, St. Mary, St. Elizabeth, Hanover and Westmoreland (Ryman 1980: 5).

After Emancipation in 1834/38, yet another exodus of slaves to Jamaica's secluded mountain areas occurred and contributed further to a more stringent continuity of African derived cultural practices. Between 1841 and 1867 further 10,000 Africans came from Sierra Leone

---

1   Sheila Barnett has commented upon the similarity between Arawak and African belief systems and worship practices (1979: 20).
2   "Shamanism," which is of North Central Asian etymological origin, is here conceived of as "an ancient kind of performance practiced by specialists in healing and trance, employing music, dance, masks, and objects" (Schechner 2002: 168).

and the Kru Coast to Jamaica and settled mainly in the parishes of St. Mary, St. Thomas and Westmoreland (Alleyne 2002: 208). These later African laborers practiced the Kongo derived folk religion which should over time become known as Jamaican Kumina, as well as the Yoruba based Etu of Hanover and Nago of Westmoreland. Alleyne highlights the importance of Maroon interrelations with these other African groups as both of their cultural retentions created a mutually enriching cultural exchange to ultimately generate the backbone of Jamaica's rich Neo-African heritage.[3] African Jamaican identity has thus come to define itself by the proud concept of *marronage*, which as the formerly defiant strategy of runaway slaves represents the African Jamaican struggle towards cultural emancipation (Alleyne 20002: 209).

Against the more assimilatory discourses of French-Caribbean *métissage* and *créolité*, Jamaican *marronage* has thus called rhetorical attention to effective black resistance in "a world and a Caribbean where there is growing hybridity and where 'white' values dominate and are still rampant" (Alleyne 2002: 194). Jamaica's national motto "Out of Many, One People," may therefore appear relative, because it in fact presents "some degree of denial of, and distancing from, the concrete reality of the dominance of black in the ethnic composition of Jamaica" (Alleyne 2002: 194). For many Jamaicans *marronage*, hence, conceptualizes a distinct Afrocentric identification, which calls for special consideration and articulation from the national side, when Alleyne concludes:

Jamaican history is replete with the struggles of the black population to assert its ethnicity in the context of resistance to slavery. Whereas slave revolts and uprisings were typical of all slave regimes throughout the Caribbean and the New World, Jamaica had more than a full share; and it was not simply a matter of uprisings or acts of rebellion and resistance, but rather of organized revolts. These had as their goals, not merely an escape by individuals from the harshness of slavery, but the desire to create a way of life based on a cultural and spiritual allegiance to Africa (2002: 218).

---

3   Cheryl Ryman coined the term "Neo-African," which according to her definition "is used to refer to those forms developed in the new world by African peoples, who draw largely on a body of cultural knowledge (African) to interpret both the new environment and cultural modes" (Ryman 1984a: 13).

And indeed, a large number of African-derived cultural practices have survived colonization and certainly support this claim for "spiritual alliance." Predominantly derived from the retention of African religions and their rituals, these are still significantly manifest in Jamaica's rich performative/performance heritage of today.

Early African Jamaican Religious and Recreational Dances

Todo el arte nace en la religión [...] pues sin una idea previa y clara del carácter consustancialmente religioso y mágico que entre los negros africanos tienen originariamente el verso, el canto, la música y el baile, estas expresiones de su arte no podrán ser debidamente comprendidas, ni en sus múltiples manifestaciones, ni en sus instrumentos, ni en su historia (Ortiz 1965: 186).[4]

Obeah/Myalism

Historically, Obeah and Myalism are the earliest two African Jamaican religious practices – documented by Sir Edward Long in 1760 – which give evidence of African-derived medicine and possessional dancing (see Long 1774). Long's descriptions, however, must be read with caution as they represent the colonial bias of his time and cultural background. Obeah has thus misleadingly been described as "black magic" and witchcraft, a tradition that was further pursued by renowned gothic novelist Monk Lewis in his West Indies journal (Lewis 1834: 91-93). As Brathwaite points out though, Obeah has likely been stigmatized by colonialist discourse in order to undermine its empowering healing, community generating, and magical/revolting effects (1993: 193-194). Whether Obeah has, therefore, correctly been reported to cause 'evil spells,' which Myalism could then successfully counteract has, as of yet, not been convincingly decided (Schuler 1979: 65).[5] As

---

4   All art is born from religion [...] therefore, without a previous and clear idea of the consubstantially religious and magical character which verse, song, music and dance have among Negro-Africans, their art cannot be understood, neither in its multiple manifestations, nor in its instruments, nor in its history (engl. transl.).

5   Cheryl Ryman supports Schuler's claim in her discussion of Jamaican Kumina by stating that "Obeah refers to the sorcery tradition or the primarily evil intentions of the specialist who manipulates the "powers" available to him through the earthbound spirits and "scientific" objects or keys, while Myal refers to the just administration and healing capabilities of Man [...]"(1984: 87).

Ryman suggests, "the form that was most likely to "go public" in Jamaica was Myal, the good" (1984: 88). Whereas Obeah, the alleged 'evil' practice went strategically underground. It appears therefore more than likely that Obeah and Myal as pre-emancipation religious practices were actually complementary rather than exclusive, traces of which may still be found in Kumina and certain Revival practices thereafter.[6]

According to Ryman, Myal traditionally "has been viewed as *the religious core of Afro Jamaican culture*" (1980: 5). Referring to Myal as a possessional dance practice, Ryman, Schuler and Patterson have listed several common characteristics in their studies, which all assume an overall positive, i.e. healing effect of the dance. Patterson, for example, argues that Myal was conducted in good faith to cause immunity against physical infliction by white oppressors as well as to impose "the power to restore life" on the dancer (1967: 186). As Monk Lewis observed in his journal of 1834:

The Obeah ceremonies always commence with what is called, by the negroes, 'the Myal dance'. This is intended to remove any doubt of the chief Obeahman's supernatural powers; and in the course of it, he undertakes to show his art by killing one of the persons present, whom he pitches upon for that purpose. He sprinkles various powders over the devoted victim, blows upon him, and dances round him, obliges him to drink a liquor prepared for the occasion, and finally the sorcerer and his assistants seize him and whirl him rapidly round and round till the man loses his senses, and falls on the ground to all appearance and the belief of the spectators a perfect corpse. The chief Myal-man then utters loud shrieks, rushes out of the house with wild and frantic gestures, and conceals himself in some neighboring wood. At the end of two or three hours he returns with a large bundle of herbs, from some of which he squeezes the juice into the mouth of the dead person; with others he anoints his eyes and stains the tips of his fingers, accompanying the ceremony with a great variety of grotesque actions, and chanting all the while something between a song and a howl, while the assistants hand in hand dance

---

[6] The difference between Obeah and Myal can furthermore be regarded as structural rather than moral, since practitioners are often versed in both traditions. Thus, Markus Coester (2004) has argued that while Obeah refers to the healing practice of an individual, Myal was practiced in groups. Margarite Fernández Olmos and Lizabeth Paravisini-Gebert similarly suggest that Myal presented but another version of Obeah, sharing its healing/medicinal function, yet being practiced in group worship rather than by individual consultation (2003: 142).

slowly round them in a circle, stamping the ground loudly with their feet to keep time with his chant. A considerable time elapses before the desired effect is produced, but at length the corpse gradually recovers animation, rises from the ground perfectly recovered, and the Myal dance concludes (222-223).

Described as a "dance ritual of 'death' and 'resurrection,'" Myal thus assumed a direct individual and social function as it was employed as a means of healing, resistance and rebellion (Patterson 1967: 190-191).[7] Schuler also points out that the dance generated "good fortune" among the participants and, moreover, that it protected them from disease and death which were believed to derive "from spiritual sources and required the performance of appropriate ritual" (Schuler 1979: 65-67). Due to the comparatively insignificant impact of Christianity before Emancipation, such ritual practice went relatively unnoticed as long as it did not disturb the alleged peace of the plantation. In contrast to the colonies under Catholic denomination, this was one of the peculiarities of the Caribbean colonies under Protestant rule, where planters up until the end of the 18th century did not care too much about the spiritual salvation of their slaves.

Once the slaves were introduced to the teachings of the bible though, the Holy Book's epistemic power was soon appropriated to their own emancipatory ends. With the advent of black Baptist preachers in 1791 and the support of the growing abolitionist movement – slave trade was officially abolished in 1807 – the end of slavery could not be protracted for very much longer. Non-conformist churches such as the Methodists and Baptists played a decisive role in spurring the slaves' Emancipation movement. While the Methodists focused on the smaller group of free blacks predominantly in the Kingston area, Baptist preachers incited the masses of black slaves during that period. Lead by African American ex-slaves, the Baptist movement succeeded for one reason, because preacher and slave shared a common experience of oppression and suffering. Furthermore, the Baptists' leader-system bore strong resemblance to that of the spiritual leaders of Jamaican Myalism. From this structural similarity emerged more and more independent Jamaican Baptist branches as both practices continuously syncretized. It is therefore hardly surprising that after Emancipation orthodox church membership was abandoned for those more

---

7   Monk Lewis' journal, for example, refers to Obeah's magic spells and the Obeah-man's frequent poisoning of water wells (1834: 221).

native versions of belief. The strategic alliance between Baptist preachers and slaves against the planter oppressor thus led to an African-Christian syncretism, which laid the foundation for Jamaican Revivalism (Patterson 1967: 214-215).

Under the influence of Baptism, Myalism underwent significant changes. Myalists, for example, adopted the Holy Spirit among their ancestors and gods in the spirit pantheon, as well as they affirmed the practice of baptism by immersion. The Holy Spirit would entrance a practitioner in Myal dance as likely as the river baptism could embody an African river spirit. In its syncretic combination of African and Christian ritual, Myalism became highly significant and in the end far more successful than the Baptist creed. As Schuler explicates:

The Myal notion of sin as sorcery, an offence not against God but against society, made it far more this-world oriented than the Baptist faith. Myal ritual offered a cure for society's ills which, since they were caused by sorcery, could be eradicated by antisorcery ritual. For this reason Myalism was far more relevant to many Afro-Jamaicans than any missionary version of the Christian faith. It attracted new followers on the north coast in the 1830s and 1840s and mounted anti-European offensives in both decades, demonstrating a continued Afro-Jamaican awareness of the major source of their misfortune in the nineteenth century (1979: 69).

The masters' hesitancy to Christianize their slaves thus turned out to be more reasonable than they might have originally been aware of: not because of the slaves' alleged ignorance, but rather because of their smart cunning. Since the bible taught humility and respect, the demand for freedom could no longer be denied.

However, after Emancipation had officially been obtained in 1834, sectionalism between the impoverished black masses, white upper and the brown middle class still posed an insurmountable obstacle to an integrative societal effort. Even worse, the church now started to ban all of the African derived religious practices as they regarded them as "heathenish" and, more significantly, a distraction from work. Obeah and Myal were attacked for their "demoralizing and pernicious influence," yet survived despite of the colonial opposition by integrating Christian saints and apostles in the African spirit pantheon (Hill 1992: 261). So while African-derived folk religion was rigorously demonized by the ministers of the established denominations, it still managed to thrive under the impact of newly arriving indentured workers from Africa after Emancipation. Kumina, next to the 1860s Great Revival, thus emerged as the two powerful African Jamaican religions, regardless of their continuous ban by the public officials.[8]

Funeral Rites

Another important element of religious cultural survival encompasses the complex of West African derived funeral rites, which in the mind of suffering slaves were believed to smoothen the passage home to Africa (Pigou 1987: 24). Even though these rites also underwent significant change through the impact of slavery, migration, and Christian missionary activities, various African forms of religious worship were nonetheless maintained. Today, those related to death are still the most prevalent. Elizabeth Pigou lists the following West African/African Jamaican beliefs that can be traced:

1. The individual has three 'components' – body, spirit/soul, duppy.
2. Death is an extended event, marking the end of mortal life, and the passage to immortality.
3. At death the spirit returns to the Supreme God and joins other spirits. This phase is perceived as being a type of journey.
4. At death the duppy or shadow wanders for several days, after which it must be laid to rest by special rites. If these rites are not carried out, the duppy may wander indefinitely and is capable of carrying evil acts, through the manipulation of sorcerers or through natural and psychic phenomena. During the interval between clinical death and the time the duppy is laid to rest, the individual is not considered fully dead. The purpose of funeral rites is to secure the safe journey of the spirit as well as to placate the duppy (1987: 24).

Dance and spirit possession play an integral part of these ceremonies. Commenting on the festival character of Jamaican funeral rites, Patterson also claims that they served as a "re-interpretation of the common African belief that on death one rejoins one's ancestors" (1967: 198). Among the common funeral practices belonged the nine-night ritual, ancestor worship and possessional dancing (Patterson 1967: 195-199).

Jamaican "nine-nights," which are preformed to accompany the deceased spirit's final departure, combine several African as well as

---

[8] Kumina and Revival will both be discussed in detail for the context of NDTC choreography.

Christian elements. To safeguard the spirit's journey, nine-night ceremonies are held by family and friends of the deceased in order to remember and entertain the dead spirit. Food is offered, sermons, hymns and songs given in order to smooth the passage from this into the other world (Pigou 1987: 25). Celebratory in nature, Jamaican nine-nights thus stress the continuity of life in death as they accompany the liminal transition phase of the spirit ("duppy") to join the ancestors. As such, these rituals are a strong manifestation of the community generating West African belief system, which unites the ritual's practitioner to his people as well as his gods, ancestors and the unborn.

"Recreation aroun' da Bood ..."[9] – The Jonkonnu Masquerade

Apart from the religious sources of African survival in Jamaica, recreational practices formed the second larger complex of that retention. While accounts of the slaves' religious rituals are extremely scarce – as they had to be held in secrecy – there is more documented evidence of their "occasional week nights and ends of dance and sing," as well as of course the well known seasonal holidays of Christmas, Easter, Crop-over and Yam festival during the last half of the 18th century (Patterson 1967: 232). The earliest reference to slaves' masquerades under the name of "Jonkonnu" has been made by Edward Long (1774: 424).[10]

---

9 The quote refers to the first line of a famous Bruckins song, first introduced a year after full Emancipation from slavery 1839. A detailed discussion of Bruckins Party will follow in the context of NDTC choreography.

10 Masquerade characters, however, had been described by Hans Sloane even earlier than that: "The Negros are much given to Venery, and although hard wrought, will at nights, or on Feast days Dance and Sing; their Songs are all bawdy, and leading that way. They have several sorts of Instruments in imitation of Lutes, made of small Gourds fitted with Necks, strung with Horse hairs, or the peeled stalks of climbing Plants or Withs. These Instruments are sometimes made of hollow'd Timber covered with Parchment or other Skin wetted, having a Bow for its Neck, the Strings ty'd longer or shorter, as they would alter their sounds. The Figures of some of these Instruments are hereafter graved. They have likewise in their Dances Rattles ty'd to their Legs and Wrists, and in their Hands, with which they make a noise, keeping time with one who makes a sound answering it on the mouth of an empty Gourd or Jar with his Hand. Their Dances consist in great activity and strength of Body, and keeping time, if it can be. They very often tie Cows Tails to their Rumps, and add such other odd things to their Bodies in several places, as gives them a very extraordinary appearance (1707: xlviii-xlix).

Ryman, however, has claimed that Jonkonnu as a "Neo-African form" could likely also have been an originally religious practice which only in its historical development became increasingly entertaining in content, as it today presents a rather symbolic/satirical than religious tradition. Since African slaves carried with them a variety of performance modes from different ethnic backgrounds, their individual heritage formed a residual presence in each cultural blend. Apart from the before mentioned rituals, performances involved mime and acrobatics as well as communal song and dance (Hill 1992: 218).

On behalf of Jonkonnu it has therefore been argued that the secular masquerade might have originally developed from African secret societies, namely Poro and Egungun (Ryman 1984a: 16).[11] In these societies the full-body mask embodies the ancestor spirit, yet it may also appear in a secular/entertainment context (Wynter 1970: 38). Because sacred and secular spheres are not strictly separated in West African cosmologies, Ryman and Wynter both suggest that an early interrelationship of religious Jonkonnu and Myal practice might have occurred. Thus Ryman states an early stage of Jonkonnu (1655-1775) that was hardly European influenced and maintained much of the original African ancestor worship tradition. Typical characters of this phase, still to be found today, are Horsehead and Cowhead, which accompanied by musicians give solo performances rather than group appearances (Ryman 1984a: 14).[12] According to Ryman's historical time chart, the second stage (1775-1838) was marked by the appearance of the set girls and other British influenced masks. At this time the masquerade reflected more of the social reality of plantation society. For example, the

---

11   Compare also Sylvia Wynter "Jonkonnu in Jamaica. Towards the Interpretation of Folk Dance as a Cultural Process," *Jamaica Journal* 4.2 (1970): 38ff.; as well as Maureen Warner-Lewis, *Central Africa in the Caribbean. Transcending Time, Transforming Cultures* (Kingston: U of the West Indies P, 2003) 223-224, where she addresses the interconnectedness of Myal and Jonkonnu practice and suggests a Kongo derived etymology of the term, which she spells "jonkunu" as according to "nza (Ko) 'world, universe' + a 'of' + kunu ~ nkunu (Ko) 'ancestors, spirits" (224).

12   The Cowhead mask can be regarded as the first masquerade wearing "oxhorns" and referred to as "Jonkonnu" (Ryman 1984: 17). Ryman describes the context of African symbology related to this figure: "In Africa, horned figures have been linked to the strength and power invested in important personages by virtue of their superior physical, political or supernatural attributes. They have most commonly been associated with warriors, funerals, initiation/circumcision ceremonies, and secret societies" (17).

set girls were strictly segregated by skin phenotype into brown, black and several shades between (Ryman 1984a: 19) and wore elaborate costume as has been documented by Isaac Mendes Belisario's 1836 sketches (see below). Also the appearance of the "House Jonkonnu," as documented, commented on the social power hierarchy. As Ryman denotes:

The 'house' bears scalloped pillars in imitation of the wooden supports used for balconies. This was a common feature of West Indian architecture and specifically of the Great House which became a symbol of power, privilege and oppression. [...] The dance and house filled with puppets (sailors, soldiers, slaves at work, etc.) embodied many of the characters and elements of nineteenth century Jamaican society and could be viewed as a microcosm of the larger, more elaborate, Jonkonnnu/Masquerade tradition that was emerging (1984a: 20).

The Red Set Girls and Jack-in-the-Green, drawn at Christmas 1836, in Kingston, Jamaica by Isaac Mendes Belisario lithographed by Duperly in 1837 (rpt. in: Nunley/Bettelheim 1988: 46).

House John-Canoe drawn by Isaac Mendes Belisario at Christmas 1836 and lithographed by Duperly in Kingston, Jamaica in 1837 (rpt. in: Nunley/Bettelheim 1988: 48).

The so-called "Actor Groups" were also part of that newly emerging tradition. They performed excerpts from Shakespeare, which subsumed "all with the recurring theme of a fight over a female, a duel to the death, quickly followed by a 'wild' dance, in which even the resurrected dead were enticed to join" (Ryman 1984a: 21). The death and resurrection theme of British plays did of course echo the similar motif in Myal practice so that a sociologically empowering blend of both sources might likely have occurred.

Koo-Koo or Actor Boy John-Canoe, drawn by Isaac Mendes Belisario, Christmas 1836 in Kingston, Jamaica and published by Duperly in 1837 (rpt. in: Nunley/Bettelheim 1988: 47).

As Wynter has outlined, West African resurrection rites transformed not only the deceased for whom they were held, but also the dancing practitioners. Myal dance became "a war ritual, and extension of the 'martial dances' danced at funerals, of the binding force of ancestor worship" (1970: 41). When in 1774 laws against Obeah and Myal were passed, Jonkonnu as the more secular – allegedly merely entertaining and therefore harmless – practice became obviously more favored than the other two in the colonizer's eyes. Furthermore, as the early Actor Groups relied heavily on mime, music and dance, a connection to the Egungun traveling companies, has also been hypothesized (Ryman 1984a: 21). It is therefore important to realize that despite the ongoing creolization process, Jamaican Jonkonnu rather reinforced its African elements than those of the European carnival/mummers tradition.

By 1825 Patterson distinguishes two schools of Jonkonnu's alleged "amusement:" the one tending towards the more African aesthetic of the "goombay" drum and dance, the other, more European in style, employing fiddle and reel to accompany Scottish dances.[13] Particularly, Christmas with the free floating 'John Canoe' masqueraders and set girl processions became an important outlet to level the social power imbalance. Slaves performed under the name of one of their more prominent white masters and thus stood suddenly on comparatively equal ground. Even if only for that exclusive moment of time, the "possession of the great house" generated a transgressive function, which Cynric R. Williams historical comment elucidates. He states:

Indeed a perfect equality seemed to reign among all parties; many came and shook hands with their master and mistress, nor did the young ladies refuse this salutation any more than the gentlemen. The merriment became rather boisterous as the punch operated, and the slaves sang satirical philippics against their master, communicating a little free advice now and then; but they never lost sight of decorum, and at last retired, apparently quite satisfied with their saturnalia, to dance the rest of the night at their own habitations (1826: 22-23).

Unsurprisingly, Jonkonnu's satirical punch-lines and role reversals became more and more important to the slaves' struggle for emancipation. As Sam Sharpe's 1831 Christmas rebellion, as well as the necessity of "Christmas Guards" to prevent the increasing danger of insurrections had shown, Jonkonnu performatively rehearsed direct rebellion and unrest, quite unlike European carnival, which rather restores than undoes its order by the end of the feast.[14]

---

13 This differentiation parallels that of Judith Bettelheim, who in her research of Jamaican Jonkonnu has distinguished between "fancy dress," i.e. European-derived and "rural," i.e. African-derived forms (see Bettelheim 1988). Gumbay drums, which are seminal to Jonkonnu, also feature in Yoruba Egungun plays (Wynter 1970: 39). Ryman refers to Gumbay as "the purest form of the once popular Myal dance, when she explains: "In Jamaica, the term Gumbay and its variants (Gumbi, Gumbay, Gumbahi, Guma, Goumbay) have been separately and collectively associated with a drum, a herb, removal of 'witchcraft' or 'sorcery' and a dance-music form linked to traditional Jamaican religious-healing practices, formerly associated with Myal" (1984b: 54).
14 Born in Montego Bay, Sam Sharpe became the leader of the late 1820s strike movement to lay down labor on the estates to call for salary and freedom. Between 25,000 to 40,000 slaves withdrew from work and fought for freedom during the "Western Liberation Uprisings" which lasted from 28 Dec. 1831 until end of March 1832 (Sherlock 212-221).

Religious and recreational practices formed the backbone of African Jamaican resistance and they should later on become the dominant expression of Jamaica's African Creole cultural identity. Since these practices arose from the slaves' folk culture, the folk-cultural domain assumed particular historical relevance, because it marked the beginning of the decolonization process and independence movement. African survivals in the guise of an adapted Myalism thus chaperoned Emancipation and the spirit of *marronage* guided likewise the 1865 Morant Bay rebellion. Ultimately, grassroots culture ushered right into Jamaican national independence. From then on, folk integrity, music and dance should increasingly be identified as Jamaica's new national icons, when dance theatre launched African Caribbean folklore onto the world stage.

Pioneers of Caribbean Dance Theatre

Beryl McBurnie (1914-2000)

In the programme brochure of a 1982 exhibition at Jamaica's National Library titled "Our heritage in Dance" the beginning of the Caribbean dance movement is credited to two women pioneers:

The 1940s represented the turning point in the performing arts of dance in Jamaica. The combined influence of people like Beryl McBurnie and Lavinia Williams, as well as the work of the YWCA and Jamaica Welfare, in bringing folk dances to the fore, all resulted in a new attitude to dance: Dance was now regarded as an instrument of self expression and self identity and as such should reflect the new national consciousness that had emerged among Jamaicans.

While U.S. born Lavinia Williams, a disciple of Katherine Dunham, had studied Haitian folklore, Beryl McBurnie, was a Trinidadian dancer who would become known as the Caribbean's "mother of dance." Though Katherine Dunham and Lavinia Williams have both credited McBurnie for her influence on their technique and U.S. modern dance in general, McBurnie has been even more influential on Ivy Baxter and the founding of Jamaica's National Dance Theatre Company. Therefore, in order to review the history of Caribbean modern dance theatre, one needs to start with McBurnie's early dance beginnings.

Beryl McBurnie had developed an early interest in Caribbean folk dance, when as a child she took part in a variety of extracurricular activities such as theatre and concerts. Discontented with the colonial education system of her local school, she soon advocated the need of a more local training. As Michael Anthony in a commemorative article for *Trinidad Express* described McBurnie's pioneering attitude:

Although Beryl was only a child when she began dancing, she apparently seemed to know exactly what she was doing and where she was going – or rather, where she wanted to go. For example, it took a lot out of her to perform the Scottish reels, jigs, and other British folk dances that the teacher at her school, Tranquility Girls', placed before them all the time. Those dances might have been delightful, but to her mind they were just a little irrelevant. For apart from their beauty of movement, they gave expression of a personality and experience that were not her own. What she hankered after was expressing, in dance, the way of life and aspects of the history of her own environment (2000: 20-21).

McBurnie's vision of Caribbean dance was consequently to be "expressive of the emotions of the folk" and set up against the prevalent "admiration of things British" of her time, when "anything smacked of Africa was regarded as belonging to the jungle" (Anthony 2000: 20-21). Supported by Carlton Comma and folklorist Andrew Carr, McBurnie studied Trinidadian folklore in order to build her indigenous dance repertoire. Growing up in the Protestant neighborhood of Woodbrook, McBurnie's father aspired to a career in medicine for his daughter, who came to attend Columbia Teacher's College in New York in 1938. Once in New York, however, McBurnie resigned from medicine and took further classes in dance and theatre arts instead. She studied at the Academy of Allied Arts with Charles Weidman and José Limon as well as at Columbia with Martha Graham and Elsa Findlay and also taught classes in Caribbean dance herself while she was there (Creque-Harris 1991: 91).

McBurnie returned to Trinidad in 1940, where she and her dance troupe presented the show *A Trip Through the Tropics*. The performances consisted of classical as well as folk interpretations in order to adhere to the still prevalent colonial tastes of her time (Creque-Harris 1991: 91). The following year McBurnie left her company to the supervision of Boscoe Holder, Geoffrey Holder's older brother and a talented dancer and painter in his own right. That way, McBurnie could continue her studies in New York, where she became known as "La Belle Rosette" and started a highly promising career to which a series of photographs by Carl van Vechten at the New York Public Library of Performing Arts still testifies. McBurnie's captivating beauty of expression on these still photographs speaks of her stage presence at the time. In 1942 Pearl Primus also took classes at the New Dance Studio, where the born Trinidadian soon joined McBurnie's company in a series of concerts (Hillsman 1984: 20-25). The program of one of these held at the Y.M.H.A. that same year consisted of an interesting mix of different folk forms not only from Trinidad, but also Haiti and Cuba. McBurnie's dancers introduced Vodou and Shango rituals as well as those of the Trinidadian Shouters, a Cuban Marriage ceremony, folk songs, calypso and drum rhythms to their New York audiences (Foulkes 2002: 92-94). McBurnie's New York based company continued to give performances at several of the New York colleges. As Alvin Ailey Dance Company acknowledged in a 1978 tribute, McBurnie's influence on the development of U.S. modern dance expression counts her among "one of the three extraordinary Black women who have had a profound influence on American dance," i.e. next to Katherine Dunham's and Pearl Primus' pioneering choreography of the time.[15]

Yet, even though Columbia University had offered McBurnie a permanent teaching position, she could not desert her island and people for too long, to whom she had already once returned briefly in 1942. Offered work as dance instructor for the Education Department of Trinidad and Tobago, McBurnie decided to return home for good in 1945. As dance instructor she successfully introduced folk dances to the schools at home and she also managed to assemble further folk material from several of the other Caribbean islands. Her travels took McBurnie to Cayenne, Brazil and Suriname. It was during this period of her own research that she met Earl Leaf, whose *Isles of Rhythm* (1948) is of particular interest for its collection of rare pictures which document some of the folk-based dances as seen at the time.[16] By 1948 then McBurnie had certainly collected more than enough of experience, training, and dance repertoire to eventually found her own dance theatre company.

The official opening of Beryl McBurnie's *Little Carib* Theatre and Dance Company was launched on 25 Nov. 1948. Special guest for the

---

15 "McBurnie: A Great Life," *Trinidad Guardian* 31 March 2000: 1.
16 Creque-Harris suggests that much of the book was in fact influenced by Leaf's collaborative exchange with McBurnie.

festive occasion was African American singer Paul Robeson, who had been touring Trinidad at the time. The foreword of the opening program Talking Drums expresses the inspiring ferment that the *Little Carib* presented to Trinidadian society at the time. Thus, one may read that the *Little Carib* Theatre was hailed for representing an "accomplishment" as well as a "symbol" of the West Indian emancipatory spirit, deeply indebted to the African folk heritage, which had been "brought into these Caribbean islands in the hell-holds of slaveships".[17] Consisting of three parts, the night's dance program opened with "Outlines and Illustrations," featuring McBurnie and her company in what appears from the arrangement to have been modeled on her New York lecture demonstration format.

Each section referred to the history and development of McBurnie's Caribbean movement vocabulary. Starting with *Early Days*, the demonstration illustrated the background of the Caribbean's different ethnic rhythms and influences ("Carib, French, African, English, East Indian") and was suggested to be read by the audience as: "An attribute of man's nature and the foundation of all art." This was followed by *Movement*, which elaborated on different rhythms ("Individual", "Life", "Native and Elements", "Primitive") and *Modern Dance*, which presented the basics teachings of contemporary dance training ("Simple Technique, extensions, contractions and releases..."). The final part "Typical West Indian Rhythms" ended on a Caribbean theme, and the evening concluded with different folk choreographies interpreting ordinary life-scenes ("The Fields", "Market Scene", "Three Peasants"), ritual dances and drumming.[18]

Not only a theatre, but educational center, too, McBurnie's *Little Carib* dance theatre presented an important innovation, which accorded to the prevalent societal debate on independence politics and the emerging West Indies postcolonial nationalism of the time. In his address to McBurnie's opening night, Dr. Eric Williams – future president of independent Trinidad and Tobago – outlined the dance theatre's social significance for the Caribbean context. Dance theatre was lauded as "the job of West Indians" in the sense that McBurnie's original interpretations of West Indian folklore contributed to the West Indies' articulation of independent "inter-nationalism," which Williams defined as the

---

17 "Formal Opening of the 'Little Carib' Thursday November 25, 1948 at 9 p.m." Souvenir Programme 1948/1988 (Kingston: University of the West Indies, Main Library) 3.
18 "Formal Opening of the 'Little Carib'" Souvenir Programme 10-11.

region's "distinctive contribution, not only to the life of our people in the West Indies, but also to the stream of that broad intellectual culture which, the more diversified it is, yet expresses the common humanity of our one, tortured world."[19]

McBurnie had started her theatre in the backyard of her mother's gallery, where she provided a stage for dance and steelband concerts to integrate those marginalized folk expressions into her more conservative neighborhood of strict Protestant upbringing. Molly Ahye described the homely atmosphere at the local gathering point, where "commonfolk rubbed shoulder to shoulder with the elite as the music after a performance became the magic ingredient for mixing" (1983: 49). In dialogue with CLR James and Eric Williams, McBurnie became part of the independence movement of her time. As her country's "ambassadress" of culture, she and the *Little Carib* Dance Theatre Company were sent to England and Canada in order to advocate her island's independent spirit. On her 1951 visit to London McBurnie was applauded. Critic Charles Archibald put her in line with Victor Reid, Edgar Mittelholzer and Derek Walcott as the artistic vanguard of the British Caribbean's "new culture" and advocates for national independence. He wrote:

These artists are proving to be correct what the politicians have been saying for different reasons – that the British Caribbean is not a secondhand Great Britain, or United States, or France, or Spain, or Africa, or India, but a region possessing its own original spirit which has only to be given its freedom to assert itself against all comers (1951: n.p.).

In her London performances McBurnie adhered to the lecture-demonstration format which proved successful in providing her audience with the ethno-historical background information of her dances, which might otherwise have too easily been consumed as mere 'exotica.' As was appreciated by a London correspondent of the *Public Opinion* in 1951:

The lecture-demonstration showed historically the influence of the different cultures upon West Indian folklore. It was brilliantly done. First, Miss McBurnie told the audience something of the origin and social significance of each dance before demonstrating the steps and movements. Starting with the aboriginal peoples of the West Indies – the Arawaks and Caribs, Miss

---

19 "Formal Opening of the 'Little Carib,'" Souvenir Programme 7.

McBurnie took the audience through the period of European conquest and settlement, showing the kind of dances introduced by the early Spaniards, such as the "Castilian"; the French "Beguine"; the British "Jig" as well as contributions in song made by the Portuguese such as the "Fado"; the Indian "Hosein festival", the Chinese and chiefly African influences.[20]

The company performed in a high quality entertainment evening, especially noted for its presentation of the African-Trinidadian Shango ritual. As the same critic concluded:

Miss McBurnie and her young dancers were very good in their rendering of street cries and street rhythms, which brought home to the audience many familiar cries heard in their homelands by street vendors but the significance of which they never before appreciated. The show was therefore not only theatrically entertaining, but anthropologically instructive even to many so-called educated West Indians.[21]

McBurnie's pioneer work in dance had to overcome similar prejudices as prevailed against folk culture and African-derived expressions in general. Her choreography *Shango* helped, however, much to overcome this notion, when it became one of the most critically acclaimed pieces of her repertoire. As Lenore Crawford in her 1958 review of the piece noted:

There was a dedicated feeling about every company member that was not apparent in some of the other numbers, a complete at-oneness with the whole presentation, plus a superb technique that reached a peak rarely equaled in the rest of the program. All these things gave an impact that left this viewer breathless from sheer excitement of a religious kind. Full proof of the force of dancing and the effect it can have was made clear. The choreography and the entire presentation, including magnificently performed music, were something rarely encountered in the finest dance companies (n.p.).

To dance Caribbean cultural folk heritage became apparently such a strong performance that it convinced even those who did not necessarily relate to that bodily memory from their own cultural background.

How much stronger then should prove the impact, when the *Little Carib* Company toured Jamaica, where similar traditions could be

---

20 "W.I. Dancer Takes London By Storm," *Public Opinion*, 17 Mar. 1951: n.p.
21 "W.I. Dancer Takes London By Storm," *Public Opinion*, 17 Mar. 1951: n.p.

found, yet were still largely neglected by the middle class strata of society. Invited to tour Jamaica for the 300-year centennial celebrations in 1955, McBurnie's visit contributed enormously to the mutual exchange of both islands that were not only to join culturally, but also in the short political Federation of 1958.[22] Inspiration from that side was very much expected, as one Jamaican *Gleaner* critic wondered about the "new impetus" her visit might provide for the local dance scene in terms of a cultural reawakening of "folk memory."[23] McBurnie's Jamaican programme *Gayap* presented the format of suites. Ahye describes those as "the exploration of themes for greater cohesion and substance" with an effort to combine "more elements into expanded synopses, which provided wider and more satisfying vehicles for expression" (Ahye 1983: 44). Apparently, there had been less of that structure in McBurnie's previous works. The show was much praised so that McBurnie returned to Jamaica only two years later, when she was engaged to teach dance at the summer school of the University College of the West Indies.

Her Jamaican dance workshop was attended by young student Derek Walcott, who undertook his studies there at the time. McBurnie's summer school should influence not only this meanwhile internationally renowned Nobel Literature laureate, but a whole generation of future Caribbean artists and intellectuals. Through Caribbean dance patterns, McBurnie introduced her pupils to the specificity and richness of West Indian expressiveness in gesture, lore, rhythm and rhyme. Moreover, her dance lessons provided this new generation of Caribbean intellectuals with a fuller understanding and appreciation of their multicultural heritage.[24] McBurnie's dances taught much more than only a few folk steps: in fact, she gave ethical advice in cultural diversity, artistic freedom and the power of expression as well. She knew though that many of her own class upbringing were still quite intimidated to wholly embrace and accept that diverse source of self-identity. As she started a lecture demonstration at the University College with the following rhetorical demand: "A multicoloured source of material exists from which we can tap, from time to time, programmes for theatrical presentation. The question is: are we prepared to accept what is originally ours, and not be afraid because it is simple and given to cottons

---

22 McBurnie, *Dance Trinidad Dance*, Booklet, n.d. 6.
23 "Spirit of the past with art of modern theatre," *Daily Gleaner* 14 Aug. 1955: n.p.
24 McBurnie, *Dance Trinidad Dance* 5-7.

and not silk? Or are we afraid because most of the vital expression of our folk material is of African origin?"[25]

McBurnie's impact on the Caribbean and, in fact, not only the Caribbean but internationally, too, was based on her vision of dance theatre as being the most appropriate representational tool to promote her culture and its development. Her anthropological research lent profound insight to each folk step in her repertoire, because it testified to a particular cultural tradition. As she explained:

> Dance is the focus in line given to a particular experience. West Indians must continue to draw on the manifold cultural influences that have gone into our historical and cultural make-up and to reinterpret them in the light of our own experiences. In this way we can make a worthwhile contribution to a West Indian way of life. Our aim should be towards creating and maintaining a universal standard. We must ensure that the artistic contribution of West Indian people should be of such calibre that it will flow naturally into the broad stream of universal culture, expressive of the common humanity of our one world.[26]

McBurnie did much to enhance that vision in her career as dance choreographer and educator of those early days. As Mollie Graham in her review of the Company's performance at Canada's annual Stratford Festival in 1958 remarked: "If there is one thing that Stratford theatregoers learned Wednesday evening, it is that there is a culture and talent in places other than Canada, Great Britain and the United States."[27] McBurnie's success thus rebutted the old time colonialist prejudice and achieved for the arts, what Dr. Eric Williams and Norman Manley fought for in politics: namely, the discovery and nurturing of a positive Caribbean self-understanding. As H.O.B. Wooding has described this stance on behalf of the *Little Carib*'s symbolical value, the company stood for the West Indies' postcolonial "self-discovery" and "love of our Islands, of our fields and flowers, of our wit and wisdom, of our pleasures and pastimes, of our sense and significance."[28]

---

25 Beryl McBurnie, "West Indian Dance," *The Artist in West Indian Society*, ed. Errol Hill (Kingston: University of the West Indies, Extra-Mural Studies, n.d.) 51.
26 McBurnie, "West Indian Dance" 54.
27 Mollie Graham, "Audience Is Delighted Here At Debut of Carib Dancers," *Beacon Herald* 18 Jul. 1958: n.p.
28 "Formal Opening of the 'Little Carib,'" Souvenir Programme 17.

La Belle Rosette, circa 1940s. Photography by Earl Leaf (rpt. in: Leaf 1948: 175).

Despite such love and adoration, McBurnie's Company remained, however, bound to the confinements of a largely volunteer effort. Insufficient financial support, lack of an appropriate theatrical space, and time for training and developing a more sophisticated technique slowly eroded the Company's promising beginnings. Dancers coming from different professions in life ("civil servants, teachers, commercial clerks and the like") could not always make the necessary time, even though they were extremely committed to their art form.[29] When McBurnie was awarded the due respect for her accomplishments in dance by Alvin Ailey Company in 1978 as one of the three influential "dames of black dance," her own beloved country could not provide the necessary funding to meet her challenging demands. The *Little Carib* was neither rebuilt nor financially supported as one of Trinidad's prime educational facilities. Yet, the seeds were sown and growing elsewhere in the Caribbean – Jamaica, McBurnie's befriended island of former federation.

---

29 McBurnie, *Dance Trinidad Dance* 6.

Ivy Baxter (1923-1993)

Born in 1923, Ivy Baxter was a Jamaican physical education teacher with a training in ballet and modern dance of the London Sigurd Leeder School, who became the first appointed dance officer of Norman Manley's Social Welfare Commission in the 1950s and later on renowned as the pioneer of Jamaican pre-Independence dance theatre. While classical ballet had been the only dance taught in the 1930s, Baxter's memoirs recall that local ballet teachers Herma Dias and Hazel Johnston had already made slight attempts at integrating folk tunes and gestures into their dances as a result of the island's "awakening of arts" (Baxter 1970: 288). Jamaican ballet thus sought to integrate popular elements from "street meetings, dances and religious activities," which leading Jamaican comedians Louise Bennett and Ranny Williams had already successfully integrated in their Pantomime sketches (Baxter 1970: 291). As a pupil of Hazel Johnston, it seems that Baxter took her teacher's words seriously, when she started to pursue her own dance career. In her official position as a young adjudicator for Jamaica Welfare, Baxter received her first personal introduction to African Jamaican folk forms. Describing her early work as dance officer, she comments on the significance of festival for the Jamaican dance theatre context:

An important feature of the Jamaica Welfare work was the festival which took place at the end of a term or year of work in a village or town. Here, in gaily decorated school rooms or under plaited coconut boughs, groups would display handiwork, preserves, and most important of all, perform Jamaican folk material, song and dance. Sometimes there were performing festivals limited to solo singing, singing by choirs, plays, choral speaking, Jamaican folk songs, and traditional dances, or dances composed on Jamaican folk themes. Eliminations would take place far and wide in the parishes in the adjoining hill country villages. It was by this means that the author began to learn about folk material when called, barely out of high school, to help judge these performances (1970: 94).

As part of Manley's community outreach work Jamaica Welfare engaged in physical education as a means to compensate at least for some of the social unrest caused by the 1930s Depression. In co-operation with the Canadian Y.W.C.A. classes in creative dance were taught. Phyllis Stapells and Bretta Powels, two Canadian physical education teachers, came to the island, where their innovative dance classes would challenge the local conception of classical dance. Due to their influence creative dance was slowly adapted from English country to Jamaican local tastes as this compositional approach "allowed the inherent movement style of Jamaicans to come through" (Baxter 1970: 296). According to Baxter, their teachings were also starting to interest people, who would have refrained from classical ballet because of their age or body physique (1970: 296).

Baxter founded her own company – called *Ivy Baxter Dance Group* – in 1950. In her early choreography she made a point in presenting stage dances with Jamaican themes and movement patterns, to which she had been introduced via her experience as dance officer.[30] Baxter had just founded her own company though, when she was offered a British Council scholarship to attend dance lessons at the London Sigurd Leeder School of European Ballet for one year. So Baxter – like McBurnie before her – left her company to someone else's devices, namely, Herma Dias' supervision, while she herself started dance class at the Leeder School in 1950/51. Though Baxter acknowledges Leeder's influence in her memoirs, it is regrettably not very much elaborated on. Judging from her later work as well as from the Jamaican dance theatre aesthetics that were to be developed after her, it seems quite evident though that Leeder's reforming approach fitted neatly into the Jamaican sensibility and political activism of the time.

Leeder's liberal approach to dance as an art form had developed from the German expressionist school of dance. Collaborating with Kurt Jooss (1901-78) from 1924 until 1947, Leeder became the co-founder of the famous German Folkwangschule in Essen (1927) and later – fleeing from the oppressive Nazi regime, both Jooss and Leeder were forced to emigrate to England – the Jooss Leeder School of Dance in Dartington Hall, Devon (1934) (Müller 2001: 119-136). Their schools followed the teachings of Rudolf Laban and to some extent the aesthetics of Mary Wigman. Focusing on the individual experience of movement, the dancer's own creative intuition was regarded as more important than the strict adherence to the traditional balletic movement canon. In that sense, "German Dance" as it was called for some time, appeared to be quite open to local re-inventions all over the world. As Jooss' creative "credo" of 1932 announced:

---

30 "Our Heritage in Dance," Exhibition Program.

Wir glauben an den Tanz als eine unabhängige und autonome Form des Theatres, eine Kunst, die nicht durch das gesprochene Wort ersetzt werden kann; seine Sprache ist die ausdrucksvolle Bewegung des menschlichen Körpers in reiner und stilisierter Form. Unsere Anstrengungen gelten vor allem dem theatralischen Tanz, den wir als die fruchtbarste Synthese von hoher dramatischer Ausdruckskraft und reinem Tanz betrachten. Wir streben nach einer Tanzkunst und einer Form der Choreographie, die gleichermaßen auf den Theorien und der Praxis des Neuen Modernen Tanzes und jenen des traditionellen klassischen Balletts aufbaut. Die Basis unserer Arbeit ist, den äußerst weitgespannten und umfassenden Bogen allen menschlichen Empfindens und Handelns in allen Phasen der unbegrenzten Wege sichtbar zu machen. Durch Konzentration auf das Wesentliche kommen wir zu unseren Tanzformen (in: Regitz 1996: 453-454).

We believe in dance as an independent and autonomous form of theatre, an art, which cannot be substituted by the spoken word; its language is the expressive movement of the human body in pure and stylized form. Our efforts concern primarily the theatrical dance, which we consider as the most fruitful synthesis of high dramatic expression and pure dance. We strive for a dance art and form of choreography, which likewise build on theories and practice of the New Modern Dance and those of traditional ballet. The basis of our work consists in making visible the uttermost widest and encompassing arch of all human emotion and action in all phases of their unlimited ways. Through concentration on the essential we arrive at our dance forms.[31]

When Sigurd Leeder decided to found his own school in London in 1947, he developed a method of dance training, which focused on the individual personality and expression of the dancer, whom he sought to raise as a self-assured artist. The experience of movement was still at the center of his teachings ("Die Lebendigkeit einer Bewegung gibt dieser Leuchtkraft, nicht die Korrektheit der Ausführung."/"The vivacity of movement makes it shine, not the correctness of execution."), yet colors (he had been known for his excellent stage decors and drawings), form, music and rhythm were considered of equal importance.

The lessons at the Leeder School consisted of dance technique, choreutics and eucinetics. As Baxter recalls her own education there, it focused on the parameters of "force, space and time" as well as "dance notation, devised by Laban; technique of dance; choreutics, the study of the use of space; eukinetics, the study of the quality of movement; and dance composition" (1970: 299). For her, Leeder training "enabled the

---

31 Translation by the author.

student to begin to see the world of movement in a new light" (1970: 299). Leeder's focus on movement as expression of self-identity was indeed an inspiration to many of his pupils. As Erika Ackermann has pointed out, Leeder's "harmony-teaching" ("Harmonielehre") freed and encouraged his students to look for their own way of movement and its appropriate form. Thus, he helped and encouraged his dancers to find and express their individual self through the medium of dance (Müller 2001: 10).

Leeder's interest in elaborate dance theatre started early through the influence of his deaf-mute play-mate Anna with whom he had discovered a secret code of danced expression. Since music was unimportant to the girl, Leeder made an effort in designing marvelous costume, gesture and mime to entertain his friend. He explains how this early beginning came to influence his later art:

Von diesem Spiel geblieben ist mir die Freude an der Bewegung und der Drang zum Theatrespielen, Werke zu schaffen, die Träger meiner inneren Gesichter sind und sie artgerecht einzukleiden. Unser Spiel bedurfte keiner Geldmittel und die späteren ernsteren Spiele hatten meistens nur sehr beschränkte Mittel zur Verfügung, und gerade die Einschränkung hat mich immer wieder angespornt und meine Fantasie zu immer neuen Mitteln greifen lassen, um schöne Wirkung aus dem fast Nichts zu erzielen. Ich weiß, dass meine Schüler aus den armen Ländern ganz besonders von dieser technischen Seite, die neben der tänzerischen Arbeit durch Beispiele gelehrt wurde, viel Anregung mit nach Hause nahmen (in: Müller 2001: 11).

What remained from this game is the joy of movement and the urge to play theatre, create works which bear my inner faces and to dress them properly. Our play did not need money and the later plays did often times only have very limited financial support; and precisely this limitation challenged my imagination time and again to make use of ever new means to achieve beautiful impression from almost nothing. I know that my pupils from the poorer countries took home many ideas particularly from this technical side, which was taught by examples beside the dance work.[32]

Leeder's notion of a "poor dance theatre" so to speak could easily be adopted by the Jamaican dance theatre movement on Baxter's return.

Seeing "movement in a new light" then, Baxter was prepared to reassess her country's rich kinaesthetic repertoire in terms of a visionary

---

32 Translation by the author.

form of Jamaican dance theatre. The mission statement of her company proclaimed to "widen the knowledge and experience of its members in dance" by developing an "idiom which would suitably and adequately give artistic expression, in keeping with life and culture of the Caribbean" (Baxter 1970: 305). Collaboration with other Caribbean dance companies, regular training, research and investigation as well as dance theatre productions were also part of that agenda. While Baxter's solid training in modern dance formed the base of her approach, it was, however, for the Jamaican folklore to refine her emerging technique. Baxter explains:

[...] the visits paid to the countryside of Jamaica in company with the early Social Welfare Officers to see and judge folk dances of Jamaica, which were being resuscitated and encouraged, contributed to my attempts to portray the spirit of Jamaica in dance. [...] I was destined to begin by creating dances and letting the research come afterwards. [...] had I known then, as I now know, the extent and depth of Jamaican folklore, I might have been afraid to start. [...] When I began, I asked of many people and was told that there were no Jamaican dances, no, not one, just a little "shay, shay" and "bram" on a Saturday night. At that time, in the mid 1940s, I had not seen Pocomania, which is now the most viewed of all the branches of religious dance. I had seen quadrille once or twice. How well do I remember coming upon the Cumina music, for the first time. Moore was doing research on African survivals in the parish of St. Thomas and as he and his colleague and I listened to the playback of tapes, I could not believe that this was Jamaican music. I was sure that he was playing material gathered in Africa. I could not catch the words – the dialect was too rapid; I could not sort out the drum beat, it was too complicated; the tunes were entirely unfamiliar. When I was actually taken to watch the Cumina memorial ceremony from eight o'clock one night to six the next morning, then my real Jamaican eyes were opened (1970: 298).

In her creative dances, Ivy Baxter brought Jamaican folk culture to the urban middle class that under colonialism had lost any meaningful connection with this part of their African history and heritage. The Baxter Company's repertoire consisted thus of three types of dances: 1. "arranged and reconstructed folk dances of Jamaica and the West Indies", 2. "creative and dramatic ballets based on folk tunes" and 3. "dance compositions general in theme" (Baxter 1970: 308).

The company performed at national and civic occasions, at shows for the Ministry of Education as well as at festivals, and later independence shows and at the National Stadium in front of "royalty and distinguished guests" (Baxter 1970: 309). Just as Baxter's eyes had been opened, she was to open those of the middle class and future generations of Jamaicans to come. The distance between city and rural lifestyle was enormous in terms of a lack of mutual understanding. When Baxter first presented her shows to Kingston town audiences, her company was met with "ridicule, distaste, and sometimes fear," because of the prevalent deprecation of folklore as low culture superstition (Baxter 1970: 298). To further and enhance the understanding and appreciation of Jamaican roots culture as significant part of the new national consciousness became therefore one of the primary tasks of Baxter's dance theatre company.

Baxter's innovative approach in creative dance enhanced the emergence of Jamaica's new public image of the time, when folk items were all of a sudden no longer limited to the secluded countryside, but became increasingly apparent in official state presentations. Baxter, for example, recalls the 1953 Military Tattoo in Kingston:

The Tattoo of 1953 formally admitted Jamaican folklore as part of the acceptable material for display to the public of Jamaica as a whole, in a government and military financed venture, to mark an official occasion. Before that, civic celebrations were characterized by sedate and patriotic songs by school children and by military displays. Burnett Webster, actor and designer, produced this section of the program with Ranny Williams, folklorist, who brought revival cult people from the West End of Kingston to lead the folk singing. Dance was supplied by the Ivy Baxter Dance Group, performing a dance, "Fishing by Night," depicting the scene of men with torches catching crayfish by the river. Original music for this dance was by Oswald Russell, a brilliant Jamaican performer and composer. Costumes and properties, designed by Burnett Webster, were colorful and distinctive. The motif of the decor was 18th century Jamaican with enormous multicoloured umbrellas as the main stage properties. This was followed by a folklore presentation by the Ivy Baxter Dance Group for the visit of the Queen and Duke of Edinburgh at King's House (1970: 104-105).

Obviously, by the mid 1950s Jamaica was prepared for the political change that the arts movement had successfully been launching into. By displaying Jamaican grassroots culture, a powerful statement of cultural independence was made that even in the presence of the British Queen and Duke was meant to tell of an African tradition standing strong and ready to take over.

Remembered today as the "quiet advocate of identification and integration," Baxter's significance for Jamaican dance theatre cannot be underestimated (Mock Yen 2001: 7). Through her international travels – she had been to schools in London, New York and Toronto – Baxter soon came to realize the importance of a Pan-Caribbean interconnectedness. More importantly, she also learned that while in Jamaica she had been a privileged member of the middle class, she was elsewhere simply perceived as "a black woman from the Caribbean – not apricot – not cinnamon, but Black," which then made her "open to issues of identity for native Jamaicans, and integration in terms of the Caribbean" (Mock Yen 2001: 9). By bringing Jamaican "history to life", Baxter's dance company not only provided the ground for meaningful self-expression, but she also managed through her dances to empower a whole society (Mock Yen 2001: 20; 14). It was thanks to her influence that the Jamaican education agenda was redefined and that, later on, dance and music became promoted as developmental tools. Dance in primary education was thus to nurture a deeper self-respect among Jamaican children, who via their own drums and dances should learn to truly connect to their ancestral heritage as well as apprehend such key skills as "collaboration, good timing, and commitment" (Mock Yen 2001: 17).

Baxter's dance compositions outlined what should in the following generation develop into the Jamaican dance theatre aesthetic. Mock Yen recalls four of her works as being "narrative in construct": 1. *Passing Parade*, 2. *Rat Passage* (1954), 3. *Village Scene*, and 4. *Pocomania* (Mock Yen 2001: 20-21). While the first explored the movement of everyday life and bustle on King Street, the second dealt with the more political issue of increased economic migration to England in the 1930s. The third and the fourth dance piece experimented more directly with Baxter's assembled folk material. As Mock Yen describes:

"Village Scene" was an enactment of how the folk laboured, loved and passed their leisure. Ivy herself danced the poignant role of a Mother near breaking point, burdened by child bearing and rearing within parameters of deprivation. [...] Pocomania, a ritualistic state of becoming a 'little mad'. We laughed at the idea of spirit possession until we who had mastered Leeder and other recognized dance techniques, succumbed to the hypnotic rhythm of the Frats Quintet singing and chanting from deep in their souls to the accompaniment and ancestral hegemony of the drums (2001: 21).

Ivy Baxter, rpt. in Sun over the West Indies by The Jamaica Company of Dancers and Singers, Howard University Intercultural Exchange, Performance Program 1961.

Baxter's choreography, furthermore, made use of simple props that derived from her knowledge of Jamaican grassroots culture: scarves and cutlass, for example, came to represent the female/male principle, while the circle and line divided movement into progression and continuity (Mock Yen 2001: 22). However, ballet was not entirely abandoned, but maintained as a worth wile technical exercise. Members of the Baxter Group were therefore also sent to attend Madame Soohi's local Ballet School (Baxter 1970: 294).

Perceived as "the vital force" to Jamaica's local dance scene, Baxter's talent and inspiration, hence, produced the cradle of Jamaica's upcoming dance theatre success. Invited to Howard University's 1961 Spring Festival, many of Baxter's former acolytes joined forces in presenting a full scale performance of Jamaican folk dance, lore and song under the common denominator of *The Jamaica Company of Dancers and Singers*. The program *Sun Over the West Indies* consisted of altogether thirteen performance acts, which presented the peak of Jamaica's talent in the performing arts at the time. In fact, many of these performers presented the core of artists to join forces in the founding of Jamaica's

National Dance Theatre Company the following year.[33] Presented were original music compositions by Mapletoft Poulle & Orchestra as well as the Frats Quintett, choreography by Ivy Baxter, Rex Nettleford, and Eddy Thomas, as well as folk tales narrated by the famous Miss Lou, alias Louise Bennett. While Baxter's own company continued up until 1967, her off-spring Eddy Thomas, Rex Nettleford, Alma Mock Yen and Joyce Campbell soon were to start their own creative dance companies. In this respect, Baxter and her later disciples should continuously pursue McBurnie's pioneering effort in their own Jamaican ways (Mock Yen 2001: 27).

From Sacred to Secular: The Institutionalization of Jamaican Dance Theatre

Re-inventing African Caribbean Ritual through Modern Dance

The body or corporeal images provide an insight into the psychic condition of the enslaved individual. The body – like the mind in the world of the slave – is numbed, impotent, inert, ultimately someone else's possession. Consequently, self-assertion is inevitably linked to a sensuous physical presence, to an active body, a standing 'upright and free,' in the words of Césaire's *Cahier*. Freedom for the enslaved is seen in terms of unrestricted physical movement (Glissant 1989: 8).

As has been shown in the preceding chapter, Beryl McBurnie and Ivy Baxter pioneered the Caribbean dance movement. Yet, in fact, the two had already met before McBurnie's visit to Jamaica at the first Caribbean Arts Festival (Carifesta) in Puerto Rico 1952 (Baxter 1970: 301). Organized by American dance scholar Lisa Lekis this event brought together performing groups from all over the Caribbean islands and had an enormous effect on the region's self-perception (see Lekis 1960).[34] For the first time, people came to realize their cultural commonality, despite the different colonial administrations. In retrospect, the festival

---

33 Compare *Sun Over the West Indies* by the Jamaica Company of Dancers and Singers, dir. by Noel Vaz and Rex Nettleford, Howard University Intercultural Exchange Program 1961.
34 Lekis accounts for several of the Caribbean dance forms she encountered during her research for the festival, yet from today's perspective her ethnographic/dance aesthetic insight into the individual dance traditions appears somewhat limited.

had marked the point of departure for an awakening of Caribbean consciousness in the entire region. Through eye-to-eye contact between the otherwise isolated island populations, dance and music performances easily overcame the colonial language divide in terms of a shared performance heritage that had successfully resisted and survived imperial oppression (Baxter 1970: 302). Astounded by the artistry of Geoffrey Holder and McBurnie's *Little Carib* Dance Company, the impact of Haiti' s Théâtre Folk-Lorique came across as particularly remarkable. As Baxter recalls: "These dancers were the first of their kind that any of us from Jamaica had ever seen. They re-enacted the ceremonies of Damballa, the snake god, complete with candles, fire, and smoke to the stimulation of the terrific drumming of Tiroro, Haiti's virtuoso drummer. Tiroro became a particular friend of the Jamaicans, and it is from him that the art of drum-making revived in Jamaica" (1970: 303-304).

Also Geoffrey Holder admired Haiti's connectedness to the African ancestor pantheon and found the Haitian heritage extremely inspirational, when compared to his home island Trinidad, where "the gods had gone because the English had killed them off" (Dunning 2001: 34). Haiti's proud tradition of being the first independent black republic outside Africa since 1804 lend energy and impetus to spur other Caribbean islands in their emancipatory arts projects (see James 1938). The discovery of the rich variety of African Caribbean folk forms thus shaped the development of modern dance in the region, when pioneers of the Caribbean's dance theatre movement started to develop their own dance techniques.

Assembling and exchanging Caribbean dance vocabulary from the islands' folkloric heritage, McBurnie and Baxter blended religious ritual with their training in modern dance. Similar to McBurnie's *Shango*, Baxter's *Pocomania* was the first Jamaican choreography to experiment with such movement vocabulary. As the dancers appropriated the ritualistic steps, Baxter, however, soon realized the need to abstract and find an artistic filter to capture the essence, yet not to perform the ritual proper in order to avoid spiritual possession on stage. She recalls that experience from her company's Puerto Rican performance:

Pocomania was based on the rhythm and ritual of the same name, and was accompanied by the Frats Quintet. In this dance, it was originally planned to have the drums stop just before the time of 'possession,' which took place in silence, just as it had taken place in the meeting which I had watched. I had never danced in this number in its entirety. However, I discovered that the same effect was produced in the dancers as took place in the real worshippers. This was not revealed until a year or so later. Many of the dancers said 'I felt light. I felt as if my head was growing, but I was ashamed to tell you.' Since then this dance has never been performed as it was in Puerto Rico. The ending was changed to prevent this happening; and, thereafter, *Pocomania* was never rehearsed 'fullout' (1970: 302).

Working with ritual movements became particularly significant, because the theatre dance innovation coincided with the Trinidadian and Jamaican quest for postcolonial self-definition. Sharing similar cultural performances, audience members from different islands were knit together by their common kinaesthetic response to the African-derived rhythms and movement patterns. Expressing one's cultural sensibility via dance thus became a powerful articulation of self-identity that directly communicated to Caribbean audiences.

In her book *Golden Heritage: The Dance in Trinidad and Tobago*, Molly Ahye describes this kinaesthetic appeal of Caribbean dance, which addresses mind and feelings as well as dimensions of spirituality (1978: 17). She furthermore characterizes Caribbean dance theatre as mimetic, because of the kinaesthetic survival of distinct cultural practices, often derived from folk festivals and religious ritual. Caribbean dance thus conveys joy, sorrow, anger, frustration, yet it can also "boost one's morale" as in former pre-/war, -hunting, or initiation context. Also, distinct dances may serve as prayer, supplication and atonement in awe of a Supreme Being. Lastly, many dances will symbolize the veneration of certain life forms, that is, for example, birds and animals; as well as introduce ancestor worship (for example the Big Drum Nation Dances) and the celebration of life, birth, death, and rites of passage (Ahye 1978: 17).

These teachings, while they are to some extent reminiscent of those to be found in modern dance, do, however, primarily rely on the religious foundation of African Caribbean movement patterns. Through the process of artistic abstraction, the sacredness of ritual dance is transferred into staged symbols and metaphors.[35] Ramiro Guerra has described this process for the Cuban context by distinguishing four stages of the theatricalization of folklore. In the first state, folk art

---

35 Joan H. Burroughs in her discussion of Jean-Léon Destiné's staged versions of Haitian Yanvalou introduces the distinction between ritually-derived body postures as "symbolic movement" and staged renderings of possession as "movement metaphor" (1995: 230-241).

serves ritual, recreational and social functions and is primarily utilitarian as, for example, in ceremonial worship and communication with certain deities. Unlike theatrical spectacle, folk art is a processual and vivid form of pleasing the gods. Only in the second stage is this material apprehended mostly in terms of its formal aspects. The musical, dance, literary, and plastic values now lose their original meaning as they are projected towards the new cultural epoch of folk revival. Guerra considers this stage as directly related to the national project, which founds its new identity on these traditional forms. However, in their revived form, these creations have become an entirely independent interpretation of the former folk retention. Following this interpretative revival, the third stage works on the stylization of the folk material, which is profoundly investigated and manipulated so as to develop a theatrical technique. Folk material is now arranged in terms of symmetry/a-symmetry, exposition/development/end, suites, narrative, theme and variation. Lastly, the fourth step can be called the original artistic creation, because – inspired by the national folk material – this innovative form has found and developed its unique style and expression (Guerra 1989: 6-15).

What differentiates Caribbean modern dance theatre thus from its modern progenitors in the U.S. and Europe, is precisely its shared African Creole background in such religious rituals as Vodou, Shango and Revival/Myal. Dance scholars Robert Farris Thompson, Kariamu Welsh-Asante and Brenda Dixon-Gottschild have argued to regard such continuity of religious practice as the foundational source of a common African aesthetic in the New World diaspora (see Thompson 1974; Welsh-Asante 2001; Dixon-Gottschild 1998). Not only do these expressions share certain formal aspects, but they also convey common ethical values and philosophy (Dagel 1999: 7-8). Robert Farris Thompson in his seminal essay "An Aesthetic of the Cool: West African Dance" (1966) first pointed out the following five key elements to be found: 1. "a philosophy of the cool"/"patience and collectedness of mind", 2. "dominance of a percussive concept of performance", 3. "West African dances are *talking dances*," 4. "call-and-response," 5. "moral function of the songs of allusion and the dances of derision" (in: Dagel 1999: 72-86). Melville Herskovits' earlier research in African American studies furthermore distinguished four different types of African retention in the New World: 1. survivals, 2. syncretisms, 3. reinterpretations, and 4. cultural "imponderables" – of which "values and automatic motor patterns" constitute the majority (in: Smith 1965: 25;

35). Of particular interest to the adaptation process of African retention in Caribbean dance theatre is particularly the third, since the notion of "reinterpretation" adheres to the corresponding value of an African aesthetic maintained even in the abstract alteration of the folk/modern blend. Modern dance thus appeared as a particularly fluctuating format which allowed for cultural permeation by African aesthetic traits, which, as will be argued here, proved so highly intriguing to convey the Caribbean's emancipatory project.

Helen Thomas' sociological reading of early American Modern Dance has already pointed out that the form was primarily regarded as an expression of American individualism and non-conformism (see Thomas 1995). The Denishawn School, out of which emerged modern dance giants Martha Graham and Charles Weidman, emphasized the student's natural talents and power of movement, thus allowing for "diversity and individuality of form" (Thomas 1995: 85). Following this aesthetic policy, modern dance mirrored its particular social environment as it derived from the life and circumstance of its immediate time and space. Its prime function was to communicate and relate to the dancers' contemporary experience. Thomas furthermore argues that the emergence of Graham and Weidman was directly related to the impact of the Great Depression and the Jazz Era. Similar to Africanist dance forms, Graham technique was solidly grounded in the earth as expressed in her floor work. She, too, would start from life experience and work through inner emotion to create dance works that would make people think. How much of Graham and other modern dance work had been – consciously or not – influenced by the African Caribbean presence though? In other words, did McBurnie's contribution of Caribbean folk elements add to the development of Graham and Weidman as much as they had influenced her?[36]

As Peter H. Wood hypothesized on the origin of 'primitivst' movement in early modern dance, it might have owed "more than it yet realizes to roots which are black, and southern, and ultimately African" (1988: 8). Bent knees, thrusting hips and pointed elbows were only the more explicit signifiers of that cultural turn, which was in fact "moving closer to the continent of Africa in body movement all the time" (Wood 1988: 8). John O. Perpener, furthermore, characterizes the "New Dance" of the 1930s as: "An artform that was individually expressive, unfet-

---

36 While the influence of Pearl Primus and Katherine Dunham's work has been recently acknowledged, McBurnie's impact appears still somewhat neglected.

tered by prior constraints, and unafraid to comment upon the emotional, psychological, and political concerns of contemporary America [...]" (Perpener 1992: 12-13). Consequently, while modern dance training was not as accessible to African American performers as it should ideally have been, it could not be completely kept from them either. As Perpener claims: "The effect of the sight and the spirit of the new dance could not be closed off as easily as a studio door" (1992: 12-13).

Certainly, the 1930s were not only the time of the Great Depression, high modernism and social upheaval, but also the Harlem Renaissance. This New York based black arts movement was in full swing at the time, propagating a concept of activist art that aimed at the perceptual change of African American identity in demand of full civil rights (Perpener 1992: 38). While the modern dance pioneers' interpretations of African and oriental folk-material blended into the modernist discourse on Primitivism, one needs to keep in mind that African American and Caribbean investigations demonstrated a rather different quality as they, too, melded into the modern form. Whereas modernism's earthbound movements were protesting against classical ballet, they still evolved from – and to some extent also remained within – that Western theatrical tradition. Caribbean dance though was earthbound form the very beginning and all that modern dance in fact achieved, was allowing these ancestral dances entrance onto the Western dominated theatre stage.

In order to gain representational access and undermine cultural hegemony then, modern dance simply presented another strategic tool to articulate African American/Caribbean identity under the guise of an accepted dance theatre tradition. Moreover, since modern dance of the early 1930s was considered a "weapon in the class struggle," as well as a means to "fight for racial justice," this appropriation appeared even the more successful, because revolutionary dance aesthetics matched the political goals and social concerns of the time (Thomas 1995: 107-109). For example, the New York based New Dance Group, which hosted Beryl McBurnie as well as Pearl Primus, had been founded in 1932 as part of the New Deal's Federal Theatre Project. Unlike many other modern dance companies of the time, the New Dance Group actually provided the African American/Caribbean emancipation struggle with a public forum, which – due to its progressive policy and training of African Americans – allowed these artists entrance onto the dance theatre stage (Foulkes 2002: 164).

To conclude, Katherine Dunham and Pearl Primus have repeatedly been heralded for their danced interventions towards African American empowerment. Including Beryl McBurnie and Ivy Baxter in this African American/Caribbean continuum, these women dance pioneers performed not only as beautifully 'exotic' stars – which of course they also were – but more importantly as "political activists fighting for their rightful place in American society" (Foulkes 2002: 168). In this respect, the 1930s and 40s have generally come to be regarded as years of discovery and self-assertion, when African American/Caribbean choreographers started to look into African-derived folk-traditions as material for their dance theatre expression. While this field-based quest was largely an interpretive reinvention for the stage, such performance dance still conveyed much of its social function and background as both were expressions of embodied liberation. Modern Dance was only the mask under which African identity could performatively claim its public legitimacy. As the following brief history of the institutionalization of Jamaican Dance Theatre through Festival, National Dance Theatre Company (NDTC) and the foundation of the Jamaica School of Dance will show, performance dance also became the prime instrument of Jamaica's cultural decolonization process after independence.

Jamaica Festival

By the time of achieving full independence in 1962, Jamaican affiliation with the British Crown had eventually grown obsolete and the (re)invention of national culture and its unifying symbols became paramount on the nation-builders agenda. Not only in regard of the Jamaican people themselves, but also in their relation to the world, an increase in awareness of Jamaican culture became a necessity that was strongly articulated in the Jamaica Festival of 1962, the country's first Independence Celebration. Building on the endeavors of Jamaica Welfare Limited, which Norman Manley had already inaugurated in 1936, Jamaica Festival continued this adult educational organization's early effort, which "aimed to carry to the people a sense of personal ability and a sense of the value of things Jamaican" (Baxter 1970: 93). Ivy Baxter's work as dance officer, for example, was undertaken within this developmental framework.

Functioning as a cultural agent among Jamaica's rural parishes, Jamaica Welfare – which after the first free elections in 1944 became first the Jamaica Social Welfare Commission and then the Jamaican Cultural

Development Commission (JCDC) – gave an administrative frame to what had in fact been an ongoing and lively tradition of rural festivals dating back to at least as early as the turn of the twentieth century. Festival in the Jamaican context meant more than a singular event of mere diversion. As Rex Nettleford has remarked in *Caribbean Cultural Identity*:

> The voluntary participation in the Jamaica Festival movement has the ring of authenticity since it reflects a long tradition of voluntary individual and community collaboration for the public good. This had formed part of the immediate post-slavery rehabilitation exercise in the setting up of Free Villages, and was later utilised through Jamaica Welfare Limited, founded by Norman Manley as a means of mobilising people around to the new national spirit in the late 1930s (2003: 94).

Moreover, as has been demonstrated already, this early mobilization of the cultural grassroots as a source of national development instigated an appreciation of folklore as anti-elitist cultural dynamic in the country's effort towards decolonization and indigenization of Jamaican cultural identity.

As also Sylvia Wynter has pointed out, festival and folk dance can be regarded as the emblem of the Caribbean's cultural self-definition. She claims that the African's survival in the face of transplantation presents "the clearest testimony to the strength and creativity of African cultures" and insists on the importance of publicly appreciating this folk heritage in the wake of Garvey's socio-political and Césaire's more aesthetically oriented Négritude movement (1970: 34). While the Eurocentric vision focussed on the exploitation of natural resources – including human beings – African slaves were caught in an ambivalence, where they would labor yet maintain a close relationship to the earth as farmers of the land. Folk culture thus evolved as "the cultural guerrilla resistance against Market economy" by asserting the slave's dignity and humanity against colonial oppression (Wynter 1970: 36). Emerging from Wynter's proposed dialectic of "plantation and plot" cultural adaptation took consequently place in form of a continuity, which transferred African festival to the Christian calendar. Jamaican society thus developed two societal superstructures: one of "Western civilization," the other of a "grassroots culture" (Wynter 1970: 36).

In line with the above argument, the conscious process of recovering the Caribbean's folk heritage has in fact emerged as a "Caribbean intellectual tradition." As Lloyd King has commented:

The theory Anglophone-Caribbean style is often implicit but certain strands can easily be picked out. If the Revolution did not materialize, one core of possibility had endured. This is what comes to be called the folk, an almost mythical entity in whom a psychodynamics of integrated selfhood survived. The folk stand for all that eluded the corruption of a totalitarian Westernization and the constitution of the folk in an elaborated discursive mode has been one of the accomplishments of the Caribbean intellectual tradition (1996: 11).

By investigating the music and dance of the rural communities, Jamaica's political elite brought the African folk heritage to the forefront of the national consciousness. From the 1962 independence celebration onwards, Jamaica Festival became institutionalized as an annual event. Also, a festival department under the Ministry of Development and Welfare was founded to administratively support its organization, headed by Edward Seaga (Baxter 1970: 106). His idea was to establish festival as a permanent institution to set up "a national stage where Jamaicans from all walks of life would have the opportunity to create their own brand of artistic expression, reflecting their life history and life styles" (in: Sherlock/Bennett 1998: 406). From 1964 until 1974 Michael Manley pursued this cultural development plan further by promoting "cultural growth as an instrument of development policy" in the nation's decolonization process (Nettleford 2003: 68-69). In fact, Jamaica Festival not only nourished such exposure, but also bridged the class division between the social lower and middle strata of society. By publicly appreciating Jamaican "roots culture," imperialist Western distinctions between high and low cultural standards were slowly eroded (Nettleford 2003: 45-46). Nettleford delineates the influence of the folk complex on the cultural process of nation building as follows:

To conceive it [the cultural process] as a manifestation of fragmented segments known as 'high art' and 'folk art' is to perpetuate some of the worst elements of Plantation society where elitist Eurocentrism lords over the collective consciousness of the African-folk and where the Great House stands in contempt of the village plot. Better if the cultural process were seen as a growth process with the source of life beginning in the roots to grow again in a never-ending regenerative process. [...] This on-going re-cycling of effort is the dynamic of the cultural process and has no place for elitism as it is understood in a class-ridden and status-conscious society. [...] It is for cultural development policies then, to bring to the people not only an understanding of the power and necessity of the roots but also a full grasp of their responsibility to nurture those roots so that they can bear fruits to enrich the quality of life through replanting and reproduction (2003: 51).

To conclude, Jamaica festival today integrates several of the island's folk expressions such as local cuisine, fashion, drama, music, dance, and arts/crafts. It still operates largely on the involvement of volunteer engagement, understood as "service to the community" – a concept that has become highly significant for Jamaican cultural development in general, because it institutionalized the revolutionary claim to the African Jamaican folk heritage as legitimate part of the new national identity (Nettleford 2003: 92-93).

Jamaican Cultural Development Commission (JCDC)

Founded by later NDTC member Joyce Campbell, Jamaica's Cultural Development Commission was inaugurated in the early 1960s. An early acolyte of Ivy Baxter, Campbell received her formal dance training under Ivy Baxter in 1951, when she was elected first officer of the Jamaican Festival Commission in 1961. In that position Campbell was responsible for the promotion of folk and traditional dance and its appreciation among the Jamaican people (see Bowen 1980). In the wake of Ivy Baxter's pioneering work, Campbell considered her early field work as the decisive moment for her personal development in dance. She recalls:

I worked for three years before going into the JCDC as dance officer with the Social Development Commission, which had used dance on a community development basis. I was exposed to these traditional folk forms from those early days on, yes. [...] It was finding yourself. For me it was getting to know my country, getting to know my people. [...] So I found my way around the countryside. I learnt about the people. It was an eye-opener, a realization of who I was, what I was, what my country was all about.[37]

Through her work as dance officer Campbell further developed the traditional dance forms – which her work first of all sought to preserve

---

37 Interview with Joyce Campbell 15 Aug. 2003.

as best possible – from their religious and recreational background into a theatre art form. Campbell had taken part in the Caribbean Festival of Arts in San Juan, Puerto Rico in 1952 and Trinidad in 1958 on occasion of the West Indies Federation. She also was among the core members of the later NDTC, who had been invited as *Jamaican Company of Dancers* to Howard University, Washington, D.C. in 1961. In 1978 she furthermore conducted in-depth research with the National Folk Dance Company in Ghana.

The Jamaican Festival continued under the auspices of the JCDC as the conscious effort to bring folk dance to the national level. The JCDC's Jamaican Festival Dance Competition thus started a cultural movement to promote this new self-awareness and development of Jamaican society at the end of colonial rule. Through the festival, dance – which beforehand had been either mere recreation or was restricted to the very few, who had access to ballet or modern dance classes – became widely known and appreciated not only for entertainment, but increasingly for its instruction of discipline, creativity and self-esteem in the communities. The festival helped to identify and delineate the traditional dances, which since 1970 became included in the school curriculum. While dance had always been an island-wide part of Jamaican life, the traditional dances were originally confined to Jamaica's rural areas and differed from parish to parish. Yet, with the arrival of the JCDC's adjudicators in the regional communities, these dances were increasingly exposed to a wider and after forty years nation-wide populace.

Most of the traditional dances were created from those African retentions which date back to the times of slavery. Among the most renowned of these dances are: Queens Party Bruckins, Quadrille, Gumbay, Nago Burro, Gerreh, Tambu, Dinki Mini, Maypole, Jonkonnu, Kumina, Myal, Revival, Poco, and Ring Games. Festival recovered those dances not only to Jamaica's public consciousness, but also from virtual extinction at times. Hence, what was once regarded as marginal came to the forefront of public acknowledgement and awareness. Ultimately, it was through the JCDC and festival that most people actually started to develop a certain pride and feeling for the dignity offered by their African heritage, which for so long had been suppressed under slavery and colonial rule. As Sherlock and Bennett have expressed, "folklore is the living memorial which the people fashioned as their answer to the castles and ruins, their source of healing, recognition of each other as shipmates on the long voyage to nationhood" (1998: 199).

Jamaican folklore as "living memorial" and "source of healing" was thus nourished and kept alive through the new nation's administrative frame. However, also in the development of the creative arts, folklore should become more and more important as the foundation of Jamaica's National Dance Theatre in the same year as independence demonstrates.

The National Dance Theatre Company (NDTC) of Jamaica

To found a national dance theatre company appeared as the logical consequence of Norman and Edna Manley's cultural policy since the 1930s, which had successfully promoted the integration of Jamaican grassroots culture. As has been shown, festival, folk dance, and musical traditions appeared to best represent that cultural shift. Also, Jamaica's Little Theatre Movement (LTM), which Greta and Henry Fowler had founded in 1941, achieved much in terms of such theatrical rehearsal of Jamaican independence. Developing the English Pantomime as a creolized Jamaican genre, Jamaica's acclaimed performer-comedians Louise Bennet, Ranny Williams, and Noel Vaz, first based their sketches on local color, political, and social satire. The genre became highly popular during the 1950s independence movement, when it was celebrated as the country's "genuine folk theatre" (Gloudon 1982: 64). The LTM's pioneering work is important in the dance theatre context, because – apart from organizing school drama festivals – it also offered assistance to emerging artistic talent. Jamaica's annual pantomime served as the country's major artistic training ground not only for actors, but also for upcoming dancers, singers, musicians, choreographers, and stage-designers. Traditionally premiering each Boxing Day, Jamaica Pantomime still attracts thousands of Jamaicans each year and its theatricality has influenced the NDTC's evolving dance theatre aesthetic as much as Jamaican playwrights Dennis Scott and Trevor Rhone.

The link between the Jamaican Cultural Development Commission, Festival, Pantomime and dance theatre was further pursued in the foundation of Jamaica's National Dance Theatre Company under Rex Nettleford and Eddy Thomas, who had both been former dancers with Ivy Baxter's Dance Group. As Sheila Barnett, dance scholar and long time NDTC member has expressed: NDTC members were first of all "a group of citizens committed to nationhood and the development of the cultural expression of their society" (Barnett 1982: 81). Founded in the wake of Jamaica's independence celebrations of 1962, the company's 'birth' date carried particular significance for the NDTC's artistic mission. As Rex Nettleford, co-founder and today's artistic director has expressed, the company's work addressed "questions of identity, of national self-respect, of new nationhood, [and] of freedom" (Nettleford 1969: 29). Touring Canada that same year, the NDTC soon became the young nation's cultural ambassador, just like McBurnie's *Little Carib* Company before them. As Edward Seaga's address to the Stratford Festival audience of 1963 suggests, Jamaican dance theatre was envisioned as the new nation's most beloved representative. He proclaimed:

Jamaica, now in her second year of Independent Nationhood welcomes any opportunity that she may be given to project to the world what have been her achievements, cultural or economic, and what are her dreams and aspirations for the future. The performing arts are an excellent vehicle through which a country can, by the medium of entertainment, present an image to the onlooker through the showcase of dance and song.[38]

Considering the complex colonial heritage, this national task was of course hardly an easy one to fulfill. In their mutual effort to build a uniquely Jamaican dance theatre aesthetic, Rex Nettleford and Eddy Thomas sought to combine the literal with the abstract in order to create a dance technique that should correspond their Jamaican based choreographic theme (Nettleford 1969: 35). As Nettleford has stated in an early interview with *Dance and Dancers* in 1965, their exploration was at first concerned

[w]ith emphasis on training, with emphasis on the exploration of movement for movement's sake, with emphasis on research into the movement patterns of the people in the Caribbean area. To find out if there was some system or a way of moving that could be developed into an art form. Mind you, all of us were exposed to the established dance techniques – classical ballet, modern dance techniques from the United States, from the Sigurd Leeder School, the old free style dance. So it was a question of how to apply these techniques in terms of West Indian movement patterns (1965: 20).

Through Ivy Baxter's pioneering work, the NDTC's more classical link of the first five years was established, while Eddy Thomas – who had been on a modern dance scholarship at the Martha Graham School of Contemporary Dance in New York – experimented with modern dance

---

38 NDTC Stratford Festival Programme, 1963.

technique. Beryl McBurnie as well as Lavinia Williams-Yarborough introduced Haitian folk forms to NDTC members, who had received various training in modern dance beforehand. Sheila Barnett, for example, joined with a background in Laban technique from the Chelsea School of Physical Education in England.[39] And Eryck Darby, who was also influential on the company's early work, had been a student at Jacob's Pillow in the U.S. (Nettleford 1969: 31).

Even though company director Rex Nettleford stresses the importance of modern dance technique and training for the beginning years, his own approach to choreography, varied from others in that he believed that "each dance does create its own technique" (1969: 31). Especially for a company in search of its own style, he argued that a balance between vitality and control should be kept in order not to "slavishly copy" but rather "find expression in [one's] own terms" (Nettleford 1969: 32). Certainly, ten years after Ivy Baxter Dance Group, the vocabulary had already been successfully expanded. As Nettleford explained:

We have the advantage of being able to refer to the vocabulary of many different techniques with a view to developing a style of our own. For whether we like it or not we are an amalgam of different techniques with a view to developing a style of our own. For whether we like it or not we are an amalgam of different cultural strains which are yet to find the coherence and distinctiveness that can be expressed in any precise terms (1968: 130).

On behalf of such further development of "distinctiveness," Nettleford held on to ballet and modern dance as "essentials" which could not easily be ignored, since he believes that they are somewhat common to all theatre dancing by "stretching across the geographical boundaries and defying racial barriers" (Nettleford 1969: 32). In this respect, the NDTC's aesthetic policy opposed the simplistic definitions of 'ethnic dance' or 'exoticism' prevalent during those formative years. More importantly, the company strove for what Nettleford calls "conscious transition," i.e. the development of a distinct Jamaican approach that emerges from experimentation with ballet, modern dance and folk movement vocabulary to create an authentic Jamaican style. Nettleford remarks:

---

39 NDTC Stratford Festival Programme, 1963.

As a teacher my own approach to training has been by way of discovering for oneself and bending some of the fundamentals of established techniques to the needs of the Jamaican dancers, never underestimating the necessity of a well-tuned instrument or of such technical proficiencies as strength, kinesthetic awareness, coordination and flexibility. But I am at the same time ever conscious of the stifling effect that exaggerated emphasis on technique can have for the work the NDTC sets itself. In a sense each dance does create its own technique, making the search endless and the creative spirit self-generating. My classes are therefore approached with this in mind, in a commitment to a judicious balance between maintaining natural vitality and imposing indispensable control. The breaking down of choreographic statements into their component parts is itself an important source of technique-building and this exercise I have regarded as essential for a company that seeks to find its own expression in its own terms (1969: 32).

Observing an NDTC class today, almost about forty years later, the western trained eye might still be tempted to recognize the modern floor work and the ballet barre first, rather than noticing the actual Jamaican input of the training. However, this impression of a very familiar studio atmosphere is misleading, and very soon creatively counteracted. The changing pattern starts with the dynamics of the NDTC's live drumming, which is immediately responded to, when the dancers exercise a variety of Caribbean movements. Caribbean dance vocabulary also dominates the progressions, which usually makes up the latter half of the class. Clearly, the drum's pounding "heart"-beat rhythm calls for a different body response than that of a softly played piano would.[40] Posture, breathing and energy release are immediately affected, because to most drumming, be it sacred or secular, there is that "dimensional" quality, which Welsh-Asante has described as characteristic trait of the African aesthetic in dance (2001: 144-151).

Since drumming in the African context traditionally served as the prime means of communication among the village members, as well as with the ancestors and gods, the presence of the singers, drums, and drummers on the Jamaican dance theatre stage establishes a cultural link from that ancestral past to the postcolonial present. In particular the use of ritual drums and rhythms such as are used in Kumina and

---

40 I owe this expression to students at Edna Manley College, who first introduced me to Jamaican rhythmic patterns, when I was looking for the NDTC class. Not knowing the directions, I was simply told to follow my heartbeat, i.e. the calling of the drums.

Revival, evoke immediate kinaesthetic response not only on behalf of the dancers, but also with local audience members.[41] In terms of the NDTC's use of Jamaican music, the influence of the African derived drum is therefore essential. However, much of the music which is considered suitable for dance will of course also owe to Jamaica's European classical tradition. While a staged NDTC program will usually contain canned as well as live orchestra music, most pieces will still be supported by the NDTC's drummers and singers, who form an integral part of the Company's Caribbean total theatre aesthetic.[42]

On behalf of the NDTC's vocabulary, Hilary S. Carty's analysis of Jamaican folk dances sums up several characteristic features of what she has defined as "Jamaican technique" (see Carty 1988). She distinguishes the following set of movement patterns:

1. earth bound movement and a low center of gravity
2. usually flat feet
3. flexed foot
4. pelvis-centered movement which allows hips and pelvis to swing independently
5. bent arms and elbows which are typical of the African-derived broken line in Caribbean dance technique
6. "cool" facial expression, body gestures are expressive only
7. isolations of shoulders, pelvis, feet, hands
8. polyrhythms deriving from African dance (1988: 88-89).

In addition, Barnett points out that a distinctly Jamaican body of dance vocabulary originated from the Festival competitions. Renowned moves, such as for example the "congo" or "pivot" step, which changes the weight sideways from one foot to the other, as well as dynamic turns and spiraling from one level to the other and the torso centered

---

41 Mervyn Morris, for example, commented in a private conversation that Kumina drumming will affect him, even though he is not a Kumina practitioner himself.
42 Because of my own scholarly constraints – which regrettably lack the sufficient music education necessary here – this analysis can unfortunately not pay the due analytic respect to Marjorie Whylie's, the NDTC singers,' and drummers' decisive contribution to the NDTC's dance theatre. However, it goes without saying that certainly their original music and song compositions form an integral and not to be neglected part of the Company's overall artistic vision.

thrust are all part of the Festival style. These patterns are both linear and circular. Barnett explains:

The Festival style is shaped by the particular use of the flat foot, the lax extension of the ankle, the relaxed flexed use of arms and feet, the ripple of the back, the use of hips and the use of groups which identify form. Teachers and community workers manipulate groups so the emphasis is on group patterns and a melting, fading, reappearing of dancers on entrances and exits and the quickly paced finale or picturesque tableau (1982: 85).

She also comments on the development of the so called "creative folk dances" which are based on material from the folk tradition, yet transferred to another level. As these dances are no longer in their original setting, they assume more of a metaphorical meaning, yet do also bear traces which will derive from the folk origin. Barnett argues to regard these as a sort of readjustment of the folk dances to the needs of today's urban people who do not necessarily share the needs of the generations past, yet partake in the common heritage (1982: 86).

Finally, up to the present day, the NDTC has continued to operate as an independent organization of voluntary engagement. Among the company's major objectives are the following: (1) "to provide a vehicle for well trained and talented dancers," (2) "to help widen an informed and critical Jamaican audience," (3) "to experiment with dance-forms and techniques of all kinds with a view to helping to develop a style and form which faithfully reflect the movement of Jamaica and the Caribbean area," and (4) "to encourage and, where possible, conduct serious research into indigenous dance-forms in Jamaica and the Caribbean area" (Nettleford 1969: 32). Relying solely on the dedication and discipline of its members who all pursue other professional careers, still nobody gets paid and performances are held for the benefit of the Jamaican community (schools, heart disease, etc.). Obviously, this concept could have worked for so long, only under the premise of what the dancing itself must give back to the individual and the larger society as can also be observed in the NDTC's commitment to the Jamaica School of Dance.

The Jamaica School of Dance

In the 1970s the combined effort of the NDTC, JCDC, the Ministry of Education and the Extra-mural Department of the University of the

West Indies promoted the training of teacher artists as educators who would be able to combine the artistic and developmental aspects of Jamaican dance theatre (Barnett 1987: 3-4). When the Jamaica School of Dance was founded by early members of the NDTC in 1970, it was first located at the Little Theatre's studio as well as at the Junior Center of the Institute of Jamaica, Half Way Tree. Training consisted of modern and folk forms, technique, and composition. Summer Workshops were also given to teachers, performers and community leaders (Barnett 1987: 4). By 1976 the School of Dance together with the School of Art, Drama, and Music became located at the Cultural Training Center. As part of the division of the Jamaica Institute, dance training was thus legitimized as an academic field with the objective that "learning, generated by the common cultural experience of Jamaicans, creates an educational link with reality" (Barnett 1987: 4). From then on Jamaican school children were consistently taught their island's own dance heritage. As Barnett describes:

Children in schools are learning about themselves, their history and culture through participation in dance programmes. Some schools offer dance as physical education and artistic expression. Children respond with body and mind to the creative and problem-solving challenges of the preparation process. Children are performing "in concert" from schools like Stella Maris and Jessie Ripoll and from studios like the Jay Teens (1963) and the Rowe-Spance Ballet Studio (1940s). A group of future artists-performers and choreographers-spectators and critics, are being disciplined through training in the dance-art (1987: 4).

As Barnett's comment shows, Jamaican dance theatre by that time had come a long way, when in fact many of the NDTC's active dancers of today are precisely recruited from the above mentioned schools and teenage companies.

Interlude II: Dance and the New Jamaica

As chapter two of this book has shown for the socio-historical context of Jamaican postcolonial society, the island's population suffered from deep social division of white upper class minority, a considerably smaller brown middle, and a disenfranchised black lower class majority. Up until the late 1920s, Jamaica did in fact not mean much to its people apart from the name on the map as Sherlock and Bennett have pointed out (Sherlock/Bennett 1998: 346). At that time, the island's African Jamaican majority had no overarching loyalties, nor collective memories or meaningful sense of community to share. Following the 1865 Morant Bay rebellion's failure onwards, Emancipation had decidedly failed to bring about the necessary political enfranchisement of the island's former slave population so that the centuries of slavery and colonial rule had left Jamaica to its own conflictuous devices. Considering the local alienation of former slaves, brown Creoles and British expatriates, there was hardly a sense of national consciousness, not to mention solidarity at that point.

Yet, as the economic pressure of the 1930s world-wide depression hit the Caribbean, it caused labour unrest which prepared the ground for socio-political change. Under the inspired leadership of Norman Manley and Alexander Bustamante a new national spirit arose, which proclaimed the reinvigorating force of the black folk culture as the binding link to form a common cultural consciousness and symbolic realm for national identification. British high culture was still dominant at that time, while African survivals were debased as witchcraft and superstition. As a consequence, education and culture became the key-issue of Manley's political reform policy, which in the late 1930s called for a "new national spirit" to promote Jamaican unity through the creative arts (Nettleford 2003: 30). In hindsight, Sherlock and Bennett have described this process of nation-building as nothing short of a "miracle," when "political revolution [...] was attended by a powerful surge of creative energy that impelled Jamaicans of all classes to think of Jamaica as 'my country' and of Jamaicans of all colours as 'my people'" (Sherlock/Bennett 1998: 390). While this "surge of creative energy" was introduced in literature as well as theatre practice of the time, I will, however, argue that more importantly than that, the dance movement in fact first institutionalized these efforts through a creative appropriation of the African Jamaican folk dance heritage as promoted by its women pioneers. Jamaican dance theatre therefore publicly performed as the prime conveyor of this new attitude, which should ultimately evolve as the New Jamaica's national consciousness to be represented by the NDTC.

Jamaica's National Dance Theatre Company has thus been consciously reaching out from the national base to international acclaim. However, skipping through forty years of reviews, international critique has also oftentimes been too easily misled (Tobias 1983: 72; Williams 1972: 40; Philp 1976: 67). In fact, critics unfamiliar with the Caribbean cultural complex may face the immanent danger of misinterpreting Jamaican dance theatre according to their own metropolitan (post)modern/classical standards. What I wish to argue in the following section though, is that despite our shared global arts community/market, we still need to be careful not to overlook the depth and significance of each distinct dance step. Thus, I would like to suggest that NDTC choreography can only be fully appreciated, if understood on Jamaica's diverse and highly complex socio-historical and cultural background. As the company's mission of self-discovery after independence implies, one needs to consider more than mere technique and proficiency in order to investigate the meaning of the dance. The following postcolonial reading of the NDTC repertoire may consequently be conceived of as a first effort towards this challenging task.

Jamaica's National Dance Theatre Company – A Postcolonial Reading of the Repertoire

Dancing Cultural Roots: Kinaesthetic Memory and the Discovery of Self

All we can ask for is that the dancer will transmit to an audience which deserves it, an aesthetically satisfying and emotionally exciting structural relationship between the elements of space, dynamics and rhythm. For those of us who want the movement patterns of Jamaica and Jamaicans to be faithfully reflected in this artform we will expect the dancer to make his art move to the pulse of Jamaica. That's as far as we need to go in nationalistic terms (Nettleford 1968: 131).

As the previous survey on Jamaica's African Creole religious and recreational practices has shown, kinaesthetic memory of these practices is essential for an understanding of the emerging Caribbean dance theatre of the 1930s and 40s. In his essay on the cultural links between Africa and the Caribbean, Harry Hoetink has furthermore described, how the African body in the context of colonization was at the same time perceived as a "vehicle of transportation, and as an aesthetic object" (Hoetink 1979: 30). Bodily practice functioned as a collective cultural marker within a minimum size unit, as, for example, in the relation of mother and child. Gestures, corporeal rhythms and movement patterns have thus been culturally encoded as traces of African cultural heritage.[1] Yet, as has also been shown, Jamaican kinaesthetic memory of African religious and recreational practices reflects such African heritage in historically selective terms, since creolized Jamaican movement patterns draw form the vast repertoire of African, Amerindian as well as European dance forms.

Kinaesthetic Memory

All conventional memory is erased and yet in this trance of overlapping spheres of reflection a primordial or deeper function of memory begins to exercise itself [...] (Harris 1967:51).[2]

The constant danger of confusing remembering and imagining, resulting from memories becoming images in this way, affects the goal of faithfulness corresponding to the truth claim of memory. And yet ...
And yet, we have nothing better than memory to guarantee that something has taken place before we call to mind a memory of it (Ricoeur 2004: 7).

More recently, Joseph Roach has referred to Circum-Atlantic cultural performances as "rites of memory," performed by the Caribbean diaspora's "anxious survivors, who now feel obliged more or less to reinvent themselves, taking into account the roles played by their predecessors" (1996: 1-2). Analyzing the relationship of memory, performance and substitution, Roach suggests to look at these embodied cultural performances as a reproduction or recreation of kinaesthetic memory, which evolves from a process of "surrogation" to imaginatively fill the "cavities created by loss through death or other forms of departure" (1996: 1-2). Important for Roach's concept is not only that he examines surrogation as it mediates between the participating cultures, as well as it negotiates between identity and difference, but also that surrogation embodies the genealogy of performance as discursive "counter-memory" (1996: 5-6). Kinaesthetic imagination is thus defined as the community's "mnemonic reserve," where "imagination and memory converge" by establishing "a way of thinking through movements – at once remembered and reinvented – the otherwise unthinkable, just as dance is often said to be a way of expressing the unspeakable" (Roach 1996: 27).

---

[1] Similarly, Roger Bastide's ethnography of African survivals in the New World argues for a prevalence of collective "motor sequences" (1971: 194).
[2] Wilson Harris commenting on the socio-cultural signifiance of Haitan Vodou trance.

Particularly, when transferred onto the national dance theatre stage, kinaesthetic memory thus builds on a truth claim, which – as Paul Ricoeur has claimed – may confuse "remembering and imagining" to a certain extent and yet, such imagined kinaesthetic memory publicly displayed will still somewhat "guarantee that something [i.e. in this context the African cultural heritage] has taken place" in order to assure one's historical existence and identity (2004: 7). In fact, Ricoeur has pointed out that the act of remembering presents the conflation of "memory-image" in form of an "incantation," which oscillates between degrees of hallucination and truthfulness (2004: 54). Ricoeur's theoretical assessment of memory in relation to history and forgetting, appears furthermore suggestive of the phenomenological impact of Jamaican dance theatre, which precisely develops its dance vocabulary from the vestiges of African Caribbean kinaesthetic memory, i.e. the Caribbean's cultural genealogy. The question, hence, arises as to what kind of "memory-images" are evoked by dance theatre in terms of their reception as either a faithful recognition of shared bodily expression, or an ideological manipulation of the same. If shared kinaesthetic memory constitutes the African diaspora in the New World, as – in Ricoeur's terms – "a matter of national self-love [...] in terms of its losses [i.e. in the case of the Caribbean, certainly the trauma of the Middle Passage]," then analysis obviously needs to assess the political implications of such performed remembrances. As Ricoeur furthermore explains, recalled "wounds to collective memory" are directly interconnected with the "work for recollection" and tied to the "problematic of identity," which appears after all as fragile an entity to distortion as memory itself (2004: 78-81). Ideological manipulation between the "demand for identity and the public expressions of memory" appears therefore almost inevitable, if not necessarily intended (2004: 82). Ricoeur remarks:

It is in fact in this role that ideology, as a factor of integration, can be established as the guardian of identity, offering a symbolic response to the causes affecting the fragility of identity. At this level of radicality, that of symbolically mediated action, there is as yet no manipulation, hence no abuse of memory. One can speak only of the silent constraint exerted on the mores of a traditional society. This is what makes the notion of ideology practically ineradicable. But it must be added straight away that this constitutive function of ideology can scarcely operate outside of the connection to its second function – the justification of a system of order or power – nor can it operate even potentially apart from the function of distortion that is grafted onto the preceding one. [...] Ideology, we may presume, arises precisely in the breach between the request for legitimacy emanating from a system of authority and our response in terms of belief (2004: 82-83).

Hence, a postcolonial analysis of Jamaican dance theatre will have to investigate the ideological underpinnings of choreography, which employs kinaesthetic memory in terms of a formerly silenced tradition and heritage, precisely, to claim its legitimacy and power in the new social order. As Loren Kruger has pointed out for South African postcolonial drama: "What is at stake in these performances is not merely the restoration or even the revision of the past, but the transformation of received material in the inauguration of a new model that might provide the basis for future restoration" (1999: 5). These theoretical premises present therefore the focus of the following analysis of selected examples from the NDTC's dance theatre repertoire in terms of its transformative/revolutionary potential for articulating Jamaica's postcolonial nationalism.

Choreographing Independence

The immediate past has attempted to destroy the influence of the glory that is Africa, it has attempted to make us condemn and mistrust the vitality, the vigour, the rhythmic emotionalism that we get from our African ancestors. It has flung us into conflict with the English traditions of the public schools and even worse it has imposed on us the Greek ideal of balanced beauty (N.W. Manley 1939).[3]

African Scenario

African Scenario (1962) was according to choreographer Rex Nettleford the company's first dance work to enunciate Jamaican dance theatre's indebtedness to the African heritage in terms of the NDTC's evolving vocabulary. Performed on occasion of Jamaica's independence celebrations, it formed part of the NDTC's inauguration show "Roots and Rhythms" (Nettleford 1985: 137). Drawing on Nettleford's exposure to traditional West African dance, his choreography explored the African "rituals, dress, music and dances" by "focussing on correspondences in

---

3 In: Nettleford 1971: 108.

traditional Jamaican life" (Nettleford 1985: 137).[4] As he has outlined the choreographic plot in *Dance Jamaica*:

> The story seems almost pure in its simplicity. A young girl enters maturity and is betrothed. Losing her loved one to war, she invokes the gods for his return. Finally he returns in safety and rejoicing. This Caribbean portrayal of ancestral rites was set against traditional African scenes of puberty, fertility, war, fetish, and masquerade (1985: 137).

While the NDTC singers undertook "serious study of the songs of the Ga and Akan peoples of Ghana" and Eddy Thomas "created brilliant costume designs based on the ceremonial dress of West Africa," Nettleford stresses right away that the company did not endeavor to create an authentic portrayal of Africa by any means, but rather attempted to show "a Caribbean vision faithful both to the essence of its ancestral sources and to the realities of the changes that naturally occurred as a result of transplantation to the Americas" (1985: 137).

Recalling the impact of his visits to Ghana and Nigeria, Nettleford expressed his intention as follows:

> There was absolutely no doubt, when I went and I saw the retention – the way people moved – it convinced me that there was a definite way in which people like us move. The other thing that convinced me was the elegance, the setting of different rhythms in the body. There was a man called Opoku, the artistic director of the Ghana Company, whom I met in Kumasi and we talked. But you know how we really communicated? We danced. We just put on the music and we danced. It was wonderful (Interview 7 Aug. 2003).

Working on *African Scenario* Nettleford became primarily interested in the aspect of "African retention in the Caribbean" in order to create "a suite type of dance" supposed to be meaningful to Jamaicans rather than to merely reproduce African source material. Accordingly, the choreography is divided into four larger compositional segments of initiation, war, invocation of the gods, and "rejoicing".[5]

---

4   In 1962 Rex Nettleford had visited West Africa, where he reports to have "renewed acquaintances in classes and repertoire sessions with Beryl Kari-Kari and the Obadjeng Dance Group in Accra, Ghana, and with Opoku in Kumasi, as well as with dancing 'societies' in Nigeria" (Nettleford 1969: 34).
5   The following analysis is based on the video-taped version of *African Scenario*, NDTC Archive CARIMAC Center, UWI, Mona Campus, Kingston.

Barbara Requa, Joyce Campbell, Monica McGowan, Rosalie Markes, Sheila Barnett, Yvonne daCosta, and Shirley Campbell in Rex Nettleford's African Scenario, circa 1962. Photograph by Maria LaYacona (rpt. in: Nettleford 1969: 90).

African Scenario opens to an a-cappella chorus by the NDTC singers on a tableau of female dancers in front of the scenic backdrop of an African village. Except for the Initiate, all of the present women dancers have turned their backs to the audience and are dressed in blue flowered skirts, red tops and matching head-ties. Only the Initiate in a white robe is facing front and as soon as the drums set in, she is the one to start the basic movement: a scant shuffle, carefully brushing the footsole over the ground and bending the torso slightly with stretched arms to her left in a swinging motion. From there she switches into a more accentuated contract/release sequence of the upper torso, which is supported by a mirroring movement of the arms as if to invite the other female dancers, who then slowly start to move as well by lifting their arms above their heads. Turning to face the audience, all female dancers shift into progressions with the upper body bent parallel to the ground in a rippling move with arms extending from leg parallel to up facing front and back, introducing a familiar step, which is still prevalent in West African modern dance.

During the next sequence, the women exit and enter from both sides with a kick jump step. Testifying to the West African inspiration, the women dancers' accompanying hand and facial expressions of this sequence are reminiscent of what Doris Green has identified as a particular feature of body segmentation in Akan dances, which employ "complex arm, hand and foot movements together with head, facial and eye expressions" (Green 1996: 15). As the drum beat increases, the Initiate moves into an inner circle, which is slowly evolving from the other dancers' progressions. With the rhythm building up to higher intensity, one sees the Witch Doctor enter from stage right in a traversing sequence of leaps. When he and the other dancers exit, the Initiate remains by herself, awaiting her Fiancé, while musically attended by the silent call of a slow beating solo-drum. Then, the Fiancé enters accompanied by a male dancer and soon the couple faces each other as, simultaneously, the assisting man and another woman start to strip off the Initiates' white robes to reveal a natural fabric loin-cloth costume underneath. When the couple's pas de deux unfolds, the drum beats become again more intense. Finally, the women and the Witch Doctor enter again, as a rising intensity takes hold of the scene, which ends with the monotonous acceleration of the initiation ritual.

After another brief call and response patterned chorus interlude by the NDTC singers – this time accompanied by hand clapping percussion, but again no drums – the second choreographic segment opens with the male dancers entering in yellow calf-length skirts, naked torsos – except of a crossed yellow cloth band encircling the back and front shoulder area – and a yellow headband, to which a tall red feather has been attached in front. As the dancers approach upstage, they come to a halt in second position parallel with arms stretched out to both sides, holding a stick in their right hand and suggesting a stance of defiant pugnacity. By the end of the sequence, this image of 'fierce African warriors ready to combat' takes up all the stage space, when last but not least the Witch Doctor steps up front from back of their midst to lead the crowd into a sequence of diagonal attack/retreat progressions from front left to back right and vice versa.

Dennis Scott, Thomas Pinnock, Audley Butler, Milton Dawes, Eddy Thomas, and Bert Rose in Rex Nettleford's African Scenario, circa 1962. Photograph by Maria LaYacona (rpt. in: Nettleford 1969: 91).

Particularly the Witch Doctor's outstanding performance asserts certain awe. His toga-like costume is covered by an eye-dazzling black and white pattern of rhombic lines, matched by his and the warriors' white facial war mask make-up as well as the almost ankle length white hair extension which fiercely flies about his body as he kick-jumps forward on one leg. Then, he suddenly lifts up in the air, turning around to land back down in a body-breaking bounce. Raising their sticks harpoon-like above their heads, the male dancers next join in a circle progression, leaping forward to abruptly rest down before the following movement sequence begins from a brief silence to announce what has come to be known as the NDTC's 'Savannah' step.[6]

When the drums set in again, the step increases in tempo and the parallel line dissolves into singular performances of more and more intense torso and shoulder ripple isolations to evoke movements from possessional dances as well as to prepare for the entrance of the female dancers, who are now dressed in white bast-fibre skirts of an ankle-length. During this scene, the female dancers exert quickly alternating exits and entrances with most of the movement centered around the

---

6 Rex Nettleford introduced this parallel to front progression step during his master class at the EMC summer school workshop 2003.

pelvis in contract release progression, passing each other several times before falling 'exhausted' to the ground with one leg lifted towards the ceiling. During this scene, each of the dancers is 'armed' with two white bast-fibre pompoms as well as wearing a white knit head-cover to hold an enormous white bast-fibre hair extension to swirl and further bedazzle the beholder's eye in a powerful display of magico-religious dance moves from a fetish dance of spirit invocation.

Rosalie Markes in Rex Nettleford's African Scenario, circa 1962. Photograph by Maria LaYacona (rpt. in: Nettleford 1969: 91).

After another brief interlude by the NDTC singers two male dancers then enter from stage left and right, stripped of their former skirts to bikini pants. Similar to the intimidating awe of the Witch Doctor's appearance, the introduction of the mask dance likewise evokes the symbolically charged, supernatural force of ancestral spirituality at this point. Being a popular form throughout Africa, the full body mask exerts specific power. As Green explains:

Although the mask is not a living object, it has a psychological significance which might be considered as a psychological disguise. When the person adorns the mask, he is transformed into the spirit or being he is representing. The identity of the mask wearer is not revealed according to secrecy of tradition. It is on record that during ceremonies, women, uninitiated boys, and girls are not permitted near the mask wearers in order to keep the identity of the masked performers secret (1996: 21).

While the mask in *African Scenario* is of course taken out of its religious background here, it still theatrically conveys much of its former transformative quality. For example, when about half of the group of women dancers enters again, they have undergone quite noticeable transformation, primarily indicated by their costume change. Crafted from bamboo strips, the costume consists of a belt-type construction to attach a magnificent circle-shaped cover, which emphasizes rather than hides the dancers' behinds as they shake their buttocks back and forth. Fertility overtones come to mind as this group is joined by the other group of women, who are still dressed in the flowered Caribbean skirts costume of the opening scene. However, they, too, have changed as their costumes are now further adorned with a broad red shawl surrounding their waists. Finally, therefore, all of the company dancers appear somewhat more 'initiated' than before, as they celebrate the "rejoicing" of bride and groom in *African Scenario*'s progression finale.

Assuming that the shawl around the waist indeed symbolizes birth and fertility, then not only have the dancers been 'initiated,' but also in a way their audiences, who by perceiving *African Scenario*'s birth/initiation ritual have been theatrically introduced to the Caribbean's African heritage. Unsurprisingly therefore, after a little more than twenty minutes of such extravagant exploration of African heritage, Jamaican audience response to *African Scenario* was quite mixed. While some people were shocked, others felt that the African movement was not yet strong enough. As Nettleford recalls:

When the work was first performed it evoked favourable responses from many Jamaicans, though some people felt that middle-class restraint had imposed itself on the bodies of the dancers, male and female alike. At least one viewer walked out of the Little Theatre in disgust – all that 'belly-rolling and back-to-Africa nonsense'. A few complained that the drumming was too much for them. [...] The approach to *African Scenario* was ritualistic and frankly theatrical – thanks to the usual collaboration of Eddy Thomas on costumes. But the work carried undercurrents of identity with Africa and this disturbed some people among the Jamaican audiences (1969: 34).

Just how disturbing the display of fierce African warrior and initiation dances must have been at the time is certainly hard to tell now, but one should remember that by 1962/63 – only a year after independence – the black power movement was still in its infancy and had not yet arrived on everybody's political agenda.

Delineating the postcolonial decolonization process, Fanon has distinguished three phases of cultural liberation: 1. assimilation of the colonial pattern, 2. remembering of origin and 3. cultural revolution. In many ways *African Scenario* suggests a reading in terms of that second phase, for it theatrically presents the quest and exploration of the African cultural heritage in Jamaican society. Fanon's argument, however, also addresses the danger of such artistic undertaking as merely articulating an estranged and banal longing for exoticism through its oftentimes superficial celebration of folk customs and traditions (1990: 178-179). Admittedly, Nettleford's approach to explore the similarity between the African and Caribbean dance heritage in *African Scenario* may at first seem to adhere to Fanon's auto-exoticism. And yet, I will argue that despite its auto-exoticism *African Scenario* does not merely indulge in the rediscovery of African heritage and ancestry per se, but explores that vocabulary in terms of the NDTC's vision of a new Caribbean self-image.

Evidently, the African heritage had always been prevalent in Caribbean movement patterns as has been shown in the previous section. Movements introduced by *African Scenario* could thus easily be identified in Jamaican Kumina, Jonkonnu, Maroon and Pocomania dances.[7] Hence, *African Scenario* appears as the outspoken re-invention of African Caribbean identity in terms of Roach's surrogation rather than an orientalist fantasy. Thus redressing Fanon's critique, I consequently propose a reading of *African Scenario* not as the superficial imitation of

---

7   Compare NDTC Stratford Festival Programme 1963. In the taped version of *African Scenario* Nettleford introduced the choreography as follows: "African Scenario, the dance that follows, goes back to the source for its inspiration, utilizing the dances of the Ga, Ashanti, Ewe and Fanti people of West Africa to portray aspects of traditional life: puberty, fertility, war, fetish and masquerade. The movement patterns portray elements of dance to be found among the Kumina people who live in the eastern end of the island, among the Jonkonnu mummers, the Maroons and Pocomania [...]" (NDTC Archive).

African initiation ritual at hand, but as the symbolic initiation of the Jamaican audience at large. Metaphorically speaking, the initiation of the girl and her marriage to the African warrior – whom she loses to war yet regains invigorated – may be interpreted as symbolically representing the rebirth of a people – "taken from Africa, brought to America" (Bob Marley) – rising the stronger from that battle ground of robbed and re-appropriated identification. As Green has described the raison d'être of traditional African puberty dances: "It is hoped that when the viewer sees such dances, they will be more informed" (1996: 20). Certainly her quote cannot be taken literally, as ritual has been theatricalized here, yet the transformative impact of the dance's original meaning remains, if not in terms of sexual initiation, but rather cultural maturation and independence.

I am therefore arguing that *African Scenario*'s quite spectacular assertion of African Caribbean identity not only irritated the spectators' eye in the very direct sense by the swirling bast-fibre pompons and skirts all over the stage, but also impacted on the audience's 'I' (i.e. in terms of a new self-awareness), because it re-appropriated the stereotypical notion of 'barbaric' and 'uncivilized' ritual in an imitative display of unfathomed vigor and strength. Far from oppressive then, such (re-)presentation in fact allowed the dancers to perform their very own imaged imagination of an empowered rather than victimized African Caribbean selfhood. Thus – at least for dance critic Michael Reckord – *African Scenario* worked as an eye-opener. When he recalls:

Thirty years ago, I was a student of ballet – had been for about three years. I enjoyed the dance genre, but in a placid, cerebral sort of way. It was mostly a head thing, though I liked the bodily exercise. Then, one night, at the Little Theatre I saw a dance which zapped my heart, kindled passion, made me fall in love with modern dance. (Paradoxically, it also made me appreciate ballet more). The work was *African Scenario*. You've heard of it, of course. It caused quite a stir at the time (1993: 2).

Apparently, *African Scenario* appealed to Reckord, because ideally, for him, "dance, like ritual, will have meaning, a vocabulary, and patterns of movement which emerge from a culture, and which strike chords of recognition in the observer" (1993: 2). One might hence suggest that precisely such "recognition" of kinaesthetic memory from African-derived movement patterns subtly ushered into Jamaica's new cultural consciousness of the time.

Considering, furthermore, that African culture was actually never that far removed from Jamaicans to begin with, the NDTC's artistic rediscovery – regardless of whether one conceives of it as being 'exotic' or not – would even in its exoticism still fulfill the important task of developing an African Jamaican consciousness in terms of a newly evolving self-articulation. To recall Anthony D. Smith's argument concerning the degree of invention necessary for the national project at this point, *African Scenario* does by no means belittle the African tradition's Jamaican legitimacy, but is rather important to reinforce it. More significant than the actual truth claim to certain traditions then, proves the question of "how far that modern public culture is a modern version of the pre-modern ethnic culture, or how far it simply 'uses' elements ('materials') from an older cultural repertoire for its own, quite novel, purposes" (1999: 52). Ultimately therefore, the evidence of African survivals throughout Jamaican folklore appears indeed to be a "modern version of the pre-modern," while at the same time using that heritage to the "quite novel purpose" of building Jamaica as an independent nation.

On behalf of *African Scenario* this strategy would accordingly be based on the sound proclamation of an African ancestry as a legitimate part of Jamaican high culture. Not only did the performance provoke mixed responses, but its re-appropriating mimicry of the Eurocentric stereotype ultimately undermined the stereotype's denunciatory power. By presenting the 'uncivilized' ritual within the frame of the very 'civilized' Western stage, the image's threatening self-deprecation within colonialist discourse was slowly eroded. Conquering the Western stage by breaking some sort of representational taboo, the NDTC's 'barefoot' performance successfully reversed the cultural hegemony. African 'wilderness' proudly presented thus undermined the discriminatory label from within: an image that Jamaican middle class *mimic men* of the time certainly needed to re-think.[8] Eventually therefore, Nettleford's choreography appears to engage the stereotypical notion of the 'primitive' precisely to the extent that the portrayed image ceases to be perceived as such. For what this mimicry of Africanness displays – a Caribbean Africanness as Nettleford quite frankly admits – is not an oppressive stance any longer, but a free appropriation of cultural pride

---

8 Naipaul's renowned novel *The Mimic Men* (1967) presented the bleak memoirs of a West Indian colonial politician in exile which at the time was largely received as the paradigmatic description of Caribbean colonial identity crisis and lack of self-definition.

and self-empowerment. Putting on the mask and beautiful costume of an imagined Africa can thus serve as an invigorating statement in a public contest over representative power.

Lastly, one should bear in mind that the assertion of black pride in Jamaica was simply setting the historical record straight, since ninety percent of the island's population are of African ancestry. Certainly, this presents a social reality quite different from that of the U.S. Adhering to white colonial standards in Jamaica appeared particularly absurd, though no less a reality. As Norman Washington Manley has described the significance of the 1960s Black Power Movement for Jamaica:

Black Power means the acceptance with joy and pride, the fact of blackness, of black dignity and black beauty. It means the acceptance by the black man of his own proud place in the brotherhood of man. It is true that although we have achieved the power of self-government and the dignity of nationhood, there still lurks beneath the surface of many minds and consciences a feeling that the white man can do more and can achieve more than we can do. It is true that the white man in order to achieve and maintain white power has taught the black man the world over to believe in white superiority. It is true that in many, many places he still so believes and leaves us with a world in which the seeds of disharmony are deeply planted and threaten us with danger all the way (in: Nettleford 1971: 379-381).

Yet, while this appeared so, Manley has also made clear that the ultimate vision for his country had to overcome such racialism of the reversed kind. And therefore he continued:

It may well be true to say that there is now and for a long time have been Black Power elements that exploit the feelings about colour that lie on the surface in the Jamaican society, where the society is divided between black and white, and brown, and disunited where matters of skin alone are concerned. This is not to be accepted in Jamaica, and it will not be accepted in Jamaica. We do not want, in Jamaica, to establish the very thing we have fought so many years to break down in our country. We do not want to establish in Jamaica the practices of America or even England or Rhodesia or South Africa we loath and despise. We realise the greatest danger that confronts the human race is race itself, and the patterns of thought that set race against race, [...] We should be proud to think that we can set the world an example by carrying through till we have achieved our goal that will come when Jamaica is an integrated community; [...] (in: Nettleford 1971: 379-381).

What Manley envisions for Jamaican society is thus precisely the utopia of Brathwaite's Creole nation, a place born on the plantation, that contested locale, where black and white first met. And tellingly enough that setting should become the departure point for the NDTC's second exploration of independence choreography in 1963.

Plantation Revelry

Plantation Revelry (1963) was the first choreography, which Nettleford in *Dance Jamaica* has referred to as one of the "social commentary" dances in the NDTC repertoire (1985: 106). Building on the LTM Pantomime tradition, the choreography evolved from typical 19th-century plantation dances. As Nettleford has summarized the plot:

The dance, which takes place in the nineteenth century, opens at the pier, where friends and workers from the family plantation gather to greet Miss Amelia, returning from England. Her arrival is awaited with excitement, and her old Nanny sings a folk melody recalling the pleasurable moments they spent together before her charge was sent to England to be educated. The second scene opens on the front lawn of the great plantation mansion. The old butler brings Amelia something to eat, while Amelia's friends greet her in a dance reminiscent of the country jigs of the period. Two working women try to attract her attention, while young men amuse her with a dance in which they imitate European gentlemen of the period. One of them acts out a mock courtship with her, much to the annoyance of her Nanny. Some of her old friends, dressed up in the costumes of Haitian set-girls, show off their attire. The men return disguised in jonkonnu (John Canoe) costumes, and the revels, heralding her return, end in frolic (1985: 107-108).[9]

Very similar to the Jamaica Pantomime model, Nettleford's *Plantation Revelry* integrates mime, music, song and dance in an entertaining, tongue in cheek mock-epic of the well known plantation stock characters: two "ladies of quality," high colored of course, accompanied by their black servant boy and the 'guarding angel' black Nanny.[10] How-

---

9   Barnett comments on the emergence of Haitian set-girls in Jamaican Jonkonnu: "In 1794, many Haitian families fled from the rebellion in Santo Domingo, bringing with them to Jamaica slaves whose influence would carry-over into the Set-Girls' Groups of the Jonkonnu by the addition of elegance and rivalry among competitors and also the creole domination of sets" (1989: 64).

10 Compare video-taped performance at NDTC archive, CARIMAC Centre, U.W.I. Nettleford reworked the choreography by introducing another

ever, Nettleford has argued that the lightly treated minstrelsy appears "deceptive" in its "simplicity" (1985: 108-109). Keeping in mind that Christmas in particular was the time of comparative free-license on the plantation – a welcome occasion of part-time role reversal, and, to repeat Patterson, "temporary metamorphosis" of the slaves' status – the class/race division between the characters on stage becomes increasingly blurred. Therefore, the ladies' encounter with the servant during the sequence after the very opening song appears actually less condescending than playful. Since the song tellingly invites the audience to "join in the fun," the spectator is asked not to take things too seriously in this dance performance of reversed role play.

Patsy Ricketts, Jackie Guy, and Beverly Kitson in Rex Nettleford's Plantation Revelry, circa 1963. Photograph by Maria LaYacona (rpt. in: Nettleford 1969: 37).

Historically, many of the slave dances were arranged according to dynamics highly reminiscent of a total theatre aesthetics. Not only was dancing accompanied by singing and drumming, but pantomimic action was also oftentimes an integral part of the game (Hill 1992: 223). A blend of African and European performance traditions, the so-called

---

female character in this later version. For an account of the pervasiveness of African American stock characters in American motion pictures, for example, compare Donald Bogle, *Toms, Coons, Mulattoes, Mammies and Bucks. An Interpretive History of Blacks in American Films* (New York: Continuum, 1997).

'plantation revelries' developed a syncretic form, which is also the basis of Nettleford's choreography. *Plantation Revelry* thus starts from the European country jig pattern and switches to the African rhythms of the Jonkonnu drums. After the brief interlude with the servant boy, two servant girls enter and make fun of the stilted moves of their mistresses by thoroughly introducing a couple of their own down-to-earth moves. "Bucking" as this section has been called, presents, in fact, a Jamaican oral tradition of song dispute, which dates back to the same period.[11] Excelling each other in performance, the women start a mock-quarrel and would probably take right after each other's throats, if the mercy of Miss Amelia and Miss Joan did not thankfully prevent them from doing so. The scene feeds on laughter and poking fun at no matter whom and for what. Consequently, the choreographer's intention appears to be less focused on portraying the racial division than actually the social interaction, which simply demonstrates very common behavior among teenage girls. While there is difference in comportment and behavior between the ladies' and their servants' body posture and dance performances, there is, however, no competitive malice to be noticed. Rather, by exchanging a couple of steps, each couple appropriates part of the other's heritage in a sharing exchange.

Likely, such harmony was historically inaccurate for most of these encounters between mistresses and servants on the plantations. However, what appears more important than historical accuracy is, indeed, the NDTC's coherently pursued Creole vision. Hardships and suffering are not the theme, when Nettleford sets *Plantation Revelry* at Christmas time soon after Emancipation. At that time, Creole society could ideally have emerged from a happy rejoicing of European and African lifestyle. And speaking in terms of performance it did: for even though it took Jamaican society much longer than Emancipation to achieve social and political integration, the cultural practices had already been aesthetically blended. As Nettleford points out:

The storehouse of Jamaican dance-lore is partly in the 19th century, when the society consolidated and found itself. Plantation revelries produced among

---

11 Compare NDTC Stratford Festival Programme 1963: "'Bucking' is an old and favourite way of fighting, particularly among women in Jamaica. A 19th century song goes 'Wha' dat you do, Mek Sarah buck you?' (What have you done to cause Sarah to butt (use her head on) you? The two women in the short mime sequence use this old technique to air a grievance."

the otherwise miserable slaves dances which they had obviously copied from their English masters, with the important difference that they underscored the music with a more complex and, to them, satisfying rhythm. So there is the Quadrille, which has its counterparts in the Spanish and French speaking Caribbean, and which could be called the national dance of Jamaica, more robust than the 18th century court dances of which it is a creolised variant, and less "square" than the wheeling, yipeeing American square dance which seems to share a common heritage. This European influence persisted among the Jon Canoe masqueraders who according to travel writers of the earlier period, were complete with powdered wigs and Georgian dress, but cut capers and went through antics which betrayed African origins of dancing (1968: 132).

Bert Rose, Audley Butler, and Rex Nettleford in Rex Nettleford's Plantation Revelry, circa 1963. Photograph by Maria LaYacona (rpt. in: Nettleford 1969: 37).

Following the above chart, *Plantation Revelry* appears to present a reconciliatory image of plantation society as the cradle of the Creole nation. Interestingly enough, it reverses the plantation pattern in one intriguing feature. Rather than having the black servants be courted by their white masters – as was more often the case – it is here black men courting the 'high colored' ladies with their dance. Reminiscent of vaudeville dances, the elegant courtship with the white hats soon leads the male dancers into the more vigorous *calinda*, an acrobatic stick-fight of West Central African origin found throughout the Caribbean islands (Warner Lewis 2003: 199-218).

As easily as European and African forms blend into the flow of the choreography, *Plantation Revelry* suggests such easy blending also in terms of the new social reality. And where better than in Jamaican Jonkonnu has this blending of two traditions been achieved? With the entrance of the Haitian set girls, the mixing of the aesthetic and the political becomes most evident, as the masquerade's tradition owes to Europe as much as Africa. Historically, the set girls were after all the first to cross the cultural divide, as the early account given by Alexander Barclay (1828) demonstrates:

The young girls of a plantation, or occasionally of two neighbouring plantations leagued, from what is called 'a sett.' They dress exactly in uniform, with gowns of some neat pattern of printed cotton, and take the name of Blue Girls, Yellow Girls, etc. according to the dress and ribbon they have chosen. They have always with them in their excursions, a fiddle, a drum, and a tambourine, frequently boys playing fifes, a distinguishing flag which is waved on a pole, and generally some fantastical figure, or toy, such as a castle or tower, surrounded with mirrors. A matron attends who possesses some degree of authority, and is called Queen of the Sett, and they have always one or two Joncanoe-men, smart youths, fantastically dressed, and masked so as not to be known. Thus equipped, and generally accompanied by some friends, they proceed to the neighbouring plantation villages, and always visit the master's or manager's house, into which they enter without ceremony, and where they are joined by the white people in a dance (11-12).

Compellingly, this almost reads like a description of the finale of Nettleford's choreography, which likely owed to the existing historical accounts of Plantation Jonkonnu for its plot line.

As has been described before, Jonkonnu survived despite colonial opposition and became probably the major Creole performance mode to represent the promise of a playfully integrated society: loyal to Queen Victoria, who had freed the slaves, and open to include everybody. And yet, Jonkonnu continued to keep a critical eye on hegemonic power and oppression (Hill 1992: 252). While Jonkonnu had declined after Emancipation, it returned full force during the 1950s. Supported by a *Gleaner* sponsored campaign, an island-wide Jonkonnu competition was held and further promoted in 1976 under the patronage of the JCDC for the CARIFESTA '76 presentation. Heralded as the embodied testimony of slave resistance, Jonkonnu received major public attention and stepped to the forefront of the emerging national consciousness, when Jamaicans of the post-independence era were increasingly coming to terms with their cultural identity. As Jamaican national consciousness turned towards Africa in the 1960s and 70s, Jonkonnu came to represent the African Creole spirit of cultural survival and tradition. And unsurprisingly so, for as Judith Bettelheim's study points out: "Jonkonnu has always reflected the changing socio-political climate of Jamaica" (Nunley/Bettelheim 1988: 44).

It is therefore hardly astonishing that the NDTC, too, should incorporate elements from that indigenous source in their dance theatre. In fact, Jonkonnu's cunning re-appropriation of the colonial insignia of power offers a perfect illustration of Bhabha's concept of colonial mimicry, when historically, as Hill points out, "[m]ilitary apparel replaced animal skins, models of ships and great houses were carried on the head instead of horns," precisely for the performers "to transfer some of that power to themselves" (Hill 1992: 236). Clearly then, the introduction of the Jonkonnu's Set Girls, Actor-Boy, the House- and Horsehead towards the end of Nettleford's *Plantation Revelry* evokes kinaesthetic memory, which owes to that performative tradition. The choice of the Horsehead is furthermore important, because the mask traditionally belonged to rural Jonkonnu rather than the city based fancy dress pattern with its Set Girls, Kings and Queens. As Bettelheim remarks: "Cowhead and Horsehead are rural, but because of their untamed power they also are revered. They scare, but they also amuse. They invoke both fear and courage" (Nunley/Bettelheim 1988: 53).

Finally then, Jonkonnu's integrated opposition of rural Horseheads and fancy Set Girls has by now come to symbolize a typically Jamaican societal ambivalence, which oscillates between grassroots 'fierceness' and a somewhat more town-based cunning refinement. Coming together in Jonkonnu, both traditions have in their own strategic performances been resisting British hegemony for so long. And yet, in Nettleford's *Plantation Revelry*, I would like to suggest, such integrated resistance is performed not only as the birth-place of the Creole nation, but also as the somewhat utopian vision towards eventually overcoming Jamaica's racial/class-based divide.

The Folk Repertoire

To be/come its vision, the Company had now therefore to move from nouveau rich or nouveau real and cellophane and cosmo cosmopolitan ... to Accompong. Back, that is, to the hills of its island's history and the shared history of our whole huge half-sunk archipelago; forward, that is, to jerk and jeng and harst, cassava bammy, rivermaid and cooing dove and engine driving; shango from imitative eleison and necrophyllic languish, to rib cage contract/ripple, sufferer and cave and kumina (Brathwaite 1985: 50).

The preceding chapters have shown how Jamaican national consciousness increasingly turned towards grassroots culture. By proudly asserting Jamaica's African heritage, dance theatre made it possible for Jamaicans to reconsider the impact and significance of their country's folk heritage and certainly the NDTC played an important role in the legitimizing process towards this social change. Through dance theatre, Jamaican folklore entered "the collective experience of the people" as significant part of their own heritage to be proud rather than ashamed of. In fact, as this consciousness slowly spread into the larger spectrum of Jamaican society, the NDTC's dance choreography became more daring and started to go even deeper into and explore more of the country's religious rites for the company's evolving movement vocabulary. Revival, Kumina, Dinki Mini and other traditional folk forms were investigated and yielded an indispensable source of inspiration. To keep in mind, while this artistic investigation owes traces to the ritual's source, it consciously separated the religious and artistic spheres. As Nettleford has expressed his concern in choreographing from a ritual base:

[...] my choreographic approach is determined largely by my concern with rooting my work in the collective experience of the people I think I know – that is by distilling the essences and attempting to arrive at the universality in a particular experience. The process often results in concealing the connection between a movement design born out of Jamaican folk forms and its distilled representation in my so-called 'serious' works (1969: 35).

Kinaesthetic memory thus forms the somewhat clandestine base from which Nettleford's choreographic reinterpretation develops in discovery of new artistic paths for Jamaican dance theatre expression. A first effort to explore this approach was Nettleford's 1963 folk choreography *Pocomania*, which he and the NDTC revived again for the company's

41st season in 2003. Portraying sequences from a "poco" ceremony, this choreography presents Nettleford's technique of abstracting the essence of the ritualistic movement. In order to create a piece of dance theatre, Nettleford's choreography thus appropriates the folk form in an aesthetic rather than ritualistic manner, yet manages to maintain its psycho-cultural iconicity and meaning.[12]

Pocomania

Pocomania, which is today more correctly spelt Pukkumina, forms part of the Jamaican Revival complex. According to Edward Seaga's research of the religion in the 1950s and 60s – which formed the basis of the NDTC's choreography – Pukkumina originated during Jamaica's Great Revival in 1860/61 and was both African and Christian inspired. As has been mentioned, the non-conformist Baptist and Moravian churches had traditionally been more inclusive than other missionary Christians and formed therefore the backbone of the Revival movement. Revival thus embraced Central African Myal possession as the unitary force between temporal and spiritual world (see Seaga 1969). Revivalism may be conceived of as an African polytheism that embraces the Christian Trinity, Angels and Saints, Prophets and Apostles, however, combining these with the African spirit pantheon of ancestral dead and diabolic host.

Pukkumina worships the so called ground or ancestor spirits, in which respect it needs to be differentiated from Zion, which focuses on the heavenly spirits.[13] Spirit possession is the center of ritual worship. Located at Blake's Pen and St. Elizabeth Pukkumina is dominated by women, although the leader ("Shepherd") is traditionally male. He is the central figure, yet the Mother, Shepherd Boy, Armour Bearer and Governess are also of ritual importance (Smith, P. 1981: 2). The Pukkumina ground can be recognized by a tall pole with a flag and is usually part of the Shepherd's yard premises with the "seal" as its most sacred center of ritual activity. Other shrine-like areas provide for other ritual objects, such as water, stones and banners. Pukkumina member-

---

12 Interestingly enough, Brathwaite in a footnote to the above quoted epigraph suggests to consider the NDTC repertoire in terms of the impact of the vocabulary's psychocultural iconicity, i.e. precisley those poetic icons of Jamaican identity, which will be further examined here.
13 Different from Pukkumina worship of the ground spirits, Zion practitioners communicate with the Holy Spirit (Ryman 1980: 14).

ship is structured as a "band" in which each member is assigned with a distinct role and function. There are three groups to be distinguished:
- Leaders
- Post-Holders
- Floor Members

Among the leaders are the Shepherd, Mother, Shepherd Boy and Governess. Post-Holders are the Rivermaid, Bell-ringer, Dove, Cutter, Hunter and Messenger. Floor Members are not assigned to a distinct function nor are they endowed with the spirit.[14]

While Revival or Poco meetings were of low prestige among people of the middle class during the 1940s and 60s, they became a highly influential source for the Jamaican modern dance movement of the time. With his 1963 choreography *Pocomania*, Rex Nettleford reintroduced the rite to the Jamaican stage in the wake of Ivy Baxter's pioneering effort. As he has stated in an article on the choreography in 1969, his focus was on "ritual and the ecstasy of individual participation in the cleansing powers of the spirit possession and of worship through dance" rather than in strictly speaking anthropological research (21). However, as a born 'country-boy,' Nettleford had been exposed to Revival ceremonies, as well as receiving his share of European classicism. He recalls this culturally diverse heritage:

As a peasant boy of six or seven living in what was then regarded as one of the 'darkest' and most folksy parts of Jamaica, I remember singing big chunks of Handel's "Messiah", Haydn's "Creation" and of course that old favourite "The Lost Chord". My grandmother and several country aunties loved the anthems and even if they sang them badly, they were exposed to some of the best liturgical music of our European culture. These same people would participate in pocomania, and I have had my dose of "groaning and shouting" as well as healing in the balmyard and the obeahman (1968: 131).

Certainly, Nettleford's familiarity with the ceremonial proceedings must have greatly informed *Pocomania*'s choreographing process, when

---

14 These descriptions are indebted to Seaga's historical research, which formed the base for the NDTC's stage choreography. Since religious practices are fluid in their development in time, part of the individual symbols in recent Revival churches have changed, while the larger meaning and movement sequences still remain the same. This observation is based on my own attendance of a Revival meeting at Apostle Sinai Church of God, Spanish Town 24th August 2003.

he sought to further translate Revival movements for dance theatre presentation.

However, while musicologist and cultural minister of the time Edward Seaga assisted Nettleford and the company in their effort to learn the movements from the Revival members, the dancers would also add artistically to the source. The program brochure of the premiere outlined the choreographed proceedings as such:

In this dance a 'poco' festival is portrayed covering the highlights of three days and nights. First there is the blessing of the upliftment table which in actual festivals is usually decked out with fruits of all descriptions, carbonated drinks and breads of all shapes and sizes. The 'bands' process in, each with a Shepherd (leader). As they approach the table they greet each other and pace the area around the table pledging obeisance. The greeting over, the Shepherds direct the lighting of the candles ("Light de light oh"), each candle costing the worshipper lighting it a small sum. Choruses are sung and the table is broken. The proceedings simmer down while the worshippers and onlookers partake of the fruits, drinks and bread on the table.
The second day is called SUNDIAL and can be considered a highpoint of the Pocomania proceedings. For then the sacrifice of a goat takes place and the worshippers begin to 'labour' for their journey through the spirit world. In this dance the Bellringer and Rivermaid are dominant features. The Bellringer imitates the sound of a bell, the Rivermaid is drawn to the pool (stage right). The Indian Spirit is introduced at the end and betrays the existence of a population of East Indians, who came to Jamaica as indentured servants to replace erstwhile slave labour after Emancipation.
The third day is usually quieter than the other two. But there can be more labouring. In the dance a short closing prayer begins to bring the ceremonies to an end (Nettleford 1969: 22).

Following the above outline, Nettleford's theatrical adaptation of *Pocomania* bears strong resemblance to Revival's African-Christian syncretism. Thus, costumes were modeled on episcopelianesque and Roman Catholic style, whereas the movement testified to the Neo-African source, even though there was no staged goat sacrifice held in the theatre space.[15]

Pocomania's Neo-Africanism is particularly evident in the following set of movements: 1. the grounded rhythm of the shuffling feet, which

---

15 The following comparative analysis relies on video-tape as well as live-performance protocols of Pocomania as it was performed during the NDTC's 41st dance season in 2003.

embodies an African-derived spirituality that the Christian costume can veil, yet not deny; 2. the vibratory or spinning movements – which are created by the rippling of the body at an ever increasing speed, as well as by jumping with feet together to both sides as the arms moved from shoulder height bent to straighten up in ready appraisal of the spirit; and 3. the grounded inching of the foot at the typical "one, two, one, two" repetitiveness. All of these elements are typically found in Revival dancing as they build up to spirit possession in the ritual setting. Particularly, the accompanying "windscreen-wiper like movement" of the upper body, appears as ready vehicle for communication with the spirit force and might easily lead even the stage dancer to possession, if the movements are not carefully enough choreographed and controlled (Nettleford 1969: 23). Important in that context is also the inhaling and exhaling of breath, which is referred to as "trumping" and produces a particular guttural sound.[16]

The National Dance Theatre Company of Jamaica in Rex Nettleford's Pocomania, circa 1963. Photograph by Maria LaYacona (rpt. in: Nettleford 1969: 11).

---

16 "Trumping" has come to replace the former term of "groaning" in more recent ethnographic scholarship.

What the dance choreography thus manages to convincingly portray, even in theatrical adaptation of the ceremony, is the movement's embodied meaning of Africanist religious survival. *Pocomania* as a study in the movement possibilities of Jamaican dance theatre experimented with Revival movement which, as Nettleford points out, not only went into dance theatre, but also into the popular dancing such as, for example, the engine jogging of the Indian Engine Spirit, which later on went into Ska. [17] As Wynter has defined the symbolic impact of Revival in the larger sociological realm:

Revivalists through spiritual 'labour' and 'work' deny the brute facts of everyday existence by their transcendence in super-reality. They establish in dance 'a putative society'. In which they are the elect, the elite. Dance turns world upside-down, liberating participants. Challenge and response syndrome leads to fact that dance as a vital and meaningful reality found mainly among dispossessed (1970: 47).

Revival rhythmical and movement patterns thus form part of Jamaica's psychocultural kinetic consciousness, which even in the stage-transferred version of *Pocomania* – as well as in Ska and Dancehall culture thereafter – will evoke distinct identificatory patterns. Obviously, Nettleford's *Pocomania* does not convey the same sort of directly enacted liberation that Wynter describes, yet the choreography still manages to portray many of Revival's core features in a semiotized way. At least symbolically, these cultural icons continue to speak of Revival's empowering force. And as such, the stage performance ultimately paved the ground for better middle class understanding and acceptance of this formerly ridiculed practice.

Pocomania as the NDTC's earliest folk choreography is therefore probably less important in terms of its rather authentic preservation of Revival movements than the actual revolutionary potential of *Pocomania*'s theatre acclaim. When many middle class Jamaicans of the 1960s did not take Revival seriously, then *Pocomania* certainly helped to enhance a larger appreciation of this cultural expression (Seaga 1969: 5). As is shown in Wynter's following comment on the prevalent anti-African stance of the middle class at the time:

---

17 Similarly, Kingsley Stewart has remarked on the prevalence of the "seal" still maintained as a notion in contemporary dancehall culture. Compare Kingsley Stewart, "Dancehall," lecture presented 14 July 2003 at Jamaica School of Dance, Summer Workshop 2003, Kingston.

Africa exists [...] without interpretation and meaning. And without its framework of meaning it repels the more Christian element who see it only as one more example of the 'sexual licence' and immoral lack of restraint of the 'lower classes'. Meaningless it reinforces their attitude of rejection and contempt which is, since this is a part of their cultural being, self-rejection and self-contempt. This attitude extends to the dances which have become 'parochialized' a means of interpretation of a religion whose wider meaning is lost. Whilst the religion is constantly experienced and expressed through the dance, its universal elements and significance are obscured (1970: 46).

Nettleford's first folk-based choreography thus presented an affirmative bond to Revivalism and put forward a positive claim of cultural heritage and identity.

From the dance aesthetic angle *Pocomania* appears furthermore important, because it was Nettleford's first attempt at distilling Jamaican folk dance vocabulary into a dance theatre technique, which appears to resemble to some extent that of method acting. To illustrate this approach, Nettleford's choreography works with the performer's kinaesthetic recollection of apprehended Revival movements to the effect that bodily evocation of such memory will lend cultural authenticity to theatricalized *Pocomania*, even though there is no actual spirit possession performed on stage. As Derek Walcott has remarked in a review of the 1960s West Indian folk-ballet:

Real bongos, shangos or pocomania dances are possessed by the faith of their cultists, who are not performing when they dance, but are enacting their belief. The choreographer, therefore, prefers to simulate such possession as closely as possible, a technique that draws the dancer closer to acting, and acting emphasizes dramatic development (1966: 5).

Such simulation, I will argue, is certainly enhanced by the dancer's embodied memory of these cultural practices, which many NDTC dancers have been exposed to from their early childhood onwards. Evocation of such bodily remembrance, hence, develops into a dance technique which lends authenticity to the movement, yet prevents actual spirit possession on stage. Such technical abstraction appears important in order not to violate the integrity of the religious practice itself, when transferring it into a stage symbol; since theatre, after all, is neither a church nor a sacred space, i.e. at least in the NDTC's context.

In another review, which antedates the premiere of *Pocomania* by three years, Walcott had already critically addressed this issue of an almost anthropological folk essentialism in other Caribbean dance theatre companies of the time (1960: 10). Apparently, Walcott found many of these performances lacking in "creative authority," yet enjoyable in "what is current stock throughout the Antilles, a prettying of 'the folk,' which is satisfying to the middle class, and amusing to the peasant" (1960: 10). In his opinion, performing folk culture for folk culture's sake could hardly survive as an art of its own, since it would need further artistic development and technique. Walcott's question appears therefore rather rhetorical, when he demands:

We are now at the stage where we are recognizing our roots, but who wants to make a career of watching roots? And can one anyhow, since they are best underground, spreading a basis for society? To cut short the comparison for good: if you pull up a young plant too early, and wave it around in spontaneous delight at your agri-, horti- or folk-culture, it stands a poor chance of growing up (1960: 10).

The difficult task for the Caribbean choreographer then, was to investigate folk culture's rich dance religious vocabulary, not to merely imitate, but rather to transform it in order to develop an indigenous dance theatre idiom. It is therefore important to contextualize the NDTC's ongoing crystallization of these field-based movements, which the company translated into a modern dance expression, precisely as to overcome Walcott's critiqued "phase of quasi-folk" (Walcott 1960: 10).

Nettleford has thus argued that he most of all sought to "capture the meaning of the psychology of subculture cultism and the fundamentals of worship" to examine Revival's deeper significance for his art (1969: 22). Approaching the cult from a choreographer's perspective rather than that of the practitioner or anthropologist, he assessed the danced ceremony first of all for its possibilities of "sheer movement" in order to transcend the "psychological and sociological antecedents of the rite and preserve in Jamaican dance theatre the treasures which must go to build up the dance as an art" (1969: 23). Against a "doctrinaire" claim for authenticity, Nettleford insists that ritual and dance theatre share a concern for people's thoughts and feelings so that Revival movement can "indeed be woven into the fabric of the country's artistic expression without threat to the deeper social and psychological meanings of the cults themselves" (1969: 23). Abstracting the "essences of existence so that they can be of continuing meaning to the people they serve" thus becomes the "very challenge offered by the cult" and posed to the choreographer (Nettleford 1969: 24). Certainly, embodied kinaesthetic understanding as well as dedicated research of these movements is indispensable to enlarge these folk religious movements dramatically, as the NDTC's 2003 revival of *Pocomania* has clearly evidenced.

Pocomania's 2003 remounting rather faithfully maintained the original choreography so that actually Nettleford's seminal work presented quite a challenge to a new generation of NDTC dancers, who – forty years after – had to carefully train not to 'catch the spirit' during performance. Observing the NDTC's rehearsal process outside the NDTC's Little Theatre Studio, I noticed the extreme difficulty of this technical approach, as a new generation of dancers apprehended the movement vocabulary from older company members and video-tape. While the tape helped in terms of the larger arrangement and composition, the basic movements were better conveyed through the assistance by the older generation of NDTC members, who had been dancing *Pocomania* back in the 1960s. As NDTC choreographer Christopher Walker – in charge of re-mounting the work and also dancing the Shepherd role – commented, the dancers' phenomenological response to the Revival movement was decisive:

[...] you have to be thinking something, there must be something consistent. So that's where I approached the remounting of it from. What were you thinking? How did it make you feel? This movement? I know, you can't remember what the movement is, but, you know, and they [older generation NDTC members] remembered a lot of it. And they would come in. They'd sit outside, details that they wouldn't remember, but seeing the rehearsal, it would jog their memory and they said: 'Oh, you know this is supposed to mean so and so...' And so that information helped a great deal and so I made notes on that, based on what I was hearing. Joyce Campbell saying, 'No, when I did that I did it so and so...' or 'I remember feeling so and so, because this person reacted to me in this way...,' which means, even though the person, who was doing that other part was not around, we kind of have the information.[18]

Indeed, it was interesting to observe how Nettleford's own input, as well as that of Joyce Campbell, Pansy Hassan, Bridget Spaulding and others helped to reshape the exact style and expressiveness of the movement. Nettleford explained that mostly due to the constraints of

---

18 Interview Christopher Walker 11 Aug. 2003.

time, field trips are not so much involved in the NDTC's actual rehearsing process any longer. Yet, as Christopher Walker also affirmed, much of that vocabulary is now taught at the Jamaica School of Dance. Moreover, Revival churches are of course renowned throughout Jamaica so that many NDTC members will have some knowledge and experience of the religion. As Christopher Walker remembered in reference to Revival meetings from his own childhood:

I grew up in the country – St. Ann, that's where my town is – and I used to see them all the time. And when they had street meetings, I would see them carrying on and, you know, I'd watch from a distance. But I'd watch, cause there was always fear of the 'wrap-head' – that's what we used to call them – 'wrap-head church.' There was always fear of it and that's because we never understood what it was, and that's because my mother was Catholic. I never understood that. But there was also intrigue. So I'd still go and watch. If my mother hears this interview, she'd gag, but I'd still go watch, because there was intrigue and I was just excited by the rhythm. And sometimes there was no drum at all, just the chanting and the humming and the grunting, and the movement of the body was just so subtle! So much more subtle than we do it right now, which for obvious reasons wouldn't work on stage, because it wouldn't carry across the proscenium. Very, very subtle. So I had been mocking that style of movement for a long time, which is a good thing, because, when I finally studied Revival at Edna Manley and went on field trips, the information was already there. Because, I was mimicking them from when I was little. But even though I was doing it in a mockery fashion, the information was there.[19]

NDTC dancers of all generations will thus usually be able to build on such kinaesthetic memories. This inherited knowledge bears a clear advantage of cultural upbringing so to speak, as it facilitates the learning process of the folk vocabulary and will easily distinguish an NDTC member's performance from non-Jamaican/Caribbean performers, who are trying to execute the same steps, yet will not necessarily manage to achieve a similar grace of perfection and identification.[20]

---

19 Interview Christopher Walker 11 Aug. 2003.
20 This observation derives from my attendance of the E.M.C.'s Summer Workshop 2003, where North American trained dance students were showing more difficulties in conveying the correct style of the traditional folk forms than students from Jamaica and other Caribbean islands, not to mention my own graceless efforts.

Kumina

Kumina, also choreographed by Rex Nettleford, but with ten years of experience later, premiered in 1971 and has since then been continuously performed as "one of the 'immortals'" of the NDTC repertoire, as *Gleaner* critic Justin Whyle approvingly expressed in the 1990s (1995: 9A). Similar to *Pocomania,* this choreography is an abstraction based on Jamaican Kumina and extracts the essential movement and rhythmic vocabulary of that folk tradition in order to translate its formal characteristics and iconicity into dance theatre. As part of the early choreographing process, NDTC dancers were first taken to the field, where they would observe, participate and research Kumina, before they actually started to work with the gathered kinaesthetic and musical material for stage adaptation.[21]

Along with the effort of the Jamaican Cultural Development Commission (JCDC) to preserve Jamaica's vibrant African folk retention, many of the early NDTC members also became researchers into the origins and meanings of their country's cultural heritage.[22] Working for the Social Development Commission at the time, NDTC founding member Joyce Campbell, the 'Kingston bread girl,' recalls:

I traveled around in some of those years with Easton Lee [...] in those early years I remember, when I found out about things like the Etu, I took JIS and went out there and filmed it [...] I can also remember the first time I saw Kumina in St. Thomas. It had rained earlier in the evening, I remember distinctly, I can see it. So the earth was muddy and I saw those feet inching the toes in the mud, and that's the basic – sometimes you don't see it now – but every time I go back to it, that's the basic, they inch along like that with the feet. They curl their toes and inch along. While they are going, there is this lateral movement [she stands up and demonstrates] in here going and the shoulders and – I was fascinated! And that was my first thing of Kumina.[23]

Jamaican Kumina ritual is considered the most distinctly African group of rites in present Jamaica. Introduced by African contract workers in the late 19th century, Kumina is a Kongo retention which focuses on

---

21 Part of the NDTC's early field work was documented on film and can be accessed at the NDTC archive.
22 Rex Nettleford, Marjorie Whylie, NDTC musical director, and former NDTC dancers Joyce Campbell, Sheila Barnett and Cheryl Ryman have conducted seminal research, to which my own is obviously greatly indebted.
23 Interview with Joyce Campbell 15 Aug. 2003.

possession, ancestor worship, song and dance (Bilby/Leib 1986: 22-23). According to Kenneth Bilby, Kumina cosmology is based on the belief that the invisible spirit world is as real as the visible world. Kumina ceremonies serve as a means of communication with the ancestral spirits via music, movement, and language. Associated primarily with wakes, entombments, or memorial services, Kumina is also practised at births, thanksgivings and invocations and is traditionally located in the parish of St. Thomas.

Kumina dancing consists of two strands: 1. 'bailo,' which is the more secular, and 2. 'country,' considered as the more African and serious dance, which builds up to spirit possession. Initiated Kumina practitioners recognize their gods and ancestor spirits in the distinct dance style. Responding to the songs and drum rhythms, the possessed dancer will execute the spirit's according steps, while each instrument connects to a certain part/centre of the body. As Marjorie Whylie, for example, has explained, the Kumina shakas will communicate to the head center, transmitting the ritual's spiritual energy, which ultimately introduces possession.[24] While the bailo dances may display a variety of possible movements, the following basic ground pattern has been identified:

The basic dance posture constitutes an almost erect back and propelling actions of the hips as the feet inch along the ground. The dancers move in a circular pattern around the musicians and centre pole, either singly or with a partner. The arms, shoulders, rib cage, and hips are employed, offering the dancers ample opportunity for variations and interpretations of the counter-beats or poly-rhythms. Spins, dips, and 'breaks' on the last beat are common dance variations.[25]

Cheryl Ryman has further specified a set of distinct Kumina movements, since she regards the dance as the ritual's most constitutive part. Ryman asserts:

---

24 Marjorie Whylie, "Traditional Music and its Relationship to the Dance," lecture presented at Edna Manley College School of Dance, Summer Workshop 15 July 2003. Richard Schechner refers to "trance acting" as a total theatre experience in which the performer surrenders to "all-powerful forces" (spirit, demon, god). As a neurobiological reaction, "[T]rance is the outcome of the simultaneous stimulation of both hemispheres (frontal lobes) of the brain" and as such considered a transcultural performance practice (Schechner 2002: 164-165).
25 See *Jamaica Journal* Vol. 10.1 (1976): 7.

The distinguishing feature of this dance form is in the second or fourth position flat-footed inching and shuffling of the feet, accompanied by a side to side or forward thrusting of the hip. For this motion, the trunk is either held upright or tipped slightly back. The undulation of the ribcage may be employed either instead of the obvious hip motion or on top of it. The dance, even in a *bailo* context, conveys a great deal of quiet intensity and is accentuated by a subtle drop on the right leg, whether it is placed behind or beside the other leg in the fourth or second position stance, respectively. The highly typical wild, flat-back spins, followed by a break in direct response to a music cue, is yet another feature of African retention in Kumina and Jamaican dance in general.[26]

During a Kumina ceremony dance and music thus form an inseparable unit as dancers and musicians take their cues from each other.

Essential to Kumina drumming are the Kbandu (battery of drums, "female") and the Playing Cast (lead drum, "male"). While the former plays the rhythm with emphasis on the first and third beats, the latter plays the more complicated and specific basic rhythms to incite the spirit. Olive Lewin has described the interaction between drumming and dancing as such:

The rhythm [of the Kbandu drums] is reproduced by the feet, while the florid and improvisatory patterns of the playing cyas [cast] drum impel movement of other parts of the body – head, shoulders, arms, hips. It also conveys to the dancers whether to proceed in the circular line singly or facing, as partner, one who is immediately in front or behind, or to spin and break before one more proceeding in single file, anti-clockwise (2000: 235).

Other percussive instruments include the Scrapers (grater), Shakas (rattles) and Catta Sticks. Accompanied by incantation, rum is spilled on the players' hands and instruments. Libations of white rum may also be offered to the ancestors, when spilled in all four directions. The ritual proceedings welcome the ancestral spirits to "return to this corporal world through the possession of the living" and "in return they provide the living with solutions to their problems, offering advice and vital knowledge not otherwise available to them." [27]

Ryman argues that Kumina ceremonies should be considered as a form of communication rather than worship of the ancestor spirits, who

---

26 Ryman, "Kumina – Stability and Change" 111.
27 Ryman, "Kumina – Stability and Change" 81-82.

are called *nkuyu* or *kuyu*. Rituals of language, music and dance channel the communication process. Yet, only as a "dance-music unit" will possession by the *nkuyu* occur.[28] Kumina possession differentiates between two types. "Mounting possession," in which the spirit controls the dancer from within and "mimetic possession," in which the spirit guides the dancer from the outside. The latter will be observed more often and can be recognized in the dancer's gestures, miming and other features of communication with the ancestor. In mounting possession, on the other hand, the dancer is directly taken over by the spirit and enticed with supernatural powers. In this case the spirit force may enable the dancer to showcase the eating of glass, burning coals or similar supernatural displays (Allen 1982: 11-12).[29] Passed on from generation to generation, this performance of the ancestor spirit's power becomes particularly important to the Kumina group, because it provides each

---

28 Ryman, "Kumina – Stability and Change" 90-91.
29 Apparently, Allen observed "mounting possession" during a field trip, which he described as follows: "[...] She was in what they call the 'myal', that controversial stage when the dancers are supposed to be possessed by the spirits. Then an elderly lady 'got out'. She grabbed a firestick out of a nearby fire and began to wield it about, sending some spectators into a quick retreat. Others who had seen many Kumina ceremonies, held their ground, certain that the woman would not harm them. But it seemed dangerous to me when she barged out of the line of dancers, rushed to a nearby kitchen and returned with a machete. She wielded the machete just as she had done with the fire. I was in no mind to receive any machete cuts in the bushes of St. Thomas and stayed wide of her. Even the stout-hearted ones like Brissett seemed nervous and uncomfortable. Then she rushed again out of the shed and proceeded to 'chop to bits' a 'bad spirit' which was lurking nearby in what looked like a butchery. On her return, apparently satisfied that she had defeated an evil spirit, she walked onto the blazing embers from which she had plucked the firestick and danced, while chanting something inaudible to me" (1982: 11-12). The 'inaudible' chant, Allen overheard, was likely to be given in Kikongo as this description appears to depict the country part of the Kumina ceremony. While Allen's report is full of the typical sensationalist vocabulary of the appalled onlooker, I consider it still important in this context, for it presents a point of view that is not only shared by some tourists and foreigners, but also those Jamaicans, who disprove of the rite as a morally harmful superstition. Thus, some of the Jamaican E.M.C. summer school participants refrained from joining the scheduled Kumina field trip in fear that it could negatively affect them. Interestingly enough though, as this report also clearly demonstrates, Kumina performance certainly speaks of a defiant power and demonstrates as such an effective cultural practice of revolt.

member with a sense of heritage, continuity and power directly linked to the African homeland.[30] As Lewin has pointed out, certain talents may be handed down from a deceased ancestor to a living member of the Kumina cult. Thus, for example, in the case of Queenie Kennedy, who inherited her distinct dance style from the spirit of Mother Margaret, another Kumina queen (Lewin 2000: 280-281).

In his study "Kumina – The Spirit of African Survival in Jamaica," Edward Kamau Brathwaite places the ritual into the context of what he calls "contact evidence of a living African presence and the consciousness of its place in the continuum: the persisting continental connection between New World and Old Africa" (1978: 46). Regarding Kumina less as a "syncretized religion," but rather as an "African/Maroon lifeform that has used the resources of Creole Christianity when/wherever necessary," Brathwaite stresses Kumina's socio-political function in terms of cultural survival (1978: 46). While the colonialist system sought to destroy the cultural link to Africa, Kumina had to be hidden from public view. However, since African religions do not separate the secular from the sacred, Kumina was not limited to a Christian 'one-hour-church-service,' but rather permeated the whole of community life. By tearing down the binary construction of two different spheres for life and death, Kumina practice manages to transcend dualistic notions of separation. Whether it be body and soul, heaven and earth or home and diaspora, communicating with the ancestors in the ritual accomplishes a state of self-forgetfulness and reconciliation (Brathwaite 1978: 46).

Music and dance in particular enhance this spiritual awareness, for the rhythmic patterns and kinetic moves generate the communication which builds up to possession by the ancestor spirit. In this respect, Kumina not only serves as a cultural link for the community, but also creates the notion of wholeness and identity within the cosmological system. Active participation in the dance and music can therefore be regarded as yet another cultural strategy that helped to overcome the psychological trauma of the Middle Passage. Kumina dance and drumming thus helped to defeat the loss and forced separation from the African homeland as entranced dancers reconnected with the ancestral spirit force. Additionally, Brathwaite stresses Kumina's particular relevance, for the Kongo-based ritual stresses the African link more than Jamaica's other religious practices do. In contrast to Revivalism,

---

30 Ryman, "Kumina – Stability and Change" 117-118.

for example, Kumina's importance relies on this autochthonous claim, which counteracts the homogenization of cultural practice under a somewhat enforced Anglo-Christian tradition of colonial provenance (Brathwaite 1978: 46). Brathwaite, however, takes an ambivalent stance towards the appropriation of Kumina by the Jamaican festival and dance movement, because he sees the danger of commercializing those more authentic forms. For example, he questions whether people will still acknowledge the ritual's complexity of meaning, once that it is transferred to the stage. Festival exposure, he is afraid, might lose the impact of the religious context and fail to promote deeper understanding and appreciation of the practice and its practitioners.

Yet, in his theatrical adaptation of *Kumina*, choreographer Rex Nettleford took care to sufficiently abstract the Kumina dance vocabulary so as to adjust it to the space and time parameters of the theatre stage.[31] As has been mentioned before, the company strives for what Nettleford calls "conscious transition:" i.e. the development of a distinct Jamaican approach that emerges from experimentation with ballet and modern dance as it incorporates Jamaican folk forms. The exploration of all of these movement techniques thus serves as a significant vehicle in a process towards an original Jamaican dance theatre style that is by no means to be mistaken as a one to one reproduction of ritual. As Rex Nettleford defends his approach against cultural purists:

Folk dancing is for participating and not as theatre dancing is, for viewing. [...] Nowhere are these [folk forms] translated wholesale on the stage. Rather, they are distilled and their essence extracted, treated, and projected. When Beryl McBurnie, the Trinidadian high priestess of dance, presents rituals of Shango, Rada Plavadoo, she presents them as an artist not as a dweller in the hills of Belmont and Laventille. The Nation Dances of Cariacou must be translated into the language of dance-theatre for presentation. Otherwise they are best left where they thrive and have their being, if authenticity is what we want (1968: 128-129).

Transferring Kumina ritual into dance theatre choreography, Nettleford thus maintained the dance's basic foot movement, yet accelerated the speed of progression, which is usually much slower in pace.

---

31 For the following analysis compare, "Kumina," The National Dance Theatre Company of Jamaica, performance video produced by CPTC/Creative Production and Training Center, Kingston.

The National Dance Theatre Company of Jamaica in Rex Nettleford's Kumina, 1971. Photograph by Maria LaYacona (rpt. in: NDTC 30th Anniversary Program).

Moreover, the NDTC's *Kumina* inserts several modern dance movements, which Nettleford superimposed on the basic Kumina shuffle. Leg extensions and port-de-bras, for example, are definitely not to be found in the ritual, yet for the stage performance, they add to the choreography's aesthetic appeal. Such explorations are taken further by the inclusion of the Warrick (stickfight) from Jamaican Jonkonnu, which Nettleford introduced in order to break the spirit inviting intensity of the dance.[32] Group formations as opposed to the ritualistic circle as well as the cross-leg jumps of the male dancers were likewise choreographed to prevent dancers from entering the state of spirit possession.[33] Maintained from the ritual, however, is the spilling of white rum to symbolically appease the ancestor spirits.

---

[32] Marjorie Whylie commented on this strategy during the 2003 Summer School Workshop. Compare Marjorie Whylie, "Traditional Music and its Relationship to the Dance," lecture presented at Edna Manley College School of Dance, Summer Workshop 15 July 2003. The "Warrick" has been identified as a stick-fighting dance that derived from the British mumming tradition, however, as has been mentioned before, stick-fighting is also a popular West Central African-derived tradition (Ryman 1980: 14; Warner-Lewis 2003: 199-226).

[33] Music ethnographer Markus Coester also noted that the spirit inviting drum key was taken out of the Kumina drumming.

Again, as Nettleford has argued for *Pocomania*, he does not intend to reproduce the ritual itself, but seeks to "capture the meaning of the psychology of subculture cultism and the fundamentals of worship" in his choreography (1969: 22). In comparison to that earlier work though, it is interesting to notice the advanced degree of abstraction here. While *Pocomania* was still closely relying on the field research, *Kumina* reinvents the ritual through the choreographer's prism into an artwork of its own right.[34] And yet, despite the increases in tempo and the "chastizing" of pelvic movements to standards of middle class "acceptability," Monica Lawrence's analysis, for example, asserts that the theatre performance still generates a truthful experience of Kumina by capturing the ritual's essential elements.[35] Largely due to the authenticity of the basic foot movement as well as the Kumina drumming, she furthermore claims that the choreography ultimately altered the social discourse on the rite, which for a long time had been culturally denigrated and neglected.[36]

To redress Brathwaite's voiced concern for commercialization of the folk forms, one might therefore want to finally take a closer look at *Kumina*'s reception at home and particularly abroad, where this alleged danger has in fact been superseded by the communicative power of the piece.[37] As the following review of the NDTC's Toronto tour in 1982 documents, theatricalized Kumina still conveys much of its spiritual force, kinaesthetically re-connecting the audience at least to the African Jamaican folk heritage at home, if not necessarily to the ancestral African gods. As Maud Fuller commented :

---

34 For a more technique-based analysis of the Kumina dance vocabulary compare Carty 1988: 22-31.
35 Monica Lawrence, M.Phil. project presentation, given on January 30th 2003 at the Cultural Studies Group meeting, U.W.I., Mona Campus, Kingston.
36 On behalf of the field to stage adaptation process, Jean Johnson Jones has similarly argued: "Undoubtedly, removal from their former contexts alters their meaning; but the movements of the staged dances maintain a cultural validity which can act as a window through which more understanding can be gained of the people who perform them" (1999: 100-101).
37 As Sheila Barnett recalls though, Brathwaite was not even critical of the NDTC's Kumina, which he elsewhere has referred to as an "icon of Jamaica and the Caribbean region" (Barnett, "Notes on Contemporary Dance-Theatre in Jamaica 1930-1979," unpublished script, n.d.).

After KUMINA had been reprised for the fourth time on opening night, the audience, having whipped itself into a state of near-frenzy, took up the strains of 'only the righteous' followed by oodles of 'boodoodum' to imitate the drumming. I saw no less than five very 'proper' ladies jutting their hips and shuffling their feet as they filed out of the auditorium with a bounce and buoyancy that had long ceased to be part of their notion of propriety. I must say – their hearts were very willing but alas! for their flesh. But such is the seductiveness of a work like KUMINA; it lures you into believing that 'you can do it too, Punchinello little fellow' (1982: n.p.).

As this example nicely demonstrates, *Kumina*'s kinaesthetic energy stirs long lost memories of cultural belonging and identity, which also appears as the communicative strength of the dance in this particular case. The NDTC's *Kumina* consequently not only obtained recognition of Jamaican African identity with local audiences, but also provided the theatre spectator with an awareness of the ritual in the field that he or she most likely would not have been aware of otherwise. In this respect then, the dance's purpose is not merely entertainment, but it also contains educational tenets. As Mervyn Alleyne conclusively confirms:

Kumina music and dance have become accepted forms of the Jamaican national culture. Kumina drumming and the Kumina 'shuffle' dance movement performed to it have become standard elements of the Jamaican dance theatre, and the Seaforth Town performers themselves are invited to perform at national celebrations. In this sense there has been a theatrification of Kumina culture which so far has not led to a dissolution of its integrity in its local setting, but which, on the contrary, seems to contribute to a growing acceptance of Kumina as part of the national identity (2002: 209).

Gerrehbenta

Based on Jamaican wakes/dead-yard ceremonies, the NDTC's third choreography to be discussed in this context is *Gerrehbenta* (1983). The work owes its name to the traditional folk form of Gerreh and its instrument the Benta, which is popular in St. Mary and made of "bamboo with a string lifted from the membrane and played with a calabash to produce a singing note while sticks are beaten at the other end" (Brown 1995: 42-46). Yet, the name is misleading, for, in fact, the choreography opens with the entrance of familiar characters from Jonkonnu and is accompanied by the typical drum and fife music of that tradition.[38] Center stage we see the impressive, quite awe-exerting mask of the rural Horsehead, who is soon surrounded by an inner and outer circle of female dancers in traditional costume and head-tie.[39] At the same time, a character reminiscent of the Jonkonnu's Actor Boy as well as a Cowhead mask take their positions on the left and right downstage corner. Both of them carry massive bamboo poles, which they rhythmically stamp onto the ground.

Similar to the Jonkonnu street parade, the choreography begins with a danced walk that is processional in character and leads the women into an inner and outer circle, marching opposite direction. The circles here are derived from British Maypole and Ring Game dancing, which both have been adapted and creolized in many of the island's folk dances and children's games. Nettleford makes again use of the jig, which he had first introduced in *Plantation Revelry* as one of the major Jonkonnu steps to be used in dance theatre. Bettelheim characterizes the Jonkonnu jig as a "travelling hopping step" with turn out knees and one leg passing from front to back or vice versa so that support and free leg will alternate (Nunley/Bettelheim 1988: 64). Typical for Jokonnu dancing – in which each character also carries out a distinct solo performances and improvisations – are apart from the processions, also the isolations of different body parts (knees, shoulders, pelvis) and the bent over torso with the shoulder "shimmy" (rotation of the shoulders). All of which owe to an African dance aesthetic, even though the jig itself is of course originally a European-derived step (Ryman 1984b: 58).

After the opening sequence, this celebratory beginning switches into the more intense drum beats of the Gerreh and Etu dance. Both forms are Jamaican funerary rite dances performed to the accompanying traditional wake songs presented by Majorie Whylie and the NDTC singers during this section. The songs are: "Kanda Tone deh blow Maw-ga," "O Timothy a Tanga Man" and "Wonda who a Zuzu

---

38 For the following analysis compare *Gerrehbenta, The National Dance Theatre Company of Jamaica*, performance video, produced by CPTC/Creative Production and Training Center, Kingston.
39 In addition to what has already been said on behalf of the mask's origin, Cheryl Ryman's research also refers to similar horse masks worn by the Efik of eastern Nigeria. Among the Buru masqueraders, she comments, the Horsehead is regarded as one of the "most feared manifestations of an evil spirit in Jamaica" (see NDTC Newsletter July 1983; Ryman 1984b: 56).

Fader."[40] Characteristic of Gerreh, which is practiced in Westmoreland and Hannover, is the use of ring games, dancing in circular pattern and a dance "in which performers are lifted as they balance standing on two horizontally held bamboo poles," as is here used by Nettleford to indicate the switch of sequence (Tanna 1987: 31). Ryman furthermore explains that Gerreh is performed during "the first two nights after the death of a person or until the deceased is buried [...]" (1980: 9). Patricia Bowen has described the dance movement as follows:

In guerre the dance steps usually carry the dancer forward and backward. There is the balance step and the shuffle as in Kumina. The balance may be exaggerated. The stress is on the supporting leg. The dancer moves forward to meet a partner, the pelvis making a figure of eight with right knee bent. Stopping immediately opposite partner, the couple continuing pelvic movements bends down, then retreat (1980: n.p.).

Etu, the other influential dance step here, also originated in Hanover and the surrounding regions. The dance, however, has been out of practice and was revived through the effort of the Jamaican Cultural Development Commission. Much of the religious intent of the dance

---

40 A recording of these wake songs and other traditional music compositions has been assembled on LP. Compare Heritage, record composed by Marjorie Whylie, Head of Folk Music Research Department Jamaica School of Music. Whylie's introduction to the recording of Jamaican Heritage music reads: "The music represents little known traditions and forms – little known that is, outside the communities where music and dance form an integral part of everyday life. In all the examples, the rhythmic impulse is very strong, even when there is no instrumental accompaniment. Voices are sometimes used in a percussive way, and handclapping and foot stomping support this norm. Instruments become, as a result of this, extensions of the body, and the interplay between rhythmic phrases and bodily response is a most interesting dialogue. The drum, as one would expect, is the predominant instrument, but most striking is the creativity and resourcefulness displayed in the use of available indigenous or discarded/recycled materials for instrument construction. The level of Africanisms still to be found in Jamaica may be surprising to some listeners, but suffice it to say that those elements in the music are but a part of the total neo-African experience and life-style of our country." Comparing the recording to the performance of the NDTC singers, one also notices a slight adaptation to a concert rather than ritual presentation as the NDTC's interpretation appears to have slowed down a little and naturally comes across as more 'classical' and 'refined' in singing and interpretation.

has therefore been lost today. Still, historically, Etu ceremonies – like those of the Nago people of neighboring Westmoreland – bear witness to Yoruba origin and they were held for several occasions such as "dinner feast, wedding or forty night memorial (i.e. the 40th night after a person's death)" (Ryman 1980: 9; 13). While a common dance style has not been recognized, some distinctions can still be made:

Generally the male dancers exhibit more strength and agility, than the women, who indulge in 'hippy' teasing movements. The dance posture is characteristically African, with bent knees, body slightly forward to erect, and flat-footed contact with the ground. Frequently, alternating feet brush the ground rapidly in response to the last beat of the drum.[41]

In Etu (Song: "Bambalala Yuwati" performed by NDTC singers) the drummers – who play a 6-8 compound duple rhythm on the typical drum set of "Achaka" (kerosene tin) and "Irre" (two-headed oval shaped drum) – and dancers work closely together. Particular of this dance is most of all the "Shawling Ritual," which is essential to the dance and is also an integral part of Nettleford's choreography.[42] The shawling proceeds as such:

The *Queen* and/or another principal female member, throws a scarf or scarves around the neck of the dancer, who is then ceremoniously 'dipped back' from the waist, 'to give him strength', and finally the *shawler* raises the dancer's arm in salutation and congratulation. Sometimes, the shawl is tied around the waist or hat, and is used to 'crown' a particularly virtuoso performance. Although only two people (dancer and shawler) are normally found in the dance area a third person may enthusiastically join the performance for a while then sit. The group dances together, marking the end of the ceremony.[43]

Looking at the choreography in light of this description, obviously the placing of the shawls as well as the hip-teasing movements of the female dancer are discernible. Correspondences between these distinct funerary rites exist and even as they are blended, as well as transformed by the NDTC dancers' modern training, they still convey the cosmological link to Jamaican traditional dances. Derived from kinaesthetic memory, these dances communicate a life-asserting, positive en-

---

41 *Jamaica Journal* Vol. 10:1 (1976): 4.
42 For a more detailed description of the Etu drums compare Ryman 1980: 9.
43 *Jamaica Journal* 10:1 (1976): 4.

ergy, which connects "body and soul(s), corporal and spiritual worlds" (Ryman 1984: 19).

Gerrehbenta thus celebrates the "procreative aspect of marking life in the midst of death," which is known as an integral part not only of nine-nights and wakes but in fact of most of Jamaica's traditional folk dances.[44] As was already mentioned, Pigou has pointed out how African Jamaican epistemology conceives of death as "a prolonged event," which encompasses three different phases: "a) the separation of the body, spirit and duppy; b) a transitional phase before the spirit reaches the spirit world and c) a final phase when the spirit, assisted by the proper rites, reaches the spirit world" (1987: 25). Similarly Wynter has remarked that in Jamaican folk belief the "dead are not the negation of life, but part of the life force" to the effect that the "folkdance of the living is made more alive by the presence of the dead" (1970: 37). Originating under the hardships and suffering of slavery, funerary rite dances were commemorating death and loss, yet celebrating the space-time continuum to the African homeland and ancestors at the same time. Such mourning therefore carries an empowering moment as the African-based cosmology unites the living and the dead through the practice of these dances. Celebratory in fashion they have stood and continue to stand for the desire to live on, to procreate and overcome. They embody remembrance in the face of loss, seeking reconciliation within the community in each individual dancing session. These traditional dances stress the social bonding among group members as much as they contribute to the affirmation of self.

This function of traditional dance becomes particularly evident during the final section of the choreography. In front of a scenic red backdrop, this sequence is dedicated to the Dinki Mini dance, the last of the folk forms influential for the choreographic process.[45] Following a Dinki Mini song, one is lead even deeper into the vestiges of Jamaican history. For the traditional Dinki Mini songs, the so-called 'digging and grave yard songs' are associated with the death of Tacky, the leader of the 1760 slave rebellion in St. Mary. According to Jamaican oral history, Tacky's death occasioned one of the great Dinki Minis in time (Tanna 1987: 27-31). Structurally, Dinki Mini songs follow an African-based call

---

44 Compare Maureen Rowe, "Roots and Branches – The Precursors," taped lecture presentation (Kingston: Library of the Spoken Word, n.d.).

45 Ryman associates Dinki Mini directly with wake dances, observing that "the more obvious pelvic activity (fertility overtones) [...] serves to pit the power of life, through procreation, against death" (Ryman 1980: 14).

and response pattern with the leader starting and the group responding as we have here from the NDTC singers. The highly popular mento music is produced by various instruments as maracas, grater, drums, guitar and sticks and has a "clear, strong fourth beat, in a bar of four beats" (Brown 1982: 45).

Similar to Gerreh of western Jamaica, Dinki Mini is primarily practiced in the eastern parts of the island. Performed from the second to eighth night of a nine-night wake, Dinki Mini cheerfully commemorates the deceased person. As a couple dance it is not only accompanied by lively mento music, but singing, ring games and Anansi stories may also be included. Climaxing the ninth night, the spirit is finally sent off to the other world (Ryman 1980: 8-9). Hazel Ramsay in an interview with Laura Tanna for *Jamaica Journal* has given a more detailed description of the dance. She explains.

[The] basic dance step [has] knees bent, moving the right foot over the left while the left foot shuffles forward. Then the right foot is placed behind the left while the left foot again shuffles forward. The hips move sideways, and even rotate while the arms are bent at the elbows, hand held palms up. Shoulders are erect and rotate backwards and forwards while the head is held straight and eyes look ahead. In a further movement, the partners may hold hands high, turn in to face each other and then face out, still holding hands. The couples then form a ring and dance counter clockwise (Tanna 1987: 29).

These characteristic movements can also be observed in the last section of *Gerrehbenta*, when the Horsehead is surrounded by couples of NDTC dancers, who engage in the flirtatious Dinki Mini dance. One more time the male and female groups of dancers enter and exit in diagonal procession, displaying the various shuffles, torso and shoulder isolations characteristic of the dance to afterward join in couples of man and woman or smaller groups of three. The last part is indeed a celebration, a party that in its ritualistic repetitiveness spreads over into the audience. While all of the company is encircling the Horsehead in commemorative appraisal, the scene slowly fades out on the NDTC Singers' refrain: "Take off you're clothes and jump in da rain a, ha [...]."

Especially the continuing presence of the Horsehead appears of particular significance here, since the mask frames *Gerrehbenta*'s beginning and ending sections. Interestingly enough, in Mande country and parts of Mali ethnographers have found a similar horse mask, which performs analogous dance steps and is believed to represent "the summation of the universe, incorporating intelligence, initiation, the spirit of life, and the wisdom of the creator," as well as "man's struggle and search for a life without end" (Nunley/Bettelheim 1988: 55).[46] Supposing that the horse mask still conveys some of that symbolic value, its prominent role in *Gerrehbenta* introduces a rather intriguing semiotic shift. Reading the Horsehead as "enactment of man's struggle and search for a life without end," the masquerader's vigorous jumps allow to re-interpret the funeral scene: Set in front of the backdrop's designed burial ground, the red lit scenery behind the grave stone no longer represents gloom, but happiness. Death is not death, but life. And it is precisely this message that the three dancers in the beginning of the last section seem to address, when they step up front, turn towards the audience and start their celebratory dance.

By choosing such clear markers as the traditional nine-night music and songs, the shawling-ritual and the Horsehead, *Gerrehbenta*'s life-affirming message is stressed. Originating from Jamaican grass roots culture, these cultural icons still carry an immense symbolic power, when transferred to the theatre stage. Easily identified by the local audience, they testify to the resistant resource of collective body memory. As Don Buckner has expressed on behalf of the impact of Jonkonnu:

Jonkonnu communicates with people, not in platitudes and big words but through music, dance, colour and drama which "tells our story". It seems to me that our strongest visual and psychological memories of what could be called an unquestionably Jamaican – Caribbean art form is embodied in Jonkonnu. It is saturated with images that stir memories in mind and muscle. I remember Mother Lundy, I remember people on stilts. I remember people being afraid, being fascinated by the procession and interplay. Fragments of memories come home to me very strongly (1993: 8).

Presenting a medley of four different folk forms, *Gerrehbenta* convincingly translates ritualistic movement into a powerful piece of dance theatre. Celebratory in nature, yet dealing with the universal topic of procreation and life in death, this NDTC choreography also derives from Jamaica's treasure of kinaesthetic memory. Publicly commemorating these traditions, dance theatre assumes a distinct role in nurturing

---

46 Similarly, Ryman points to the mask's mystical association "with the ruler or any person of importance" in Africa, as well as she highlights the prevalent horse and riding imagery connected to spirit possession (Ryman 1984b: 58).

the larger community's self-understanding. As Brian Heap, arts' critic for the Jamaican *Gleaner*, has commented on the significance of Dinki Mini in the NDTC's 1998 *Gerrehbenta* performance:

There is a very distinctive 'cripple foot' step from the Jamaican dinki-mini which is now widely accepted indeed integral, feature of the Caribbean dance vocabulary. Hence it has become a part of NDTC's repertoire, which serves as a powerful metaphor not only for the struggle of Caribbean peoples against adversities, but also for the triumph of the Caribbean spirit. [...] inspired by indigenous death rituals which celebrate life, gerreh, ettu and dinki-mini, pit us once more against the ultimate adversity. And that cripple foot step, that triumphant shuffle, becomes the means of overcoming everything that life can throw at us. [...] the healing forces will always seek to overcome. Crippled spirit, cripple foot, one can heal the other, apparently – at least so it seems in art (5c).

The National Dance Theatre Company of Jamaica in Rex Nettleford's Gerrehbenta, 1983. Photograph by Denis Valentine (rpt. Caribbean Beat Nov./Dec. 2002: 52).

In this sense then, *Gerrehbenta* (re)assembles kinaesthetic memory into a socio-political statement of empowerment. Against stereotypical notions of dance as having no meaning, being lascivious and whatever else colonialists such as Sir Edward Long have mistaken this practice for, it in fact testifies to quite the opposite: a very well thought through strategy of secrecy, camouflage and spirit that only the initiated fully understands. In terms of the African Jamaican identity claim, such dance theatre performance of traditional dances surely proves of undeniable importance.

Bruckins

Bruckins choreographed by Joyce Campbell and Barry Moncrieffe in 2002 presents yet another repertoire piece to showcase Jamaica's rich dance heritage, very much in line with the efforts of the JCDC's annual festival. The original folk dance is celebratory in nature, accompanied by speeches, parading, dancing and feasting. Etymologically "bruk" may refer to 1. not having money, 2. "the typical dance movement which gives the appearance that the body is broken at the waist" – in that sense also "to break free" – but can also 3. simply relate to forms of social gathering.[47] According to oral history the first Bruckins took place in 1834 at Muirton's Works Yard. As the story has been told by Kenneth Bryan in 1984:

Now at this time there was some upheaval in St James and as was typical at that time, slaves heard on the grapevine about anything that was happening among slaves anywhere in the island. It is difficult to say just how the news travelled, but usually it was the house slaves who overheard conversations of their masters who spread the news. When the slaves in East Portland heard of what was happening in St. James they became unwilling to continue working and got together and started singing and dancing. They were jumping up and down using their machetes like swords and they made music with old pans, graters and bamboo. The owner allowed them to carry on dancing for a while, then he gave order to get back to work. But this was not easy for they assumed that others in the West Indies and in St. James were free. This, however, was not true.[48]

In fact, only four years later by the year 1838, freedom was really in effect and greeted by the famous Bruckins song "Jubalee" – "by far the most important of the songs:"

Jubalee, Jubalee dis is de year of Jubalee
Queen Victoria give me free, Queen Victoria
Give me free, dis is de year of Jubalee

---

47 "Bruckins Party," unpublished paper, African Caribbean Institute, Kingston.
48 "Bruckins Party" 3.

Jubalee, Jubalee, Jubalee, Jubalee.[49]

Mention of Queen Victoria here, clearly signals the dance's acknowledgement and celebration of Emancipation. Other Bruckins' songs include: "Recreation," "True a Noble Chairman," "Walk in Deh," "Heel and Toe," "Mango Blassom," and "The Frack the Queen a go wear."[50]

As there are two sets, one red and the other blue, Hill and others have placed the emergence of Bruckins in the context of the Jonkonnu masquerade complex. After Emancipation, Hill argues, Bruckins evolved out of the decline of the public Jonkonnu festivity, which came under pressure from the local authorities, who made a constant effort to subdue the tradition. Also, because the 'brown' upper class did no longer identify as much with the masquerade tradition as they used to, Jonkonnu became largely a lower class cultural practice. Celebrating Emancipation day on August 1st, former slaves commemorated their freedom day in due fashion and Bruckins added a new dance to that festivity, which in satire, rebellious spirit and social comment was very much in line with Jonkonnu tradition. Hill explains:

Moving from the public streets to the barrack yard and the village compound, the August 1 celebrants developed other types of events to mark their day of freedom. [...] to the black underclass, especially those who still worked the land, it was a day to recall, the day on which Missis Queen had set them free after more than a hundred years of enslavement. They formed ad hoc associations; they erected bamboo sheds with thatch-covered roofs in which they gave banquets, made speeches, sang songs of freedom, played their fifes and drums, and ended with lively dances that were called 'Bruckins' (1992: 253).

Also Joyce Campbell in her essay on "Jamaican Folk and Traditional Dances," suggests that the origin of Bruckins' Party is African and derived from the Jonkonnu Christmas processions. She asserts:

Bruckin' Party is a set dance – Blues and Reds performed in a sort of contest with each set trying to out-dance the other. Talks reveal that in the past the costumes were more colorful and were usually kept a secret until the dance was performed. A Bruckin' Party would start at night in one yard, then they would march on the streets to another yard where the Bruckins would end at daylight. The dancers represent Kings, Queens, Princes, Captains, Soldiers,

---

49 "Bruckins Party" 4.
50 "Bruckins Party" 4.

Trainbearers, etc. in each set, complete with swords and crowns for the Kings. The men dance with sticks described as "razzling the swords" (1976: 8-9).

Accompanied by the "rattling" and the "bass" drum, music and singing are an integral part of the dancing. Most of the songs stem from oral tradition and are passed down from generation to generation. Some words are directly related to Emancipation and Queen Victoria ("August Morning come again/This is the year of Jubilee/Queen Victoria set us free").

Bruckins – as it has today been canonized by the JCDC's annual festival and as it is also performed in the NDTC's choreography – starts with the procession of the red and blue sets singing:

De Queen a com in [3x]
Oh yes, a beautiful sight.
Red Queen a come in [3]
Oh yes, a beautiful sight.
Blue Queen a com in [3x]
Oh yes, a beautiful sight.[51]

The dancers are dressed up in finery and execute very stately steps and dips, which originally derived from the European Pavanne. Each set has a King and a Queen and courtiers called grandson and granddaughter. Carrying swords in their hands and wearing crowns on their heads, the dancers, however, have adjusted the "upright stance of the Europeans" by tilting back on the diagonal and fully flexing the foot.[52] Highly competitive rivalry reigns among both groups as each set seeks to outdo the other in performance by the end of the procession. Among the renowned movement sequences are: "Bruck, Siloh, Benup and Kneel-Down-Bow-Down."[53] Originally located in Ressington and Portland, Queen's Party and "Teameeting" were related forms also performed to celebrate the Anniversary of Emancipation from July 31 to August 1 (see Bowen 1980). In the staged adaptations, however, these do no longer appear. As becomes evident once more, the cultural significance of Bruckins and its masquerade competition of kingly sets

---

51 For a more detailed musical and song analysis compare Lewin 2000: 114-115.
52 Compare Carty for a more detailed discussion of Bruckins dance vocabulary as technique (1988: 58-65).
53 "Bruckins Party" 6.

appears to somewhat mirror that of the Jonkonnu masquerade complex. Here, too, formerly silenced and disenfranchised groups of the population appropriated stately power by disguising themselves with the insignia of hegemonic rule.

Interlude III: Dance and Self-Discovery

By artistically exploring material from Jamaica's kinaesthetic memory, the NDTC has laid the foundation of a distinct dance style that not only reflects the country's African heritage, but managed to display it on a nationally significant level. As Loren Kruger in her study on the national stage in England, France and America has pointed out, theatre oftentimes functions as "the appropriate site for nation building" as well as the "battleground of intersecting fields on which the legitimacy of national popular representation is publicly contested" (1992: 6). Considering Jamaica's social make-up at the time of independence the project of national reconciliation, as well as the question of precisely which values could be claimed as Jamaican after the fall of the British colonial hegemony, were certainly considered pressing issues. Already with Ivy Baxter's pre-Independence audiences, the process of re-identification with Jamaican grassroots culture had set in, when she first confronted her middle class audiences with their African ancestry. To those, who V.S. Naipaul had characterized as colonial "mimic men," the NDTC's *Pocomania* must have come home as quite a shock, yet also as a revelation. National dance theatre in Jamaica thus emerged as what Kruger's analysis has conceived of as a "site of struggle among competing attempts to legitimately define the appropriate relationship between theatre and society" (1992: 6).

Negotiating Caribbean identity via dance theatre proved particularly intriguing, because of its cultural ambivalence. While the early NDTC members were contested for their 'bare-foot' dance, they still conquered the national scene, i.e. traditionally the site of hegemony. As Kruger remarks, staged identification remains doubled and cannot easily be claimed by state power, since "the institution of theatrical nationhood appears as both a cultural monument to the legitimate but nonetheless exclusionary hegemony [...] and a site on which the excavation and perhaps toppling of that monument may be enacted" (1992: 6). Hence, national dance theatre in Jamaica operated subversively from within the Western theatre frame by appropriating modern dance as much as the proscenium stage, yet dancing quite African rhythms and beats. Thus, Ivy Baxter's Dance Group as well as Eddy Thomas' later Dance Workshop and ultimately the NDTC integrated those local performance modes into a theatrically effective dance 'mimicry,' which performed according to western standards on behalf of stage set and some of the training, yet expressed what was truly discovered on their own. The NDTC's conscious claim of folk culture and its performative traditions soon evolved through the backdoor, if you will, as the legitimizing force of national identification after independence.

When the theatre stage traditionally was a space of the upper middle classes and in the beginning British dominated, it changed into the space of the people with local performance traditions, comedians and the NDTC taking over in the early 1960s. The NDTC's creative appropriation of African Jamaican ritualistic dance movements for the theatre stage thus introduced a variant of ritual theatre, which Hill has defined as secular rather than religious in significance. In fact, he asserts that it was due to theatre and festival performances that eventually "the educated middle class joined forces with the less-educated underclass in the preservation and appreciation of an indigenous cultural form" (Hill 1992: 281). Folk-based choreography is therefore of continuing importance in the NDTC's repertoire, because it presents an identificatory as well as politically integrative societal forum.

Moreover, folk vocabulary still forms the base from which much of the NDTC's more experimental or abstract modern choreography evolves. Stylistic elements from the folk such as polyrhythms, rippling back and pelvic movements as well as the respectability of the bare feet on the concert stage have been the merits of the NDTC's conscious effort to (re)present that part of Jamaican history with pride and dignity. In this respect, Caribbean folk-based choreography has taken a powerful stance against the stereotypical notion of the alleged "culturelessness" of the African tradition which for too long had dominated not only the stage but also Jamaican public life. As Ryman has so pointedly expressed:

For the Maroon (Asante), the other "Africans" – Kumina (Kongo) and Etu (Yoruba) people, Revivalists, and the Rastafarian, their dance and all that informs its content and context, is the act and activity of creating a world that lends dignity, self-identity and a measure of control over one's life. To the extent that the mainstream society remains non-viable alternative to the strength of that offered by the African ethos in the traditional dances, they will survive as vibrant and dynamic agents and catalysts of African retentions and the Jamaican culture (1984: 21).

'Dancing Cultural Roots' in the Caribbean context thus outlines a performative paradigm that not only keeps kinaesthetic memory alive, but points the body towards a self-assertive expression of Jamaican heritage and future.

In Celebration of Diversity – The NDTC's Caribbean Dance Vocabulary

We ought to root our work in the collective experience of Jamaica and in the other West Indian territories – always trying to get to the essences, the universality of a particular experience. By doing this I think we will be able to communicate with audiences both at home and abroad. We will continue for a long time to have a variety of styles with an underlying thing – I cannot even describe it – a thing evolving which will put a stamp on us (Nettleford 1965: 21-22).

We have movements much like the Graham contraction and release in our own traditional dances. But there is at least one great difference. Graham looks inward into caves of the heart; our dance looks outward into sunbursts.[54]

As has been shown in the previous chapter NDTC dance vocabulary prides itself on a strong folk dance tradition, which even in the more distinctly modern works of the company shapes the NDTC's unique style.[55] Cheryl Ryman has codified the NDTC's "Core Vocabulary Structures" as consisting of ballet, modern and folk elements. Her list contains the following elements as the most prevalent: 1. contraction and release, 2. rippling back/body waves, 3. arched/hyper-extended back, 4. ribcage shifts, 5. hip-side thrust, 6. lunge, 7. spiral, 8. change of back, 9. flat back with side extension on the floor, 10. low crouched turn, 11. off-balance side extension and 12. catch step (see Ryman 1982).

---

54 Rex Nettleford in an interview with Jack Anderson (1980: n.p.).
55 Daniel Lewis defines the term "style" on behalf of the diversity within modern dance expressions as follows: "[...] style determines how a movement or step is executed; that is, what muscle action achieves the movement, what the timing of the movement is and what kind of quality of expression is given to the movement" (1984: 35).

As her list indicates modern technique is juxtaposed with African-based folk forms which together form the basis of the NDTC's innovative blend of movement vocabulary. Nettleford, furthermore, has stressed:

The straightforward repertory of actual traditional dances is one thing. But the technical discoveries are strong in terms of the way Caribbean people move, whether in ritual, for recreation, or in reaction to everyday concerns; whether in jumping for joy, crawling with fear, writhing in pain, standing frozen in fear, or shimmying with anger. Very few of such locomotor responses are peculiarly "Black" or "Caribbean," but Caribbean people do express these emotions in body language that betrays a way of releasing energy and a vocabulary of "dance" that is distinctively different from that of other cultures (2002: 81).

Careful not to place a racial label on the NDTC's vocabulary, Nettleford avoids the politically laden concept of "black dance", yet insists on a culturally distinct style variation that emerges from Jamaica's unique historical background.[56] In line with Victor Turner's anthropological concept of social drama the NDTC's cultural aesthetic thus appears to mirror the self-reflexivity of Jamaica's African Creole public performances (1990: 9-13; 1992).

According to Turner, social drama embodies the performers' "social ties, the power of their symbols, the effectiveness of their legal and moral controls" as well as "the sacredness and soundness of their religious traditions" (1990: 9-13). Dance and theatre thus present an "active or 'magic' mirror" of the society's social drama to the extent that it "influences not only the form but also the content of the stage drama" (1990: 9-13). Moreover, (dance)theatre serves as a "metacommentary,

---

56 "Black dance" historically referred to the legitimizing struggle for the acceptance of an Africanist aesthetic within US modern dance, which had been constructed as allegedly white. However, the controversy arises from the term's evocation of a racialized dance history that traditionally conceived of "white dance" as "light, ethereal, and refined," whereas "black performance" was connoted as "dark, brutal, exotic" (see Dixon-Gottschild 2003; Fischer-Hornung/Goeller 2001; Myers 1988). Whether "black dance" is a useful category to describe a particular cultural impulse in Africanist dance, however, appears highly contested. In fact, as this study also seeks to demonstrate, it appears that most black performers today choreograph from highly complex sources, best described by the alternative paradigm of hybridity/creolization discourse.

explicit or implicit, witting or unwitting, on the major social dramas of its social context (wars, revolutions, scandals, institutional changes)" (1990: 16-18). Applying Turner's model to the NDTC's stage adaptation of folk aesthetics and dance vocabulary, the latent impact of the folk forms' social drama so to speak is always present – even if only subtly so – and must be accounted for in order to achieve a culturally informed understanding of the complex meaning of Jamaica's unique dance heritage.

As has been shown in the previous chapters, Revival, Kumina, Etu and Dinki Mini steps, chants, music and rhythms embody kinaesthetic memory of a historically distinct background: the living testimony of African survival in Jamaica. This dimension of spiritually empowering presence informs not only the NDTC's folk choreography, but also each of the company's more abstract works.[57] NDTC repertoire owes much of its originality and distinguishing style to this input of folk connoted dance movements. As dance scholar Susan Foster has pointed out, a performative aspect underlies each dance technique/school of dance training in so far as it develops/constructs the theatrical dancer as a particular "body-of-ideas," i.e. a map which creates a distinct "body topography" to evoke an idealized body image (1997: 238-239). Dance technique thus shapes the dancer's body according to the teacher's aesthetic/cultural sensibility. By focusing on the training of folk forms, the NDTC training has overtime established a "body topography," which stylistically distinguishes the company's original choreography from other modern dance works. As Foster also makes clear, technique "represents a given choreographer's or tradition's aesthetic vision of dance [...] to fashion an expressive self that, in its relation with the body performs the dance" (1997: 241). In this respect then, the NDTC's Caribbean movement vocabulary also articulates certain body parts in a rhythmical arrangement and fashion precisely to convey a unique expression of identity and self – thus presenting an inherently modernist concept.[58]

The concept of "body topography," apart from its metaphorical implications, also applies quite literally to the NDTC's dance vocabulary.

---

57 For a detailed list of African Jamaican dance vocabulary compare Cheryl Ryman, "A-B-C of African Retentions in Jamaica: Dance," unpublished typescript (Kingston: African Caribbean Institute, 1978).
58 According to Foster modern dance historically "promoted the body's movement as material substance to be worked into art, [and] assumed an irrevocable connection to a self" (1997: 256).

Commenting first on the expressiveness of life experience, Nettleford asserts the geographical impact as a second important source of the company's emerging style and technique:

Caribbean folk dances, particularly those still danced by an older generation, emphasize the body's center as if to celebrate life itself. These dances seem to recall a period when procreation and childbearing guaranteed men and women a sense of place and purpose. Building strength in the legs and feet is critical: strong feet and toes are needed for earth-centered movements, and sinewy calves will be resistant to the strains of marching and shuffling. Strong knees are requisite for attitudes of obeisance to the gods during ritual ceremonies, and strong thighs support a torso rippling horizontally while possessed of a particular spirit. The flexed foot is useful as symbol not only of hoe and pickax but also of resolution, strength, and earthiness. The arms, like other parts of the body, must be able to describe the curve of mountains, the flow of rivers, and the ebb and flow of oceans, just as in other traditions the movements of swans and the shapes of Gothic cathedrals, skyscrapers, and pine trees piercing the winter sky have found correspondences in dance attitudes (Nettleford 1985: 176-177).

In developing this Caribbean based dance vocabulary, modern dance offered itself for several reasons. Sondra Fraleigh, for example, in her phenomenological discussion of modern dance regards "freedom and individuality as the existential context of modern dance" (1987: xxiv). Throughout the form's historical development from an expressionist to a non-expressionist phase, modern dance has continuously elaborated on the notion of discovery.

Intrinsic to this approach is modern dance's "open (or free) aspect of method," which, Fraleigh claims, "resulted in many and widely varied styles" (1987: xxxii-xxxiii). Modern dance traditionally emphasized the spirit of inventiveness and change "through a questioning attitude and way of working, rather than assuming without question the already established models" (Fraleigh 1987: xxxiii). Fraleigh, furthermore, underlines the fact that dance in general, more than any other art form, "represents our expressive body-of-action and its aesthetic idealization". She insists that "dance draws upon both the personal and the universal body" with a tendency towards the latter. Dance thus testifies "to our bodily lived existence, our mutual grounding in nature, and our shared bodily acculturations" (1987: xvi). In this respect, modern dance simultaneously presents unique individuality and the universal human condition. As a result, Fraleigh considers it no accident that modern dance proved particularly "open to cross-cultural assimilation" and therefore occurs in various stylistic adaptations throughout the world (1987: 87).

While this is admittedly so, I would, however, stress that these creative transformations of modern dance vocabulary in the postcolonial Caribbean, amount in fact to much more than a mere assimilation. I rather suggest that what quite co-incidentally interconnects the two, are several striking parallels between modern and traditional dance forms. When modern dancers sought for a unification of the lived and staged experience of their assumed reality, African festival forms had never known a strict separation of these spheres to begin with. Within the African cosmos of dance, bodily presence is experienced as a lived totality of different epistemological levels. The dancing body thus encompasses the individual, ancestral spirits as well as a variety of deities. Phenomenologically speaking though, dance has always been described as an inherently spiritual act, which not only in religious folk ritual context, but even in secular formats may lead towards self-dissolution in terms of a liminal transition, i.e. the felt/experienced unity between a body-subject and body-object status. The more focused a dancer becomes in his/her movement, he/she will achieve what Fraleigh refers to as "present centeredness," i.e. a sense of unification of the danced action and presented image (1987: 41-42). The religious implication of Caribbean folk dancing thus parallels to some extent the notion of a mystical union prevalent in early German and U.S. based modern dance. Likely, this feature presents one common aspect of dance theatre's worldwide claim to universality.

Drawing on dance as "a fundamental (if not the fundamental) aesthetic vehicle for expressing personal and collective inner worlds" the Graham school of modern dance philosophically paralleled the function of dance to that of religion. Accordingly, religion and dance both offered "concrete form to the unseeable spirit of mankind, the hidden essence of human life" (Helpern 1994: 4). The dancer's body was conceived of as the prime instrument to convey inner expression. Starting from this fundamental position, modern dance developed ever new modes of training to deliver that particular self-embodying/revealing statement on stage. As Louis Horst has described modern dance's beginning efforts in the primitivist terms of his time:

The pioneers in modern dance and their successors recaptured the relation that the primitive has to his body – an intimacy with the muscle tensions of daily movements which had been lost to modern men. This is not at all the ballet dancer's awareness of line, of speed or balance, and dramatic portrayal of a role. It is, rather, an inner sensitivity to every one of the body's parts, to the power of its whole, and to the space in which it carves designs. The great quest was to find ways to attain this sensitivity, and manners in which to discipline it for communication (Horst/Russell 1977: 19).

Adhering to a Jungian concept of collective unconscious and primordial archetype, modern primitivism's quest for "ancestral footsteps," however, touched American Indian or African dance aesthetic – if at all – only on the surface. Rather, Graham's "inner landscapes" appeared to offer an interpretation of those 'primitive' forms in terms of a liberation from U.S. culture's repressive, guilt-ridden Judeo-Christian/Puritan upbringing. By seeking the "truth of movement" in somebody else's footsteps – whether Amerindian, Asian or African – Graham embodied in fact more of the West's long lost yearning for origin than that sought after notion of an ancestral, i.e. continuously lived cosmological connection.[59] Alas, she, too, fell into the trap of a probably well meant, yet still somewhat patronizing Orientalism.

According to Horst, modern dance relied on primitivism primarily as a "background source" for dance study and creative inspiration. Graham-inspired modern dancers thus conceived of "primitive culture" in terms of an exoticist mysticism rather than truly acknowledging its highly complex dance vocabulary. Modern dance study of "earth primitive," for example, was described in quite derogatory terms. As the following excerpt demonstrates:

For an Earth Primitive study, movement can be experimented with which will suggest the mysterious powers that abide in the earth. Such a dance study invokes the mood and creates the texture of the primitive in his relation to the world beneath him. The dancer is alertly sensitive to the feel of the

---

59 Wole Soyinka comments on the racist implications and faulty designation in Jungian thought. Rather than to frame primitive thinking within the parameters of Darwinian evolution and Freudian psychoanalysis, Soyinka argues that one needs to acknowledge the Western lack of appropriate vocabulary. He claims: "What we call the mythic inner world is both the psychic sub-structure and temporal subsidence, the cumulative history and empirical observations of the community. It is nonetheless primal in that time, in its cyclic reality, is fundamental to it. The inner world is not static, being constantly enriched by the moral and historic experience of man" (1976: 35).

earth under his feet. It is the genesis and grave of all living things – areas and oriented to the floor. They can be clumsy and animalistic. They can be brutal and threatening. They can project the lyricism of wonder, or the tenderness of the giver of life. They may have a drum-like percussiveness. But always they are simple and meagerly articulated; lean and taut (Horst/Russell 1977: 62-63).

While this Western misconception engendered quite astonishing dance works of considerable artistic merit, one should never forget though that these North American choreographers actually told their audience more about the social strata which they came from, i.e. in the majority white Anglo-Saxon, than the cultures, which actually inspired their new modern movement discoveries.

Africanist cosmology and aesthetics, by contrast, do not separate between worlds as much as Western based traditions tend to do. The overall conceptualization is rather one of integration. As Green points out: "African dance is the integrated art of movement that is controlled by her music which is governed by her languages" (1996: 13). Therefore, African dance presents "a source of communication through which it is possible to demonstrate emotion, sentiment, beliefs and other reactions through movement," all of which appear to clearly assume the function of social drama in Victor Turner's sense. Among the decisive elements of the African dance vocabulary Green lists jumps, body segmentation and pelvic contractions, all of which can easily be found in the NDTC folk-based repertoire (1996: 15). So, as has been shown before, African-derived movements were indeed evoking already existing echoes in the bodily memory of the descendants of former slaves rather than expressing an auto-exoticist fantasy.

Notwithstanding the common lineage between traditional African and Caribbean dance forms, the new world dances of the African diaspora form an altogether different canon. As P. Sterling Stuckey points out, a "new history of dance" had inevitably emerged from the violent rupture of slavery (1995: 51). Jamaican dance theatre aesthetic may therefore structurally recall the group dances of Ghana and Nigeria, as both tend to perform preferably in "lines or circles, with the circle being more prominent in recreation dances and the line formation prominent in war dances" (Green 1996: 18-19). And yet, African and Caribbean dance forms share, genealogically speaking, the same ancestral perspective. Encompassing the omnipresent spirit force, which interconnects the living, unborn and dead, African and Caribbean dance forms function as "a way of life, a source of communication, and history reenacted through movement" (Green 1996: 26). African and Caribbean dance forms thus share the holistic approach towards a dance/life unit, which parallels a similar vein in modernist primitivism at least to some extent. Yet, examining this affinity more closely, one will find that each cultural tradition expresses its own particular (hi)story quite independently.

Shifting the analytic paradigm from "dancing bodies" to "bodies in movement," J. Lowell Lewis' anthropological analysis of embodied movement practices has furthermore remarked that "genres or types of human activity are more culturally diverse than human bodies (however construed) themselves are" (1995: 226). The argument puts forward "the question of how body movements are patterned, formed, and divided in different cultural worlds"(1995: 226). Lewis thus raises the issue of style and particular cultural aesthetic. As differently framed cultural spheres do not appear mutually exclusive, they often times share "deep iconic patterns or schemata that inform many social domains and therefore are central to the recognizable, distinctive, stylistic unities of given cultural systems" (1995: 227).

In the context of this study, Africa appears as the Caribbean's major aesthetic reference point for such shared iconicity. Therefore it will be useful to take a brief look at the African art historical background for a better understanding of the iconic transfer between the two cultural regions. With the aim of crystallizing an African-based aesthetic, Robert Farris Thompson in his seminal work *African Art in Motion. Icon and Art* (1974) was among the first scholars to investigate the integrative aspect of African arts. His analysis places dance as one element among many which taken together form what he refers to as "worlds of artistic happening" (Thompson 1974: xii). At stake is not merely a different emphasis, but rather a different conceptualization. "*Danced* art" thus intertwines different aspects from sculpture, crafts, music and dance by reinforcing their mutual impact on the aesthetic perception of the art work in time and space. Transcending the European genre confinement, African art can therefore hardly be grasped by such separation. In order to correctly address the complexity of such totalization, Thompson therefore suggests to "start with the shared norms of performance" before one actually begins to decode the meaning of any given element (dance, sculpture, music, chants, etc.) in singular (1974: xii).

Looking, for example, at African sculpture, Thompson remarks that one will encounter a focus on forms of arrested movement rather than an excessive interest in anatomical accuracy. Parallels between sculpted body posture and choreographed dance movement can easily be identified, as in "the relation between the bent knees of the black dance and the identical expression of flexibility in the corpus of black sculpture." (Thompson 1974: 5). Among the "criteria of fine form" in African art, Thompson also lists "ephebism," i.e. the "bending quality" of a youthful vitality in sculptural stance and dancing, as well as the concept of "balance," which defines the peaceful interrelationship of human beings in almost ethical terms. Thompson defines African aesthetic as a "mediating force," which balances "identity through the merger with a larger social whole" (1974: 27). As opposed to Western representations of individualism, African dance focuses on the integrative power of the circle, the "generalization of humanity in the dancing ring" (Thompson 1974: 27). The typical call-and-response pattern, for example, mirrors this social unity in its formal aspect. Moreover, Thompson points out that plastic art and motion are intertwined to the extent that "phrasing the body transform[s] the person into art, make[s] his body a metaphor of ethics and aliveness, and, ultimately, relate him to the gods" (1974: xiv).

Kariamu Welsh-Asante describes such deep respect for the transcendent in terms of an inherent dimensionality within the African aesthetic. Following Thompson's basic outline Welsh-Asante distinguishes seven shared "senses" that stylistically link the new world's African diaspora to the continent. They include: 1. polyrhythms, 2. polycentrism ("It is this multiple existence of polysenses that is the African's signature in dance. The representation of the cosmos in the body is a goal."), 3. curvilinear ("The structure is always related to experience, message, theme and feeling."), 4. dimensional ("The dimensional aspiration speaks to the supernatural in space, the presence beyond the visual presence."), 5. epic memory, 6. repetition, 7. holism (2001: 144-151). Joseph M. Murphy (1994) has furthermore defined "working the spirit" as the central commonality of Caribbean religious practice. In his analysis of Haitian Vodou, Brazilian Candomblé, Cuban Santería, Jamaican Revival Zion and U.S. Black Churches, he stresses, for example, that "ceremonial spirituality" equals "community service" in the sense that the spirit is worked not only to praise but also to empower the practitioner (1994: 7). This notion of "service" and commitment to the community, I would like to recall, is also at the heart of the NDTC's voluntary engagement. As Rex Nettleford suggests, embodied spirituality may even serve as a means of "safe transit" into the rather disquieting environment of the 21st century, when he claims:

[...] modern man's need for safe spiritual transit at end-of-century is leading to a search for modalities to reconnect much that have fallen apart. One may find some clues in the ever-present element of unity in African dance [...]. There is unity in the juxtaposition of the secular to the religious, of sacrifice to play, of ritual (in the sense of structured procedures), to improvisation, of the obligatory to the novel, of the naturalistic to the abstract, of tragedy to comedy and sadness to laughter, of this world to "other worlds," of man to woman (virile men dance the roles of women in masquerade without fear of their sexual credentials ever being dragged into suspicion), of ancestral/traditional to modern/contemporary. Adaptations abound (1996: xviii)

The Caribbean dance aesthetic is consequently based on the culturally diverse texture of its people and is as much modern as it is ancestral. Coming back to Fraleigh's idea of the expressed/experienced combination of individual input and shared universality in movement, Caribbean dance hence embodies a nucleus of diversity, which can indeed hold claim to universality. As Nettleford suggests:

For Dance, I feel, remains the most eloquently non-partisan of the theatre artforms. It stretches across the boundaries of race, customs and politics and religion, linking peoples of the world through a common idea rooted in the sheer power of movement. [...] The world then is our source in a very real sense and the dance can do as much as bring to Jamaica and the Caribbean something of the outside world as it certainly can take Jamaica and the Caribbean to the outside world (1968: 130).

How this cross-cultural communication of Caribbean identity has found its way through a postcolonial appropriation of modern dance will be analyzed in the following reading of the NDTC's modern Caribbean dance theatre repertoire.

Rex Nettleford's Aesthetic of Caribbean Dance Theatre

Ritual of the Sunrise
There is a force of exultation, a celebration of luck, when a writer (read "an artist") finds himself (herself), witness to the early morning of culture that is defining itself, branch by branch, leaf by leaf, in the self-defining dawn, which is why, especially at end of the sea, it is good to make a ritual of the sunrise. The noun of the Antilles, ripples like brightening water, and the sound of leaves, palm fronds, and birds are the sounds of a fresh dialect, the native tongue...[60]

Presenting a signature choreography of Rex Nettleford's more abstract Caribbean dance theatre works, I propose a reading of *Ritual of the Sunrise* in this section which regards the choreography in the context of Fraleigh's notion of "discovery" in modern dance. As I have outlined her argument in the previous chapter, discovery is understood not only in terms of developing a vocabulary, but also in terms of introducing a stylistic prototype, which Sheila Barnett, former NDTC choreographer, has referred to as the Jamaican "Festival Style," i.e. a composition of creative modern variations on the folk-based dance material.

Ritual of the Sunrise divides into four sections: 1. "Sunset-Prologue – lone voice walling hope," 2. "Discovery sequence- shaping of vocabulary," 3. "Self-defining sequence (dawn)" and 4. "Ritual-Jouvert, High Mass-Sunrise."[61] Introduced by a hymnal tone and the solemn voice of a choir singer (Veronica, Noiet de Temporal, Sal Negro), the scene opens on a tableau set of eight female dancers. Crouched onto the floor as if to evoke small packages, their bodies appear as mere shadow silhouettes. The spectator can only distinguish several dark spots – reminiscent of shells maybe – on the blue lit stage. Then, the dancers slowly rise to their knees and lift their arms in a reverential akimbo gesture. They take a brief break before the signal of a single drum beat incites them to instantly crouch back down to the floor, from where the group changes position into a flat back extension.

---

60 This quote by Derek Walcott reads as epigraph to the choreography. Compare "In Celebration of Diversity. The National Dance Theatre Company of Jamaica UK Tour 2001," NDTC Tour Program.
61 Compare "In Celebration of Diversity. The National Dance Theatre Company of Jamaica UK Tour 2001," NDTC Tour Program. The following analysis is based on live-performance and rehearsal as well as video-tape support.

The following sequence leads the female dancers through a variation of several sculptured positions: from statuesque kneeling, to sitting and bottom turns, as well as standing upright with bends to both sides, turns and smaller units of retreat and advance in which, for example, the dancers move forward in unison with arms lifted and the torso subtly rippling back and forth in a devotional gesture of piety. Throughout the scene, a yellow light beam slowly increases in intensity so that it illuminates more of the dancers' white dresses. Also, the dancers keep moving in unison: two rows of three and a pair of two, which several times changes in arrangement from back to front. The scene ends with all of the dancers in flat back extension back on the floor.

Reflecting on the choreography's title and epigraph, the first sequence indeed creates the impression of early morning sun beams breaking through the clouds, if you will. Music, costume, lighting and movements in ensemble suggest iconic postures and gestures of worship, as well as the notion of constant flow as a subtle wave movement projects its kinaesthetic energy through the dancers' bodies into the theatre space.

The National Dance Theatre Company of Jamaica in "Discovery Sequence" from Rex Nettleford's Ritual of the Sunrise (rpt. in: NDTC 40th Anniversary Program).

In a first assessment, this floor-based composition certainly appeals to a correlation with the archaic impulse in modern dance. As Horst has described this idea:

The archaic period growing very gradually out of the primitive, gives birth to something new – aesthetic consciousness. The tribal artisan or dancer who petitioned the gods in primitive ritual becomes the artist breaking through the ritual, conscious of formal beauty for the first time. He is completely absorbed in the newly discovered aesthetic ideal, and this absorption makes for an intensity and awareness of detail, of color, line, texture and design. A creative passion supersedes his emotion as a mere worshipper. The craftsman who fashioned forms for service evolves into the artist who creates them because they are beautiful (Horst/Russell 1977: 69).

Horst's evolutionist model is of course highly problematic. However, leaving his modernist bias aside for the moment, one could still argue that the ritualistic "archaism" of *Ritual of the Sunrise's* opening sequence consists in the stylized abstraction of movement, color and music, which in totality create not only an archaic, but also ritualistic overtone, of which angelic, sea spume, purity, dress code of Vodou worshippers are but a few possible connotations to interpret. More importantly even the thematic correspondence: for archaism within modern dance, as Horst explains, is connected to the notion of giving birth and the direct expression of the creating human spirit.

Aesthetic consciousness as opposed to allegedly 'intuited' worship represents thus the transition from the ritualistic to the aesthetic phase in terms of the primitivist/evolutionary discourse. No longer a worshipper of gods, modern man thus becomes "the craftsman" to create in his own image. Adhering to similar formal principles yet deriving from an Africanist perspective of creation, Nettleford comments on such similarity between both forms:

The emphasis on weight in the negotiation and shaping of many a movement-pattern finds kindred association with the fall-recovery, tension-relaxation complexes of some schools of American modern dance, as does the contraction-release complex, usually identified as a Martha Graham invention, but organic to all African dance, which predates American modern dance by a few centuries. Movement is moulded more often than attenuated. It is as though the material being worked on is clay rather than steel. Arms flow like rivers and torsos undulate like the outlines of rolling hills or the ebb-flow of the surrounding sea. These are technical foundations in the preparation of the body as the instrument of dance expression (2002: 88).

So while both approaches are modern in the sense that they assess movement in terms of developing a secular technique of artistic expression rather than to portray embodied ancestralism, the approach varies in that American modern exploits/appropriates a somewhat orientalist fantasy, whereas Caribbean modern develops an aesthetic, which is kinaesthetically recollected. In terms of "discovery" the opening sequence of *Ritual of the Sunrise* thus speaks of the Caribbean's aesthetic awakening in modern terms: "the early morning of culture that is defining itself" on the base of the Caribbean's unique cultural heritage as it is expressed in the Walcott epigraph.

Taken as inspirational source, Derek Walcott's poetics lend themselves to an interpretative reading of *Ritual of the Sunrise*, because as a Caribbean writer, he, too, is concerned with the discovery and definition of a self-expressive vocabulary. For Walcott, the Caribbean does not strictly speaking have a history in terms of an artistic canon or aesthetic, that is at least from the perspective of a Western dominated teleology of empire. Rather Walcott conceives of history as "the Medusa of the New World:" a complex entanglement of cultural amnesia and loss (1974: 4; 6-7). According to his literary philosophy, however, this should be neither considered a source for constant mourning nor for "jaded cynicism which sees nothing new under the sun" (1974: 3). On the contrary, Walcott's "truly tough aesthetic of the New World neither explains nor forgives history," but asks for "an elation which sees everything as renewed" and claims the freedom for "the re-creation of the entire order, from religion to the simplest domestic rituals" (1974: 5).

The loss of cultural memory is thus redeemed by the appreciation of the here and now in terms of creative "rebirth" and "cunning assimilation" (1974: 7). Much of that sensibility Walcott finds represented in the image of the sea. As he explained:

When somebody asks you where is your history or where is your culture, or what have you done, the question comes from a presumption of people who believe that history represents achievement [...] History is only an aspect of the kind of territory, one of the territories that they dominate. So if someone asks me, as a Caribbean person: 'Where is your history?' I would say: 'It is out there, in that cloud, that sky, the water moving.' And, if the questioner says: 'There's nothing there,' I would say: 'Well, that's what I think history is. There's nothing there.' The sea is history (1996: 24).

What the Caribbean artist thus shares with "modern man" in the West, is the same sort of "displaced, searching psyche" with a tendency to concentrate on the presentness of experience rather than opting for insecure transcendentals (Walcott 1974: 24). In that respect, the "sea of history" and the dance suffer from the same sort of a-historicity, for the dance, too, only exists in radical presence.

As Maxine Sheets-Johnstone has explained, dance is "truly ekstatic" in the sense that it defies fixation at any given moment (1980: 22). Dance only takes place in creation, which makes it so extremely difficult to trace. Similar to the image of the eternal sea then, dance evades ideological rigidity. Whether in terms of a cliché portrayal or objectified existence, one can never fully take hold of a dance's meaning/identity, for as a "form-in-the making" dance is already evanescing the moment one starts to contemplate.[62] So in that sense, dance not only embodies a radical presentness, but a radical annunciation of freedom, too. However, in terms of the Caribbean sensibility this freedom should not be misnamed a bleak existentialism, for the outlook is rather optimistic. As Walcott concludes:

The Caribbean sensibility is not marinated in the past. It is not exhausted. It is new. But it is its complexity, not its historically explained simplicity, which is new. Its traces of melancholy are the chemical survivals of the blood which remain after the slave's and the indentured worker's convalescence. It will survive the malaria of nostalgia and the delirium of revenge just as it survived its self-contempt (1974: 18).

In analogy, the NDTC's Caribbean dance vocabulary also emerges from such "chemical survivals," which celebrate the discovery of being alive and creative despite the historical hardships.

Coming back to *Ritual of the Sunrise*, the new day dawn – evoked by the slowly brightening light beam throughout the opening sequence – symbolizes precisely "the ritual of the sunrise," when the dancers rise from the blue lit darkness of an imaginary sea towards the symbolical sun. "Walling hope," as the sequence is entitled, the dancers' bodily recovery from the annihilating flood so to speak leads them straight into the sun beam of a next morning, tellingly entitled: "Discovery sequence – shaping of vocabulary." The transition between the two dance episodes is indicated by the entrance of the male dancers, who are also dressed in a somewhat more extravagant white costume (one leg bare, the other in white leotard and a frilled sash as surrogate shirt) and in-

---

62 Sheets-Johnstone defines: "Since movement is never complete at any one instant or point, never fully there, consciousness exists its body in movement as a form continuously projecting itself toward a spatial-temporal future; hence, as a form-in-the-making" (1980: 36).

troduce more announced body ripples and Yanvalou steps, derived from Haitian vodou worship.⁶³ As one of the Haitian ritual's most common dances Henry Frank characterizes Yanvalou as follows:

The Yanvalou is a dance of supplication in honor of Agwe, the deity of the sea and Damballah, the snake god of fertility. In the execution of this dance the worshippers try to mime the undulating movements of the snake and the waves of the sea by moving gracefully, forward and back, their shoulders and the upper part of the body. The participants are often dressed in white during ceremonies honoring Agwe and Damballah. There are two types of Yanvalou: Yanvalou Doba (back bending) where the dancers bend forward and the Yanvalou Debout (straigth) where the dancers perform upright. The latter is in honor of all the deities of the Rada rite (2002: 111).

Introducing the Yanvalou at this point interconnects the image of the sea with that of fertility and by opening that dimension of a spiritually informed movement pattern, the sequence seems to suggest ritualistic worship as the prime nutrient of Caribbean dance vocabulary. Drawing from that source, the scene metaphorically recalls the invocation of the ancestral spirit force as the guiding principle of Caribbean dance movement.

From this rather solemn beginning, which indeed may be characterized as a certain melancholy over a loss of origin, the third part "Self-defining sequence (dawn)" playfully engages with the exotic image of the Caribbean tourist resort: the female dancers enter first in costumes adorned with ornamental flower bouquets, worn as corolla, and colorful skirts of layered fabrics in green, blue and pink variations. Next enter two of the male dancers in fancy bird costume, wearing a single feather, as well as glitter and gold. Such a splendid panorama easily suggests the island's tropical flora and fauna – the paradise, which people especially from colder climates would certainly expect to see from a Caribbean National Dance Theatre Company. Accompanied by

---

63 Burroughs describes the adaptation of the ritual dance movements by non-Haitian dance theatre practitioners as follows: "It is commonly held among non-Haitians that the rhythmic structure of Yanvalou is 6/8 time, and that the most basic elements of the dance occur with the execution of three steps. They are best described as step-together-step although when they are notated according to the rhythmic structure of Yanvalou, there are pauses between some of the steps. As these movements are executed by the feet a simultaneous undulation of the torso that seems to emanate from the pelvic region occurs" (1995: 9).

the obligatory steelband and flute music, the glamorous display is enhanced by refined lighting which wins over its audience as it pays tribute to the well known Carnival and Jonkonnu tradition. Yet, as has been mentioned before, the simplistic exoticism of the scenery may be misleading. For example, in the beginning of this section three male dancers enter in a powerful twirl, which sets their red cloth costume ablaze. Slightly bedazzling in apparition, the movement adapts the ancestral power behind African masquerade forms. In Yoruba Egungun, for example, red cloth represents protection against disease (Thompson 1974: 219). Similarly, the harmless appearing bird costumes of the two following dancers pay tribute to African animal masks, while being of course a very real element of Jamaican geography. Clearly though, with the time and local detachment in mind, those references to African ancestralism remain at best a subtle hint.

Collaborating with choreographer Nettleford on the costume design for his works, NDTC chief costume designer Arlene Richards usually attends rehearsals as she seeks to grasp the idea behind the dance, which she will then try to bring out in the costume. Commenting on that process for *Ritual of the Sunrise*, she explained:

Ritual of the Sunrise [...] that's all about the birthing of a culture, the maturing of a culture and so different aspects of the dance represent different stages of development. The very opening is the birth and the dawning and so forth. And usually that is in the spiritual sense, so I chose white to represent that. [...] but then, when a culture really begins to unfold, then all the varying colors, colors of personality of the people all those things begin to unfold. So I just use nature as inspiration [...] But first, I remember speaking to professor, and I'm saying to him, 'This is called Ritual of the Sunrise, but where is the sun?' And the sun influences so much and it's life and it's energy and it's the source, so I wanted something to represent the sun in there. So I did these things with all the rays when the guys come in with the gold [...] and then out of that come all the varying colors [...] and then came the birds, and he really was working on a theme with birds, because he had the peacocks in there. And so I just used exactly where he was going to just develop it further.[64]

So for Richards the red costume actually represents "bursting sunrays" rather than the ancestral mask which I found the costume alluding to. What this shows then, is that such costumes and masks have by now so fully adapted to the changed environment that today they bear witness

---

64 Interview Arlene Richards 23 Aug. 2003.

to new forms of self-expression. However, what has become paradigmatic of the Caribbean carnival spirit and is expressed in the abstract medley of modern dance forms, Dinki Mini steps, Kumina turns and Yanvalou struts, can in terms of the Caribbean aesthetic – to quote Walcott once more – be defined as follows:

> A race in exile and slavery loses its language quickly, since it is not in a position to communicate or to make itself understood, but has to understand orders. But it preserves, both for a communal identity and for defiance, its ancestral rhythms. Banishment may have increased rather than lessened the fierceness of some of those dances [...]What is there to celebrate, since even joy has its springs? The answer is that he is celebrating a man's right to be happy and free while he is alive; his right to become what he wants, to do what he wants, [...] He asserts that this is possible: in fact, that it is necessary. It is a tribal ritual now that, like all tribal cycles, especially those based on single crops, as ours once was on cane, buries and resurrects its kings and queens and then dances in votive frenzy (1965: 4).

As "ritual[s] of appearance" Jamaican dance theatre and Carnival thus share the same "sense of joy," since celebratory elation is at the heart of both art forms.

Celebration has of course generally been claimed as the "universal impulse" of dance throughout the world, since dance embodies identity as an "indivisible physical and spiritual whole" and thus cherishes the joys and sorrows of life (Fraleigh 1980: xvii). In the experiential totality of body/mind movement, dance may even transcend the confinements of present time and space. While this fundamental truth of dance practice applies to dancers all over the world, it has of course become particularly prominent in the Caribbean, where African cultural identity was largely maintained in social and religious dance festival forms. Caribbean dance celebrates cultural survival and freedom of expression, for which not only NDTC dancers, but also their lucky audiences have every reason to "Give Praise" – as announced in the lyrics of the song, which fittingly accompanies the choreography's final section "Ritual-Jouvert, High Mass-Sunrise."

Ritual of the Sunrise thus ends with a sequence of progressing line formations and circular patterns, which recall structural elements from Revival, Dinki Mini, and Kumina, while accompanied by David Rudder's 'High Mas' music score to underline the NDTC's Trinidad connection.⁶⁵ With over twenty company members on stage, the reappearance of entering and exiting dancers creates a mosaic pattern which resembles the topography of ebb and flow of the Caribbean seaside as well as that of the islands' soft mountain curves. In fact, as the epigraph from one of Derek Walcott's poems suggests, the Caribbean's luscious geography appears a source of inspiration for voiced poetry as much as danced movement: not only the noun, but the body, too, "ripples like brightening water, and the sound of leaves, palm fronds, and birds." The traumatic image of the sea – historically representing the loss of the Middle Passage – may thus turn into a lastly redemptive one: waters to wipe clean the muddy sands, leaving behind an untrodden beach, blank for new beginnings.

Cave's End
Journey of a lifetime
A light at the end of the tunnel
Always...⁶⁶

As has been shown, the Caribbean genesis is a prevalent motif of Nettleford's choreography, which informs many of his epic dance compositions. From *Plantation Revelry* to *Ritual of the Sunrise* and the more recent 40th anniversary *Cave's End*, the Caribbean topos of an evolving Creole nation appears as the driving force of the choreographer's imagination.⁶⁷ Paying tribute to Jamaican musical icon Jimmy Cliff and his vision of "dread," i.e. "hope in despair," the selections from Cliff's *Journey of a Lifetime* form the musical score and central theme of *Cave's End*. Similar to *Ritual of the Sunrise*, this choreography, too, evolves from the evolutionary image of a metaphorical journey from darkness towards light. While *Ritual of the Sunrise* was carried by an overall lyrical impulse, expressive of a particular aesthetic sensibility, *Cave's End* allows at least in some sequences for more of a social-realist reading in terms of danced comment on contemporary Jamaican society forty years after independence.

Cave's End starts with a "Prologue," which introduces the Haitian Ibo step to the rhythm of South African traditional music (Ulwamkelo

---

65 Compare NDTC 40th Anniversary Program 2002.
66 Epigraph to Cave's End, NDTC 40th Anniversary Program 2002.
67 Another important work on the same vein is Nettleford's *The Crossing*, which is a dance theatre composition on the Middle Passage.

Iweirokneli).[68] The scene opens on a group of dancers, who stand in the upstage left corner, assembled in a tight cluster which is arranged according to sex (female dancers in front, men in the back) and height. As the music begins, the blue lit stage is illumined by a single light spot from the left side, which irradiates the dancers' body contour and thus rears the impression of a mosaic of differently shaped individuals. Dressed in rainbow-colored unitards all dancers start executing the same basic step: a ribcage shift with arms akimbo and a quick flat to demi-pointe rise of the foot with simultaneously bent knees switching to both sides in demi-plié. On top of this basic movement one dancer after the other raises an arm and finally spreads out the fingers of the raised hand as if to make a statement of 'hello, here I am.' To top the sequence off, all of the dancers roll their upper bodies half-circle backwards in a hyper-extension or alternatively the group in ensemble shifts in a body wave to the left.

Next, all of the dancers move forward in unison, isolating the torso and changing direction after every two steps so that eventually the group will have come full circle by turning to side, back, side and front. This formation is repeated two times. As the music switches from the percussive opening into a more melodic tune, the male dancers separate from the group as they perform balletic turns in two pairs, progressing forward from both sides of the group which itself remains in place. The multi-armed and legged body of the beginning thus disperses into singular bodies performing individually. As the music has switched from percussive into melodic tune, the movement, too, has adapted from the folk-based Ibo step and torso ripple to modern balletic idiom. This alternating pattern is maintained for the rest of the sequence, which, however, does not strictly adhere to that first introduced correspondence of music and movement. In fact, one can also find modern movements accompanied by percussive instrumentation later on. Yet, both styles form part of the Caribbean tradition and that is

---

68 Rex Nettleford, "Jamaican Dance Theatre – Celebrating the Caribbean Heritage," lecture presented at the Jamaica School of Dance, Summer Workshop, 10 July 2003. See also NDTC Fortieth Anniversary Program 2002, where Rex Nettleford lists South Africa "from the days of apartheid to contemporary life in freedom" to the "various 'connections' [which] are significant in the NDTC's nurturing and development since 1962." The following analysis is based on live-performance, rehearsal and video-tape support.

what should be expressed here. As Nettleford has defined the Caribbean aesthetic elsewhere:

Europe's melody here seems to have found new challenges from Africa's rhythm, creating vibrations – unprecedented and, to some, awesome. Sometimes the drum tones are deep, steady and haunting. At times they take on a rapid, breathless, frantic sequence of seemingly unstructured polyrhythms. At other times it is that dry, sustained and high-pitched sound called 'ciye' by the Haitian voodoo drummers, as if coming from choruses of castrati deprived of their manhood in the wake of bondage. The operative words here are 'as if'. For the realities of the situation point to possibilities of a cultural fusion rich and cohesive in its diversity (2001: 210).

By choosing a South African musical composition – which precisely matches the above mentioned syncretism – Nettleford's "Prologue & Invocation" section of *Cave's End* reinforces his persistently announced artistic vision in terms of forming Jamaica's National Dance Theatre Company over the decades. In fact, what is expressed in the blending of "Europe" and "Africa" is not only an aesthetic solely confined to the Caribbean, but one that shares echoes with postcolonial societies and their liberation struggles all over the world. The "Journey" in terms of an ongoing quest for self-definition therefore continues, of which the solo dance of the second part gives an ardent demonstration.

The transition is marked by a black out during which the audience listens to a traditional drum insert accompanied by the following voice-over as the stage light slowly goes up again: "Out of the darkness came forth light/all life begins in darkness/and we're all moving towards the light/so stop with me on this journey of a lifetime." Led by two dancers in expressionist modern dance vocabulary, the sequence introduces the dance's guiding principle, which ballet mistress Arlene Richards, has assessed for her performance of the part as such:

What the dance is really saying is that we are all on a journey. And it's a journey of a lifetime it really says. It speaks about this hope, but it is also speaking about moving into what I would call a level of consciousness, that you are moving towards the light. So you're coming out of darkness and you're moving towards the light. And you can apply this for all American societies where you move into the light and so for me, yes, it is a journey of moving towards this consciousness and that's how I approached the work. And you know it's funny that you say that, because it has now become even more important for me personally in life this kind of a statement where you move towards a consciousness and a consciousness not necessarily anything religious, but just in terms of how we as a person approach our relationships with people and whether art allows us an enlightened position you know, which is really a position of love and peace and harmony. And that is how I see that figure moving towards a greater end, where there is that kind of freedom of expression.[69]

Arlene Richards in "The Journey" from Rex Nettleford's Cave's End, 2003. Video Still.

In performance the floor oriented solo – during which the dancer struggles her way upwards in relevé, turns and outreaching arm movements – conveys much of that rather personal statement of a move towards (self)consciousness. This rather abstract notion seems to be embodied also by the presence of three female dancers, who, for several times during that sequence, enter and exit upstage parallel as well as they cross diagonally. Forming a sort of background composition to the solo performance, they appear as the dancer's three muses, who in their dresses of softly tinged, rainbow-colored rays symbolically allude to the spiritually enlightening force; especially towards the end, when the blue lit backdrop changes color from orange into deep red. What is interesting to observe in Richards' modern dance interpretation here, is an earthbound elucidation, which actually never quite takes her off the floor. Despite the harmonic melody, one is thus never completely lulled into the airy lyricism, but strangely aware of the dancer's inner struggle and work. This "journey" – so the dance seems to say – is not always an easy one, but very well worth the trouble.

---

69 Interview Arlene Richards 23 Aug. 2003.

Accordingly, the "Street Vibes" episode presents – in a slightly self-ironic mode of expression – typical macho postures danced in a rather vigorous jazz idiom: bouncy walks with rotating shoulder and arm work, kicks and jumps to display self-assertive manhood, likewise shared between the six gang members in street-wear and the two policemen in black uniform on stage. The "street-fight" thus carries a rather humorous tone, which appears quite in contrast to the violent reality of gunmen roaming Jamaican streets. While the police is usually conceived of as the enemy and in Rastafari terms part of the system of Babylon, the choreography presents them mockingly as a part of the people awfully in need to be re-integrated. Presenting a powerful cross-fertilization of Caribbean and U.S. American street dance aesthetics, the sequence indulges in the cliché idealization of the "tough" and the "cool" image of male/macho-prowess, typical of those gang communities. What Nettleford refers to as "male indulgences" though has a rather negative flip-side, namely that it makes women the "burden bearers" – confining them to a social role they do not really want to represent.

Thus, the second episode – "Revival" – addresses women's quest for liberation in an abstraction of the Jamaican Revival folk idiom. Dressed in the already familiar costumes of the three spiritual muses of the "Journey" part, the dance builds on the prevalence of Revival rhythms in Cliff's music. Forming a continuum of the dance-music unit in Jamaican popular culture, not only dance choreography, but Jamaican popular music from Reggae, Ska to contemporary Dancehall, too, are all greatly influenced by the folk rhythms generally and Jamaica's Revival church in particular. "I am not here to be a burden bearer," as Cliff's lyrics proudly proclaim, therefore recalls the continuity of the sufferer in Jamaican society and his/her proud claim to better Jamaican living conditions. As has been shown before: Revival has played an enormously important part in embodying that tradition of resistance and survival, which the "Revival" sequence of *Cave's End* clearly pays tribute to.

Thus the dance subtly suggests the familiar Revival step, which, to remember, was first introduced to the Jamaican dance theatre stage by *Pocomania*. However, the reference to the forward/backward tilt as well as the off-balances and the typical head-wraps is quite abstract. And I would even go as far as to say, probably only apparent to an audience 'in the know.' While a foreigner might have difficulties to place this modern abstraction, Jamaicans will clearly be able to uncover the off-stage cultural reference. And those who have seen *Pocomania* forty years earlier, might even find direct reference to that earlier piece in *Cave's End*. For example, when the group of male dancers enters in file and they each swing a shawl-substitute, extending from their Revival-like head-wrap, the costume suggests the Revival Shepherd's cloak.[70] And then there is also another even more explicit hint, in which the male dancers for a very brief moment take up the exact same position as was choreographed for the ending of *Pocomania*: the Shepherds standing together in off-balance.

The National Dance Theatre Company of Jamaica in "Revival" from Rex Nettleford's Cave's End, 2003. Video Still.

Especially the comparison between this very early work of Nettleford's choreography to *Cave's End*, which is a rather contemporary composition, demonstrates the refinement of abstraction, which the field movement has undergone over a time span of forty years. As I have argued before, I would not think that as a non-Jamaican, one will easily detect the Revival background here. The NDTC's folk imprint thus creates a certain eclecticism of the company's Caribbean dance theatre. As Arlene Richards has explained:

We have our own material. And I think that it is very important that we use our own material and that is what distinguishes us from another group and another country. And so in any country, I believe, that your modern dance is gonna be eclectic. It's going to be some of this and some of that and is going to be a nice blend and fusion. And so that is what I do in my work because I

---

70 Rex Nettleford, "Jamaican Dance Theatre," lecture EMC summer workshop 2003.

think that is what is going to distinguish it from anything else that you've ever seen, if you take it and, oh boy, where is that coming from? It's the folk material [...] for example, in my work it's very slow, it's very, very slow. In a ritual it would not be done at that kind of pace you know, so I change it just a little bit and incorporate it in the work. Cause I think that it is important that we do that. And I also think it is important that we maintain the essence of our folk material and we have sufficient folk material in an almost pure artistic sense.[71]

The folk forms' empowering message thus remains a constant in Jamaican dance theatre, a sometimes more outspoken, sometimes extremely subtle, yet always continuously present force to be counted on as it has carried a people on their life-journey.

Correspondingly, "Looking forward," the fifth section of *Cave's End*, explores the underlying message of Jamaican Dinki Mini. Recalling that Dinki Mini derives from Jamaican nine-night funeral rites, the dance perfectly matches Cliff's message of "hope in despair," introduced by the song of this section. Commenting on the impact of the rhythm and movement for this sequence, Nettleford states:

The dance here progresses into what the lyrics say – one has to be forward-looking and the dinki-mini rhythm utilized by Cliff is here ideal. The body becomes free, the mood is even joyous and hopeful in the middle of what could be despair. It is danced in different groups to emphasize the importance of the collective endeavour on the journey.[72]

Introduced by lead dancers Arlene Richards and Abeldo Gonzales-Fonseca the section starts on a balletic tone, yet soon switches into the 'healing cripple foot' step of Jamaican Dinki Mini, which was already introduced in the chapter on *Gerrehbenta*. As with the Revival section before, this allusion to the folk repertoire is furthermore evoked by a group of three dancers, two men with a woman in the center. Performing the basic Dinki Mini traveling step, they move diagonally forward in a playful attitude, turning and swinging their arms in an audience inviting gesture. The Dinki Mini's celebratory mood is thus taken into the choreography as an expression of elation and happiness. Alternating with more balletic turns and extensions, the couple is juxtaposed by group formations of dancers, varying of seize. Thus, we first have a

---

71 Interview Arlene Richards 23 Aug. 2003.
72 Nettleford, "Scenario Cave's End."

group of four dancers with two men in the back and two women in front, which is followed by another group of six female dancers already in costume for the final section of the dance.

"Change," as the finale is entitled, introduces another set of original costumes, which consist of white 'disco' unitards, reminiscent of 1970s fashion with a rainbow-colored ray of glitter on the torso-top. As the lights go on, all of the company is on stage, lined up in file behind each other and marching forward with accompanying shoulder rotation, arm swing and an African-based head isolation. Arriving at the front of the stage, the whole group switches into Yanvalou steps. The following sequence then alternates between the male and female group of dancers, as each group performs a variation of Jamaican modern variations in unison, i.e. modern blended with folk abstractions, until the lights fade back to the blue lit beginning and the dancers exit again from where they came: upstage left. Having completed the journey, so to speak, this last part embodies the dynamic of change in life. As Nettleford describes:

The journey having been made – "towards the light", the entire stage becomes the destination – well lit, celebratory and redemptive – albeit with a full understanding that change is the dynamic of all life and living. Everything changes for life to go on, completing as it were the cycle which began with formlessness and progressing to form, place and purpose – water-foetus-child-adult! An understanding of this "life-in-motion" is itself a liberating force. The contained energy of the performance of this is intended to depict the tension that exists between the cause for exultation and the wisdom of restraint without cynicism or lack of will.[73]

Performed for the NDTC's fortieth anniversary *Cave's End* thus presents the company's coming-of-age process, since each of the choreography's parts documents a particular stage of developing vocabulary as well as aesthetic consciousness. Playing on Jimmy Cliff's traditional rhythms and hymnal tunes, the blending of Europe's melody upon Africa's rhythm could not have been more fittingly presented. *Cave's End* ultimately announces the state of the nation forty years after independence: a global entity adapting to cultural changes from Europe to Africa via the Caribbean, Canada and the United States.

---

73 Nettleford, "Scenario Cave's End."

Eduardo Rivero: The NDTC's Cuban Connection

Sulkari

In an exchange collaboration with Cuba's National Modern Dance Company, NDTC dancers since the late 1980s have also been trained in the Cuban technique of contemporary dance, as it was first developed by Ramiro Guerra. Similar to the NDTC's own training, Cuban contemporary dance also emerged from the early teachings of German expressionist dance, which allowed for experimentation with daily life movement as well as choreographic freedom of self-expression. Yet, as was already briefly introduced, Ramiro Guerra also explored African Cuban folklore, which he incorporated in his technique on top of the North American modern schools and the discovery of isolations which helped to merge both forms (Mousouris 2002: 56-72). Paralleling Jamaica's cultural decolonization process, the Cuban modern dance movement also accompanied a period of cultural re-definition: Cuba's cultural revolution of 1959. At that time Ramiro Guerra installed Cuban modern dance as a small department of the Cuban National Theatre, where the first national efforts to investigate the country's rich musical and dance folklore were undertaken.[74] Coming out of that tradition, Eduardo Rivero, who since 1988 is director of his own *Compania Teatro de la Danza del Caribe* in Santiago, emerged as one of Cuba's most distinguished modern dance choreographers. And it is his work as choreographer and dancer that became most influential on the NDTC.

A student of Ramiro Guerra and former member of Cuba's National Modern Dance Company, Eduardo Rivero had started choreographing his own works by the 1970s, exploring further the African Cuban heritage of his country. In his artistic development Rivero became more and more interested in the process of abstracting movement from African Cuban ritual, very much in line with the efforts that were undertaken by Rex Nettleford and the NDTC. Emblematic of Rivero's dance technique is his choreography *Sulkari* (1981), which blends elements from ballet, Graham-based modern and Cuban folk dance vocabulary.[75] Particular to *Sulkari* is furthermore, the direct impact of African sculp-

---

74 Interview with Eduardo Rivero 13 Aug. 2003.
75 For a more detailed description of Eduardo Rivero's dance technique compare Gene Cumberbatch-Lynch, *An Analysis of the Rivero Modern Dance Technique* (State University of New York, College at Brockport: Unpublished MFA Thesis, 2001).

tural patterns, which informed much of the movement abstraction of the piece.

In 1979/80 Eduardo Rivero passed *Sulkari* to the NDTC and thus introduced the Cuban Modern Technique to the NDTC repertoire. According to Carson Cumberbatch, who was cast as one of the three male leads in the first NDTC production, the Cuban technique shares several of its fundamental exercises with NDTC vocabulary. Starting with barre exercises and adapted ballet positions, a Rivero class will usually continue with center work, Graham floor exercises and progressions of axial movements from African Cuban folk material and other sources (Cumberbatch-Lynch 2001: 22). While most of Rivero's floor exercise is Graham influenced, it has increasingly incorporated Caribbean dance aspects. Over time Rivero's training thus built a distinct mode of energy release to create far more flexible rib cage moves and a less stable hip than in conventional Graham technique. Cumberbatch explains:

Mr Rivero to translate his vocabulary of dance to a Cuban style and technique, studied the Cuban folklore, i.e. the way the Cubans walk, stand and move, to develop the Rivero/Cuban technique. This is based on movements of hip and spine, shoulders and neck to develop the rippling of the back. The ripples begin at the base of the spine, travels through the entire spine, right up to the back of the head... The rippling back or body waves which is so typically Caribbean, captures the flow of the sea, rivers and the undulating mountains, along with the ripples of the arms (1986: 31).

In this respect, then, Rivero's development of a Cuban technique or style variation of modern dance is indeed comparable to the NDTC's training and vocabulary. As Cumberbatch also notices, this consistency of Graham technical influence makes for the actually rather stylistic than technical variation between the two companies. He lists the following commonalties between Cuban and Jamaican modern technique/style:

1. hyper-extended back
2. contraction-release of upper torso (which is an original African dance feature even though it became so prominent for Graham technique)
3. ribcage shift in second position parallel demi plié or straight
4. spiral/cross sit, followed by fall to floor
5. rippling back/body waves in flat back position in demi-plié

6. spirals (three-dimensional curve, moving around central axis) around upper part of body
7. change of back
8. lunge (transference of weight from one leg to other)
9. side thrust of hip
10. slide to ground
11. off-balance leg extension on floor
12. stepping from one knee from a closed to an open position (1986: 31).

Breathing, kneeling in devotional reverence, the hyper-extended hands (praise), lifts and flexed foot, and the rippling back are also shared components of both schools of training. However, due to the structural and organizational differences of the institutionalization of modern dance in Cuba and Jamaica, there are also notable differences. For example, there is a stronger ballet retention in Rivero's work, likely dating back to his first dance training with Alicia Alonso and the National Ballet of Cuba (Cumberbatch-Lynch 2001: 3). Moreover, his unique stylization of African sculptural patterns into dance movement differs to quite an extent from Nettleford's livelier, more relaxed and energetic dance compositions.

The video-taped version of the NDTC's 30th anniversary performance of Rivero's *Sulkari*, begins with three female dancers entering the stage diagonally from upstage left to backstage front, accompanied by Rivero's arrangement of traditional Afro-Cuban drumming and the NDTC singer's solemnly melodic humming. As the three female dancers step forward with the typical bent knees and hyper-extended back of Rivero's dance vocabulary, they exert the signature ripple of his technique, which starts in the back through the spine and extends from there into the shoulder girdle and arms. Arriving front stage, they turn around to step back center stage, where each dancer subsequently performs a technically highly proficient solo. These solos demonstrate the versatility of Rivero's unique modern dance style, which introduces superbly toned shoulder ripples, reverential knee turns, and pliés with flexed hands and bent joints. In combination with the purist brown ballet suit, the strong-featured eye make-up and the powerful 'Afro'-style hairdo and white shell-necklace, the composition evokes an overall sculptural, almost carved image of Yoruba inspired archaic postures.

According to this pattern, the male dancers enter in the next sequence, each carrying a wooden stick which is rhythmically stamped onto the ground. Bare chested in bikini-pants with only a shell girdle resting on their hips, their toned bodies are, similar to the women's bodies, on display. As they lift the stick or bear it like a yoke on their shoulders, it symbolically changes from occupational tool to heavy burden and aggressive weapon. Despite the stylized abstraction of the danced movements, it would actually be quite hard not to think of the typical warrior/hunter/provider triad here, when these gorgeous male bodies exert their beautiful, acrobatic leaps. Not enough though, the stick, becomes even more heavily loaded in symbolic meaning, when pointed upwards from between the dancers' legs. Now, clearly it carries some sort of phallic connotation, considering that through all this macho prowess, the female dancers sit in the back and watch.

The National Dance Theatre Company of Jamaica in Eduardo Rivero's Sulkari, 1980. Photograph by Maria LaYacona (rpt. in: Nettleford 1985: 148).

In accordance with Nettleford's *African Scenario*, one could easily read this scene as another approach towards the Caribbean's African heritage from the Cuban perspective. As such it is a powerful choreography, particularly because of its technical versatility. Yet, while *Sulkari* carries ritualistic overtones, which are evoked by the African Cuban traditional drum score and folk singing, the oppositional arrangement of three female and three male dancers almost enforces a reading in gender terms.[76] Rivero's modernist stylization of African Cuban folk material emphasizes the toned muscularity of his dancers, which in its

---

76 Such a reading is further supported by the dramaturgical note in the NDTC's 30th Anniversary Program, where the dance is described as: "A dance of exaltation in fecundity and fertility, so that through the man-woman relationship the life of man will continue [...]."

heroic gender portrayal may at times appear somewhat problematic, or dated if you will. Thus, his stylized gender portrayal creates an image of the black male dancer, which evokes a modernist Darwinian type of the masculine. Ramsay Burt has critiqued this same representation of essentialized masculinity also in the work of Martha Graham, José Limón and Alvin Ailey, and the Graham foundation is likely responsible for that same notion in Rivero's work, too (1995: 132-134).

Gene Carson and Denise Robinson in Eduardo Rivero's Sulkari, 1980. Photograph by Maria LaYacona (rpt. in: Nettleford 1985: 121).

Rivero's aestheticized display of male prowess appears unsettling, because it enhances an image of macho hyper-sensuality, which is in pictorial accordance with a prevalent racial stereotype. As Burt points out, "non-white masculinities appear from a dominant, white point of view to be in touch with 'essential', 'natural' masculinity" (1995: 128-129). Perceived as such, they pose a representationally unsettling counter-image to the white male spectator, who might feel threatened, yet at the same time awkwardly fascinated by the portrayed hyper-sexuality of the racially construed Other. However, to defend Rivero's work, one has of course to admit that, when I, for example, was watching *Sulkari* as the special performance of Rivero's *Compania Teatro de la Danza del Caribe* at Kingston's Little Theatre in the summer of 2003, there were neither that many white men nor white women present to feel optionally appalled or enticed; except for the casual handful of tourists who usually will find their way down to the theatre from the nearby New Kingston hotel area. And one can assume that the same is true for the company's performances in Cuba, which makes their performance situation a different one compared to that of the Alvin Ailey Company in the United States, for example, which performs to a somewhat half white, half black audience.

Yet, being of course a white woman myself, what I found personally disturbing – and this statement I am afraid I can only make as a very subjective one – was precisely that knowledge I share with Ramsay Burt and other academic critics from our Lacanian film class theory. Suddenly, several questions formed in the back of my head, while contemplating Rivero's work: Had I been made so very aware of stereotypical minstrelsy that by now, whenever I see a black performer with bulging eyes it will remind me of O'Neill's *Emperor Jones*? Curious, if other people would share my concern, I was however to be surprised by the general enthusiasm and applause the performance received. Stepping out into the lobby during the break, I overheard comments like "Wonderful!" and consequently no longer dared to voice my critique, as the same sort of racial discourse intimidated me, as a white European, to 'once again' voice a critique that could come across as patronizing. Another question: Was I over sensitized? But what actually did *Sulkari* then (re)present?

The National Dance Theatre Company of Jamaica in Eduardo Rivero's Sulkari, 1980. Photograph by Maria LaYacona (rpt. NDTC 40th Anniversary Program).

Especially the last section of the dance, when the male and female dancers engage in a sequence of pas de deux configurations, erotic spectacle seems to overshadow the ritualistic impact. Considering, for example, the following episode, when the female dancers first slide down the stick, which is firmly upheld by the men, and then kneel submissively down in front of their partners, do these danced actions not suggest a sexualized reading of the scene? Triumphantly lifted on the males' shoulders, these women dancers become trophies rather than goddesses, it may seem. However, unlike the example of feeble looking ballerinas, these 'exotic' women remain quite self-assertive and strong in their fierce gaze at the audience. Puffing their cheeks in a stylized imitation of possession, they do indeed convey extraordinary, yes perhaps even frightening power. As Martha E. Savigliano has pointed out on behalf of the "political economy of passion" and its relation to a colonizing desire:

Passion and Desire do not move in plain opposition to each other. They circle one another in an ambivalent, unbalanced dualism in terms of power. Desire is invested with legitimacy, the authority enjoyed by those in power. Passion's power lies in its illegitimate nature precisely because it is imputed to nature, to the primitive, to the irrational. Hence, Passion's power resides in 'empowerment,' in seeking to partake (part-take) of some crumbs of the power held in legitimate hands. Passion's power is akin to a terrorist maneuver that asks for containment. It is wild, inhuman, beyond conquerable nature – that is supernatural – and must be subjected to the workings of the civilizing/humanizing Desire (1995: 10).

So to suggest a hesitant conclusion from my reading here, maybe what I was first misled to read as a stereotypical, almost derogatory sexual dependency/victimization scene in Sulkari's partnering of male and female dancers is in effect a rather empowering stance.

What appears as ambivalence in Sulkari is thus its juxtaposition of gender neutral African based ritual to the exotic/erotic modernist archaism: for neither are Rivero's dancers African sculptures per se nor are they actors in the role of men and women in a 'primitive' village scene. Rather, Rivero's modern dance technique translates an abstract idea of that cultural power. As he has commented:

The bended knee is the same as in African sculpture. The strength in the face, in the eyes and the lips and cheeks are very strong expressions of African culture and what we called the phenomenon of possession. In Cuba this is very strong in the Afro-Cuban culture of Yoruba rituals. Observation made in respect of these rituals reveal a living sculpture, with strength in the face, and the expression of these people. That is a great strength for when you see a Yoruba sculpture or carving you are seeing a Yoruba possessed person. And that strength that you see in the culture and that you see in a possessed person, that is inside Sulkari. Sulkari is an art form that goes on stage, the dancer cannot be unconscious, i.e. be possessed, and come out of themselves on stage. The dancer must have the same strength of the sculpture and the possessed person, but very controlled, extremely controlled. And that is the strength of Sulkari. That is why in my class we used so much the breathing, and all these elements, which we find in African dance and African retentions in Cuba (in: Cumberbatch-Lynch 2001: 25).

Rivero's abstraction of possessional dances thus seeks to symbolically convey the quintessential expressiveness of African Cuban ritual. As Susan Vogel has also remarked, on behalf of the aesthetic foundation of African sculpture: unlike 'naive' mimesis, African sculpture rarely imitates people or animals for what they are in themselves, but rather it conveys abstract "ideas about reality" (1986: 12). Hardly naturalistic therefore it should rather be interpreted as "the result of a highly intellectual and abstract process of translating ideas, concepts, and values into physical form" (Vogel 1986: 12). In this respect, the dancers' bulging eyes and puffed cheeks are not intended to convey the derogatory minstrel stereotype, but rather the power of possession. However, even if such an aesthetic may speak differently to a Caribbean audience than to one abroad, i.e. me in this case, the problem of the stereotype remains as "white definitions of gender and 'Otherness' intervene" (Burt 1995: 130). Transferring this ambivalent stance to *Sulkari*, the interrelation of the stylization of ritualistic ecstasy and power on the one hand with a clearly gendered erotic connotation on the other are somewhat both present: in-between traditions there can never be just one reading it appears.

Congo Layé

Arsenio Rafael Andrade's *Congo Layé*, the second NDTC choreography to be briefly mentioned in this context, also employs the signature elements of the African Cuban technique, yet to a stylistically rather different effect. Intended as a "Eulogy to my ancestors, to my blood, to my motherland Africa," choreographer Andrade announces quite clearly the agenda under which he wants his choreography to be read. A former member of Eduardo Rivero's company in Santiago and a graduate of the National School of Dance in Havanna, Arsenio Andrade moved to Jamaica, where he joined the NDTC as principal dancer and also teaches dance classes at the Jamaica School of Dance. In comparison to *Sulkari*'s rather statuesque composition, *Congo Layé* by contrast presents the same technical elements in a far more energetic accentuation and ensemble based composition. Accompanied by music from Conjunto Ballet and Folklorico Afrocubano, the pace and rhythm set are already much faster and as the ensemble of female dancers appears on stage, they lift their arms in an aggressive posture as if pointing a spear towards the audience. They, too, puff their cheeks, however, as their warrior make-up signifies, the expression seems less ambivalent than in *Sulkari*, since the whole narrative of the dance is an already familiar and yes, probably also a meanwhile somewhat topical one.

Congo Layé once more explores the African heritage in Caribbean dance by interpreting the African Cuban movement vocabulary in terms of a defiant warrior stance. Embodied in acrobatic jumps, turns and lifts such technically spectacular arrangement hardly fails to win an audience and probably, in this respect, it is an assertive gesture every Caribbean choreographer needs to make at one point in the career. Power and tempo mark the female as well as the male group of dancers who engage in confrontational and competitive juxtaposition. In this respect, *Congo Layé* demonstrates that the Cuban technique may potentially form the base of various dance interpretations. While *Sulkari* is rather contemplative and solemn in expression, the same technical foundation in *Congo Layé* becomes an energetic vehicle to conjure the defiance within African dance practice in the Caribbean. Thus, indeed, the Caribbean's rich folk heritage re-invents modern dance to stylistically quite unique interpretations and appropriations, depending on the choreographer's imagination.

The Caribbean Modern Interpretations of Clive Thompson

Of Sympathy and Love
Born in Jamaica and an early acolyte of Ivy Baxter, Clive Thompson pursued most of his career as a dancer in the United States. A mainstay with first Martha Graham Company during the 1960s and then Alvin Ailey American Dance Theatre in the 1970s, his work as a choreographer naturally owes to these strong technical foundations. As Thompson explains, it was in particular Graham's approach of character, which had a lasting impact. He recalls:

Martha works from the moment. [...] She works on that in her imagination, speculating on the reasons why, and this is a wonderful approach to dance and theatre, because you get involved in character. The characters unfold and become real individuals. From the moment the curtain goes up you're telling, reliving the story right till the curtain comes down. It all unfolds with you, by you, on the stage. As opposed to telling stories just by wonderful virtuoso movement, I enjoy virtuoso movement, but movement for me, is not enough. I think this is my Graham background. I think the artist must be able to add meaning to the movement. In Graham, there is nothing wasted. No gesture added and then thrown away. There's a cause, and you're always aware that you're communicating to that audience (in: Mclain Stoop 1978: 82).

This approach of character is particularly evident in Thompson's recent *Of Sympathy and Love*, which he choreographed for the NDTC's 41st dance season in 2003. A duet for two male dancers on the biblical Lazarus theme, the dance divides into two solos and a brief pas de deux at the end. As Thompson reflects on the choreographing process:

This idea, the idea of Lazarus, the Lazarus theme has been in my head for long, long time. It's one of my concepts that I've been going over and over. And one of my concepts was that I didn't see Jesus, I just saw a white light and I heard the voice saying that sentence. And I see, I was seeing Lazarus back out of that cave at one time with cloth hanging from him, because I didn't want it to be cloth, but to represent decomposed flesh and the face covered.[77]

Starting from that original idea, the choreography begins with a blue lit stage floor and the empty space, which is first entered by the music:

---

77 Interview with Clive Thompson 21 Aug. 2003.

single piano keys set the solemn, almost sacred mood into which the first solo dancer in the character of Jesus enters.[78]

"Jesus wept" from John 11:35 has been interpreted as a sign of Jesus' humanity (May/Metzger 1973: 1304-1305). And it is this human aspect of the Christ figure that Thompson's choreography of the solo seems to also focus on: entering from the side wings of the stage, the dancer directs the focus of his movement in a vulnerably open relevé with arms upheld and an upward look as if in appeal to his God/Savior. Then, he turns towards the audience in that same posture, whereby he establishes himself as the link between both spheres. On his knees, the dancer apparently measures his psychical burden in a bodily arm gesture, which in staccato retardation drops from a relevé to shoulder height. In Graham oriented movement vocabulary, the solo introduces its character through a series of gestures, which – supported by the purist white costume – evoke an expression of lament and endurance. Repeatedly, the dancer, for example, covers his head protectively under crossed arms, while simultaneously bending the torso horizontally over. Technically refined balances and turns, furthermore, create an image of balanced beauty and grace – Christ's humble humility, his human pain and forbearance of suffering.

Mark Phinn in Clive Thompson's Of Sympathy and Love, 2003. Video Still.

---

78 Albert A. Johnstone has described how "ludic symbolism" via a narrative correlation of props, movements, lighting, etc. generates the "dancer-character relation" in dance theatre (1984: 171-172).

Choreographer Thompson is highly demanding of his dancers, because, as he has said, mere expertise in technique is not quite enough. So what Thompson demands of himself, he also expects to see from his dancers, whom he challenges to find in their dance not only technique but more importantly a means of communication. As he has described the elation, which derives from this transcending moment of technique into expression: "It's wonderful to know that you've transcended yourself, become a character, and shown, as in a mirror, a part of humanity for the audience to see the reflection of mankind."[79] Reassessing the "Jesus Wept" solo from this perspective, the dancer's expertise consists precisely in achieving such transition, when the audience can indeed partake through the movement gesture in the emotional expressiveness of the dance.

The second solo, "Lazarus Come Forth" from John 11:43, was inspired by Thompson's discovery of the Native American musical arrangement. In this case, the finding of the music re-shaped the original outline of the dance. As Thompson recalls:

The concept than changed and there were two solos. The first solo of Jesus, "Jesus Wept." The second section are rituals performed on the sacred ground, the burial ground, the holly ground [...] it's not unlike what happens here in the Caribbean or what happens in Africa, or Brazil or there in Germany, in various parts of the world as spiritual manifestation of the people. Not just black people, all people, all [...] mankind, where the spiritual manifestation just takes different forms. And when I heard this music, I said: 'Ah!' And it solidified.[80]

The transition from the "Jesus Wept" part of the dance is introduced by a loudspeaker transmitted voice-over: "Lazarus Come Forth," after which an upstage light beam goes up immediately on the hand of the second male dancer, accompanied by the sound of a vigorously pulsating heart beat. Stretched out on a bench and clad in flesh-colored rags, the focus is solely directed to the dancer's hand, which moves along his lifeless body as if an independent entity almost. This is a captivating scene to follow as the hand touches the chest right above from where the heart is located and sucks the upper body into an almost violent contract release, similar to that of an electric shock reaction. Yet, 'Lazarus' is still not back to his senses as the hand further inches along to the

---

79 Interview with Clive Thompson 21 Aug. 2003.
80 Interview with Clive Thompson 21 Aug. 2003.

back of the head, lifts it to the chest, sets it back down, moves to the knee, contracts and releases again, rests down and lets the body relax briefly, before the whole body contracts in a tense upward move to instantly crush back down.

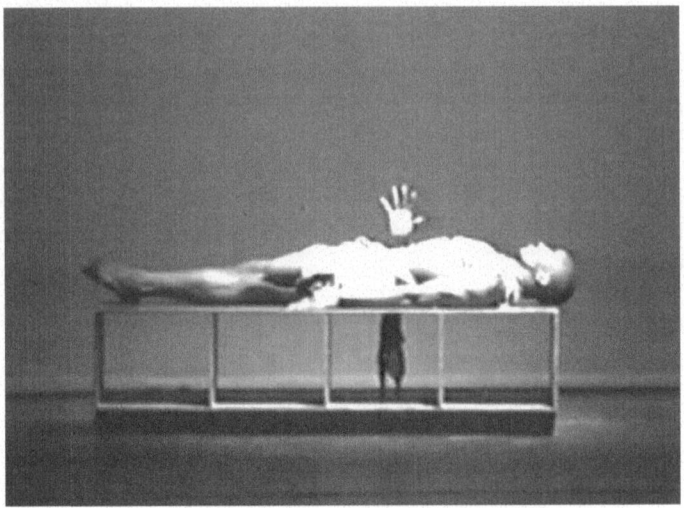

Marlon Simms in Clive Thompson's Of Sympathy and Love, 2003. Video Still.

From there, the dancer engages in riskier positions, as, for example, turning on the bench, lying on the stomach, extending the leg, etc. to eventually leave the bench behind. And then, he moves ever so free to explore the whole space of the stage, to extend and balance, to jump and turn, almost as if he had never danced before. Thompson comments on the development of this scene:

When I had Marlon there the first time, I knew I wanted to go into the cave, I didn't want the bench, but we rehearsed with that and the bench, it's a prop from a previous work, it worked, because you don't see the bench. It just suspends. The blue you really don't see, I realized today. It doesn't need a lot of décor, because the movement is so strong. Especially, when I see the hand, now the light comes in too slow, when he says: 'Lazarus, come forward...' The light has to come up then, because it goes right into a heartbeat. And the heartbeat is the opening. [...] I love the moment, when you just see his hand appear. And it doesn't look as if it was joined to him at all. Only afterwards. [...] I used the image also of spirit moving through his body, but the power was in his hand, because it's the hand touching these things and bringing the energy. The spirit was just moving through the hand.[81]

Thus, apart from bringing the energy to the dance, the "moving spirit" also surprisingly appears as the link that connects this inherently modern dance work to a Caribbean sensibility, as it speaks of the redemptive impulse that is so prevalent in the religious syncretism of Jamaican Revival as well as the other folk retentions.

As has been restated throughout this analysis, the liberation aspect of Christianity has been a constant motor of African Jamaican resistance, which is also at the heart of the Lazarus theme. Thus, towards the end, both dancers join in a brief pas de deux, where the dancer of Lazarus is lifted on the Jesus dancer's thigh – a lean on, supportive position – after which the dancer of Jesus leads Lazarus for a few steps. Finally, they each take second position relevé, arms lifted and facing backs opposite each other. While Lazarus looks upward to the back, Jesus looks straight into the audience, again establishing that bond between the godly presence and human sphere that was already introduced in the beginning. A deeply religious work, *Of Sympathy and Love* technically owes to Thompson's Graham foundation, yet at the same time Thompson and his two dancers make it distinctly their own expressive creation. Enhanced by the Native American soundtrack – its ancestral voices and wind blows – *Of Sympathy and Love* not only speaks of the gospel's story-line (which in my reading comes across far more explicit than it was actually experienced during performance), but also of that spiritual infusion of breath energy which is so much part of the Caribbean ancestralism. As such Thompson's choreography successfully defies national and cultural boundaries and yet expresses his own unique imagination.

Interlude IV: Dance and Cultural Diversity

While the North American modern dance school technically shaped Thompson's physique as a dancer, the Caribbean impulse did, however, remain the base of his individual dance interpretations. Thus, Thompson's presence in the "Fix Me Jesus" section of Ailey's signature piece *Revelations*, carries a Caribbean stance unlike that of dancers who

---

81 Interview with Clive Thompson 21 Aug. 2003.

had performed the part before. Asked for the Caribbean input in his work as dancer and choreographer, Thompson remarked:

I have a very conscious way in Alvin Ailey's Revelations, Rex will always say that he has never seen "Wading in the Water" or "Fix Me Jesus" performed the way Sara Yarborough and I did it. We are both Caribbean people, she being from Haiti and I'm being from Jamaica. And especially, even with Judy during the white section, when I come down dancing and I'm dancing with Mari Kajiwara, who's Japanese, she's coming very straight up and down, and I'm, it's very subtle, but you see the movement of the pelvis as the hips are going. It's a Caribbean thing. It's not necessarily black as in African, but it's Caribbean and it's definitely Jamaican. So you see the folk forms that we have, that one grows up in, which surround you. It's not necessarily conscious – it's just there, you get it, if you look, you go either to, or you hear a Revival meeting, my parents did a lot. Or you go and you see the people dancing and singing, and I didn't know what it meant, but I was there and got caught in the drums and the tambourines and the singing and you look at that thing and see that. All those things are there and in you. When you become more conscious now, then you realize, what you were doing: 'Oh, that's a Dinki Mini and that is a something, but you already know it. Cause it's been there.[82]

Based on the work of two of the prime American modern dance companies, Thompson's work certainly appears more indebted to that tradition than Rex Nettleford's more folk-oriented work, even though Thompson's *Folk Tales* of the 2003 season also investigated that latter idiom in an entertainingly self-ironic manner. Hence, as has been shown throughout the previous analyses, both traditions easily blend into each other with quite fascinating stylistic results. Moreover, since the NDTC's repertoire has successfully blended the North American schools of modern dance with their own explorations of Caribbean folk material, as well as the Cuban Technique, the common cultural sensibility of the African diaspora's dance expression undeniably shines through.

To conclude, modern dance pioneers such as the women already mentioned as well as the later generation of men in the Caribbean and the U.S. have mutually enriched their dance vocabulary by adding that Africanist perspective, which the very early modern dance had lacked, or at least not publicly claimed. As with McBurnie's early beginnings in

---

82 Interview with Clive Thompson 21 Aug. 2003.

Trinidad, the Cuban example of Ramiro Guerra and later Eduardo Rivero, as well as the NDTC's work in Jamaica, the Caribbean shares a 'black history' of dance very much in line with Alvin Ailey's American Dance Theatre.[83] Not only did the Caribbean pioneers have the same vision of modern dance to announce their own cultural experience of diaspora, but also were they Renaissance women and men with a clear humanistic dedication to the social and educational outreach of dance theatre into their larger communities. As Clive Thompson has summarized this universal outlook within modern dance:

I tend not to think of our audience as the man who just pays a few dollars to come in and enjoy. I think of it as humanity, and we're all part of the whole human thing. You should be taken away a bit, but not necessarily into fairyland. You must be able to see some of reality, some of man's struggle, some of our history, some of our joy in the theatre, at times (in: Mclain 1978: 83).

Therefore, as has been demonstrated by the example of the NDTC's creolized dance technique, such crossing humanity is indeed achieved in their celebratory dance of cultural diversity – undeniably Africanist in gesture, but also an expression of our shared humanity in the world.

Next Generation's Re-Inventions: Jamaican Dance Theatre Goes Global

A new generation of students has emerged whose environments oscillate between the local and the global; whose enjoyment of cultural practices find the modernist concepts of popular and high art a straight jacket irrelevant to their lives; and whose experiences and identities transcend those mononationalisms. For these students, the narrowness of the canon of western theatre art dance is being challenged; not to overturn it, but to gain a more balanced perspective on the practices of dance and codified movement systems in human society (Buckland 1999: 3).

This study of Jamaican dance theatre has thus far focused on the historical development of Jamaica's National Dance Theatre Company

---

83 Compare Thomas F. DeFrantz' insightful study of Alvin Ailey's America Dance Theatre Dancing *Revelations. Alvin Ailey's Embodiment of African American Culture* (Oxford: Oxford UP, 2004) and Jack Mitchell, *Alvin Ailey American Dance Theatre: Jack Mitchell Photographs* (Kansas City: Andrews and McMeel, 1993).

within the frame of postcolonial nation-building, emerging vocabulary and identity formation. However, a new generation of Jamaican choreographers has meanwhile matured, whose dance theatre works clearly demonstrate a new development. Starting with NDTC ballet mistress Arlene Richards, these young choreographers – with exception of Arsenio Andrade, who joined the NDTC and the Jamaica School of Dance staff from his home country Cuba – have been trained in the NDTC vocabulary and are so to speak original 'products' of that school. Interestingly enough, despite the NDTC's strong folk dance background, their recent choreographic work appears increasingly oriented towards modern/contemporary dance expression. While this generation will still integrate Jamaican folk vocabulary to a considerable extent, it appears no longer the primary concern of experimentation. Rather, today Jamaican folk dance heritage presents to them but one – alas, in terms of 'rootedness' very important – of the many dance vocabularies out there. In a way, this survey of selected choreography shall finally outline rather than conclude that with this generation of promising young dance choreographers – the children of the 'new Jamaica' – Caribbean dance theatre continues to re-invent itself, precisely to fit the artists' contemporary needs of diverse identity expression.

Arlene Richards – *Cocoon, Renewal of the Spirit*

Starting dance lessons in high school, Arlene Richards won a scholarship to attend dance classes at the Jamaica School of Dance in Kingston. Many of her teachers there were members of the NDTC at the time. Richards took classes with Tony Wilson as well as Patsy Ricketts before she joined the NDTC in 1978.[84] When she received her dance training at Edna Manley College, she recalls that her teachers put a strong emphasis on folk forms. Dancing *Pocomania* and *Kumina* with the NDTC later on, she thus came to assess Nettleford's choreography as an art form rather independent from the religious ritual practice, which helped her as a practicing Christian to overcome a certain reservation towards the ritualistic dances of another religious denomination.[85] However, Richards' own choreography does not abstract on the ritualistic background of Jamaican folk dance vocabulary, but rather employs these forms in entirely new configurations. For example, her choreography *Cocoon*

---

84 For biographical data compare NDTC 30th Anniversary Program.
85 Interview with Arlene Richards 23 Aug. 2003.

deals with extraterrestrials, whereas *Side by Side* has explored the emotional entanglement of two sisters. While both works will also incorporate NDTC vocabulary, it may be easily overlooked, for Richards transfers that vocabulary to her more topical, contemporary themes. Similarly, her more recent *Renewal of the Spirit* also relies heavily on theatrical narrative and modern dance vocabulary, which in terms of declared 'Jamaicanness' does not articulate itself quite as strongly as the NDTC's earlier works. And yet, I will argue that Richards choreographs Jamaican dance drama in the best sense: for her story-telling compositions create colorful stage imagery, characters and conflict, comparatively seldom seen in dance theatre today, but very much in line with the tradition of Jamaican ritual and masquerade.

The National Dance Theatre Company of Jamaica in Arlene Richards' Cocoon, 2003. Video Still.

Cocoon, for example, presents the discovery/encounter between the inmates of an extraterrestrial 'spaceship' – created by the seven female dancers covered under a satin balloon – and two supposedly 'human' male representatives. Introduced by the futuristic electronics of the canned music, the opening scene is dominated by that estranging image of the cocoon as it mirrors the 'alie/n/ation' of the dance characters on stage. Certainly, the image of the cocoon on top of the synaesthetic sensation of the music presents a stunning stage metaphor to play with: a birthing shell, a ship of transport, transcendental force, bounded yet without boundary between time and space, etc. The satin prop works wonderfully here, for it allows the dancers to explore and actively engage with the flexibility of the fabric during that scene. By pressing her face against the satin, for example, a dancer creates the astonishing imprint of a ghostly mask; or, also, by briefly standing bent over butt out, another dancer points to the life-force within the cocoon as simultaneously a radiating light beam illuminates the satin's silvery surface from the top. Finally, in a repeated move from the beginning, all of the dancers lean back outward again so as to flatten down the balloon's volume, 'shedding that outer skin' with arms, elbows and fists fighting against the malleable tissue, swirling in a circle flow-wave from dancer to dancer, before one after the other actually breaks out of the prison/capsule/cocoon.

In fetus-position or gliding along backwards, the dancers singly roll out from under the satin and either assume what appears as a wriggling beetle perspective, or, even more curious, they perform a tedious, dragging crawl by moving forward from contract fetus to stretch release, reminiscent of a snail or other amphibian species. Tinged in soft-colored blue light, Richards has choreographed the scene as surrealistic underwater-world, reminiscent of a dry-swimming symphony of uninvestigated movement possibility on back, knees and side-stretch, subtly accompanied by the electronic sound dribble of drum and pan-flute acoustics. Interrupted by the intruding noise of unintelligible whispers, the dancers suddenly stand up – as if 'possessed' – and execute a sequence of robotic walks and angular moves as if directed via remote-control or that voice from off-stage. From the organic amphibian crawl then, the audience is instantly confronted with highly mechanized marionettes in line formation and pairs, lunging to both sides, exerting jumps and handstands of disoriented obeisance.

The National Dance Theatre Company of Jamaica in Arlene Richards' Cocoon, 2003. Video Still.

And while the futuristic aspect of the choreography, costume and music could not have appeared farther remote from ancestral African rites thus far, the episode that follows appears strangely reminiscent of familiar Revival ritual. In fact, as one of the 'robot'-dancers falls 'sick' on the ground, the group – not unlike the historical descriptions of Jamaica's powerful myal-men – starts to exert a healing ritual supposedly designed to bring back the dancer's spirit. First encircling the entranced/lifeless body with conjuring gestures, the group dancers finally lift her up above their heads to acclerando music. At that moment, a glaring red light fills the scenic backdrop and increases the emotionally tense atmosphere of the sequence. Produced by the unsettling sound effect of the unintelligible voice, the dancers respond somewhat unwillingly to that elusive force in space. So while this sequence does not deal with the specifics of Jamaican ritual by any means, the underlying theme of supernatural power, deadening threat and remorseful healing remains strikingly similar.

Moreover, the scenic imagery is to great extent evoked by Richards' congenial costume design. Since she has been quoted earlier, yet to briefly repeat, her costumes seek to underline the message of the individual work. In *Cocoon* this approach proves particularly convincing, because of Richards' assured apprehension of the materiality of her props as well as the color design. While the women are dressed in white-bluish water-colored diving-type suits, the two men wear pink, flesh/ribcage-colored unitards and matching bathing-caps. Depending on the light, the women's costume may create iridescent effects of manifold blue variations. Lighting and costume thus become integral elements of the overall composition to successfully create *Cocoon*'s impression of 'other-worldliness.' The choreography's narrative hence evolves not only from the dance, but such binary opposition of color, costume and lighting, too, which in totality convey the dramatic tension of the scene.

Following the brief exposition of character and conflict, the next sequence then stages the encounter between the two worlds as a romantic pas de deux of the two men and two women soloists. Dream-like in atmosphere the choreography here consists of technically versatile lifts and balances to underline the eroticism of the love theme, followed by a group formation finale of the ensemble. While the romance lyricism of the scene appears a bit kitschy perhaps, it proves at the same time to be luring enough in its utopian promise and quite enjoyable to watch: 'If only 'alie/n/ation' was ever overcome that easily –' Yet before one steeps into such sentimentality, the finale's again humorous tone of squatted 'kangaroo bounce' and 'flamingo head' isolations is already taken up again. Alien creatures indeed these dancers may become, if they venture freely into unfamiliar movement territory. Unfortunately, such imaginative paradise is quickly lost, as again the unintelligible voice intrudes and another space-ship pops up right onto the red illumined backdrop. To the distorted sounds of an e-guitar the friendly visitors are being called back home, finally ascending the violently flickering space-ship projection.

Cocoon surprises, because of Richards' quite candid use of pop-culture elements. Her colorful costumes, trick-scenery and electronic sound devices draw freely on the abundant fund of film, news-release, TV and stage theatricality. Engaging playfully with that diverse material, she creates dance theatre that is easily accessible to audiences from all walks of life. In almost less then twenty minutes, Richards' *Cocoon* thus manages to take her audience through a dense tour de force of fantastically allusive dance-imagery: from outer-space right down to the beginnings of evolution through African Caribbean ritual and romantic courtship. As a matter-of-fact, *Cocoon* re-enacts no less than the whole mystery and drama of life, where – whether it be a sacrifice to ancestral God or revengeful Cyber-Spirit – the ultimate secrets remain untold. As Richards' epigraph to *Cocoon* tellingly suggests: "The Universe – all that is – vast, varied, yet to be explored. What if ...? Would you ...?"[86]

The National Dance Theatre Company of Jamaica in Arlene Richards' Cocoon, 2003. Video Still.

---

86 Compare NDTC 40th Anniversary program.

By entering the psychology of alterity from the extraterrestrial vantage point, one might even go as far as to find her treatment slightly self-ironic. Certainly, the landing of 'extraterrestrial' beings is not that new to the Caribbean. After all, the region has survived several attacks throughout its turbulent history. And if the visitors have not come from Mars quite yet, than certainly from strange European and North American crusades. Personally, I only need to recall the gigantic ships harboring on the Jamaican sea-shore off Ocho Rios to picture a somewhat different, but no less surreal scene. Richards' creative power, hence, appears to operate from a cunningly internalized cultural sensibility, which is after all truly Jamaican. And last but not least, her marvelous stagecraft and affinity for theatrical means surely owe a lot to folk traditional aspects – as, for example, Jamaican Jonkonnu – without explicitly having to portray them as such.

The other work I will briefly discuss in this context is *Renewal of the Spirit*, which Richards choreographed for the NDTC's 41st season in 2003. As the *Gleaner* has pointedly summarized, "*Renewal of the Spirit* is a dramatic dance which deals with a man who loses his faith and a woman who subsequently finds hers" (2003: C4). Given away that much, the choreography would not appear all too exciting, if it was not for the beautifully arranged costumes and original ensemble dances. Referring back to the same critic's review, the costumes were praised for their authenticity as portraying the "surplices and cassocks worn by priests and garments worn by nuns" (2003: C4). And it is in fact mainly due to this naturalist realism of the costumes that a certain reading is provoked, despite of the rather neutral modern dance vocabulary. Therefore, I, for example, found it quite hard not to think of the choreographed 'priests' and 'nuns' in terms of the all too familiar dramaturgy of tacky German TV series, according to which a priest will also 1. fall in love, 2. from grace and 3. straight down to the 'devil,' which in a nutshell breaks down the underlying suspense of Richards' dance drama.

In a series of melodramatic 'dance events,' *Renewal of the Spirit* thus presents two excelling solos by the protagonist lovers – the priest and the beautiful woman, he falls in love with – as well as their highly romantic pas de deux of astonishing lifts and passionate modern expressions. Sinners in the hands of a vengefully loving God though, the priest is struck down by lightning from the heavens, while his lover will return to the compassionate arms of the church. Beautifully represented by the following ensemble performances, Richards' choreography next presents her audience with group formations dominated by the spiraling ebb and flow of mourning priests and nuns as during the funeral scene. Finally, *Renewal of the Spirit* concludes with an ancient, yet no less surprising theatrical effect: the deceased priest's 'duppy' reappears as a truly frightening deus ex machina in form of a masterfully crafted puppet effigy.

The National Dance Theatre Company of Jamaica in Arlene Richards' Renewal of the Spirit, 2003. Photograph by Wiston Sill (rpt. in: The Gleaner 30 July 2003: C4).

Admittedly, such tense melodrama presented itself quite unexpectedly. Not being used to dramaturgical correspondence between TV and dance theatre conventions, I hastily placed *Renewal of the Spirit* into the pop cultural entertainment/diversion box. Maybe one could name it 'dance theatre soap,' if that genre existed. Yet, as *Renewal of the Spirit* was performed almost every night during my stay with the NDTC's 41st season in 2003, I was fortunately given many a chance to revise that preliminary conclusion. As it turns out, to read the dance solely in terms of the topical seduction theme does justice neither to the choreography's excelling soloists nor to the finely choreographed and costumed ensemble performances. To begin with, I believe that at first the concept of dancing nuns and priests in conservative Catholic costume irritated, not because of cultural estrangement, but rather owing to an over-familiarity at least on my part. For one, I was reminded all too well of what actually wearing these 'costumes' feels like from childhood mass service, not to want to imagine to try and dance in them. Thus referring back to my own experience, made me wonder all the more, why would you choose to portray such an issue as a 'scandalized' priest in Jamaican dance theatre? Considering Catholic celibacy somewhat ridiculous for my own cultural upbringing, I found it even more astounding in the Jamaican context.

And yet, when I learned more about Jamaican Revival Churches and even attended one of their services in Spanish Town, Catholicism does not even have to be the issue here. Regardless of the actual denomination portrayed, Richards' choreography started to make sense as the connection between dance, spirituality and faith moved to the foreground. Assessed from that Jamaican cultural background then, the choreography's religious message of spiritual deliverance did not appear that limited a viewpoint at all. As Richards has furthermore explained to me:

I think the dance speaks to your spirit and your religion and what you believe in and how you remain faithful to it or not. [...] As to – if I committed myself and I had chosen this path, how do I stay faithful to it and if I don't, if there are consequences. What happens, if I don't? And that is really what the work is teaching about, it is not, you know, targeting anybody at all. And we have always used dance to do that.[87]

So what slowly occurred to me after this interview, as well as the increasing study of Jamaican folk forms, was the noticeable prevalence of that (Neo)African spiritual dimension, which really infiltrates so many levels of the Jamaican cultural sensibility. Not only in the folk-legendary 'duppy' and religious rituals, but also in the popular dance, music and apparently even Anglican churches, the concept of the 'spirit' permeates Jamaican identity perception.[88]

When I now consider Richards' choreography in retrospect, then *Renewal of the Spirit* is precisely remarkable for that articulation. Regardless of whether one finds the plot significant or not, there are definite elements which despite the overall modern dance vocabulary will speak of that Jamaican kinaesthetic trace. Not only in the body ripple or the resurrection of the deceased priest's spirit/duppy as an effigy puppet, but also in the funeral scene before, which was actually inspired from contemporary Jamaican wake ceremonies and the elaborate décor of the dancehall. As Richards remarked:

---

[87] Interview with Arlene Richards 23 Aug. 2003.
[88] Compare Interview with Arlene Richards 23 Aug. 2003, where an audience member apparently had told Richards that he identified the performer as a danced portrait of his Anglican priest.

[O]ur popular culture is greatly informed by our traditional folk forms. Greatly. Especially over the last five years, our dancehall culture, the movements are instated by what happens. I don't know, if it is, because so many people die. That sounds terrible, but there are so many wakes, they get accustomed to the movements and I've seen it more and more coming into the dancehall. [...] But I was influenced by that dancehall culture, too. The funeral, because there is that thing that you go to a dance funeral and you come out in your very finest. All your gold and glitter and everything comes out at the funeral. It's no longer this very solemn black thing, you know. I mean, this is a celebration.[89]

The degree of cultural cross-fertilization between folk forms and modern, popular and highbrow, life and stage, etc. appears thus as the hallmark of Richards' choreography. Despite the folk traditions' comparative 'invisibility,' I hope to have convincingly shown that it still contributes to her work's overall communicative power. Not only aesthetically, but also in terms of her artistic engagement. Richards wants her dance choreography to address issues that concern and affect her immediate surroundings.[90]

While this may not adhere to fashionable postmodern trends, I consider her work important precisely because of that. Thus, even where one would not be necessarily made aware of it, Richards' Jamaican sensibility is still present in a subtle way. In fact, Richards 'resistance' to mimic what she does not believe to be meaningful, expresses a renowned Jamaican attitude, which in tradition goes as far back as Jonkonnu, where dance theatre and costumes were also designed to purport distinct social statements. As Richards has commented on her own artistic approach:

A lot of companies are moving towards a postmodern kind of way of dancing. But that's not acceptable to us. I don't think we can present it as a Caribbean people that is so colorful, I don't think we could present it to anybody at all. I mean sometimes they go, 'Oh it's not sophisticated!' But we can't present it to anybody. So it's not acceptable, because if you go and do it like that, then everybody has the same dance, you know. But life is interesting, because then we're hearing: 'Oh you shouldn't be taking on so much of...' Whatever it is, you know. Because then, there are also people still thinking that we are 'Caribbean' and we should still have the grass skirts, or little loin cloth, or something. So that's why it's important that we have to know who we really are

---

89 Interview with Arlene Richards 23 Aug. 2003.
90 Interview with Arlene Richards 23 Aug. 2003.

and hold on to that. And work with what we really have in a very positive and confident way.[91]

Far from naive, therefore, Richards purposefully creates dance theatre for a broad range of audiences. Easily accessible, her work is emotionally moving rather than intellectually challenging perhaps, yet as such it adds to the overall appeal and diversity of the NDTC's genuineness. And if people will see different things in her marvelous scenery and dance design, then that has also been intended, since Richards' danced 'statement' is very far from doctrine. As she will ultimately claim: "[i]t's there for you to interpret it."[92]

Arsenio Andrade – *Epilogo*

Arsenio Andrade's choreography *Epilogo* is a dance/performance tribute to Malcolm X. Composed for three male dancers, the choreography begins, when the curtain rises on a blue lit backdrop. The three dancers stand in a triangle freeze arrangement with two of them downstage corners and one of them upstage center. Dressed in black satin pants and tank tops, they have their backs turned toward the audience and face the backstage wall. As excerpts from Ossie Davis' "Euology for Malcom X" are delivered over loudspeaker from off-stage, the upstage dancer makes his first move, while the other two remain still. [93] Accompanying the solemn lyrics of: "Here – at this final hour, in this quiet place – we have come to bid farewell to one of our brightest hopes...," the solo dancer first reaches up relevé, then turns around into a lunge to the right, one arm extended upward, the other pointing down, rising briefly on demi-pointe, falling into a bottom turn and finally continuing the sequence by stepping towards downstage center between the two others. Framed by their backs, the soloist reaches up again, both arms

---

91 Interview with Arlene Richards 23 Aug. 2003.
92 Interview with Arlene Richards 23 Aug. 2003.
93 Ossie Davis delivered this speech at the funeral of Malcolm X on Feb. 27th 1965 at the Faith Temple Church of God in Harlem, New York. For the original speech given compare www.americanrhetoric.com (04.03.20005). Davis' speech was also reworked for Spike Lee's 1992 movie Malcolm X. Also the choreography's final song "Revolution" by the Rap/HipHop band Arrested Development, which Epilogo introduces during the third part, was originally composed for that film. Whether the film, however, was in fact an inspiration for the choreography has not been verified.

lifted, before he steps back into a half-frontal standing freeze. Meanwhile the lyrics have continued:

[...] extinguished now, and gone from us forever. For this world is where he worked, where he struggled and fought – where his tribe was and his people now are – it is, therefore, most fitting that we meet like this to share these last moments with him.[94]

This introductory adagio solo is taken up in flow by the second dancer, on the upstage left. Turning inwards, he faces front, swinging both arms in a half circle outward, extending the left leg into an arabesque pointing his arms to the side stage wings. As the lyrics proceed:

For we have ever been gracious to those who have loved us, who have fought for us and defended our honor even to the death. When they asked us what we find to honor in this stormy, controversial, bold young captain – we will smile. And we shall answer and say to them: Did you ever talk to Brother Malcolm? Did he ever touch you? Did you ever have him smile at you? Did you ever really listen to him? [95]

Simultaneously, the dancer continues pirouetting first position and then adding another arabesque, this time oriented opposite direction than the one before. At last, he addresses his partner, the third dancer, with an inviting gesture for him to take up and resume. While the speech carries on:

Did he ever do a mean thing? Was he ever himself associated with violence or any public disturbance? For if you did, you would have known him. And if you knew him, you would know why we must follow him: Malcolm was our manhood, our living black manhood! That was his meaning to his people. And, in honoring him, we honor the best in ourselves.[96]

This last accompanying solo consists mainly of defiantly controlled athletic postures such as hyper-arched back bending, lunges and a crouched knee-fall – slightly reminiscent of ancient Greek discus-throwers – as well as a final stand with back turned towards the audi-

---

94 For Andrade' personalized adaptation of the speech compare video-tape version of Epilogo, NDTC 41st dance season 2003.
95 Compare video-tape version of Epilogo, NDTC 41st dance season 2003.
96 Compare video-tape version of Epilogo, NDTC 41st dance season 2003.

ence, both arms crossed behind the head and fists pointed to the center of the shoulder girdle.

Eventually, the first scene ends with all three dancers back on their beginning triangle position. While the speech concludes – "And you will know him then for what he was and is – our prince – our black shining prince! – who didn't hesitate to die, because he loved us so" – the dancers, who are now facing the audience, slowly pull up their right arms inwards into an upheld clenched fist, before they finally rearrange the triangle in orientation so that, on the very last beat, they face again the upstage left exit by reaching out and pointing off-stage with upheld heads.

Through juxtaposition of performed lyrics and danced movement, this introductory scene starts on a highly elegiac, yet distinctly powerful tone as the speech's rhetoric elegance is matched by the dancers' grace of movement. Since the single solo sequences demand exact control and concentration, the soloists furthermore translate Malcom X's praised personality traits into their dance, as both demand extraordinary discipline, self-forgetfulness and dedication to the cause. Reaching up and pointing direction thus appear as the prevalent movement motifs and may be read as suggestive emblem of Malcolm X's iconic significance as a cultural leader of the African American Black Power movement. Also, the dance not only reinforces the lyrical praise of Malcolm X as a revolutionary role model, but presents the idealized image of 'black manhood' directly on stage via the tightly built bodies, perfectly synchronized focus, balance and pointed directedness of the dancers. Quite purposefully, Malcolm X's political slogans of 'black power' and 'black is beautiful' are thus transferred to the proud exhibition of the male dancers' eroticism and strength.

The second part dramaturgically moves from the elegiac commemoration directly into action. Choreographed from everyday movement, the very first sequence allows the dancers to walk around freely. Their walks rely heavily on bounce steps and dangling arms, – the 'cool' posture/attitude of street gang members – when they step up front stage and directly address the audience in a defiant stance, shouting out one after the other:

A: People, understan'! This is for all my ancestors who were raped, killed and hung.
B: Because of their plight for freedom and dignity.
C: They died for me, the died for you.

B: Yes, this is for them. You know that today in the year 2003, we're still fired up and we're still talking about revolution.⁹⁷

With neither music nor voice-over accompanying this sequence, the 'action' solely rests on the dance performers, who appear as revolutionary agitators during this scene. At the end of the last line, they retreat back to the upstage left corner, where they take position in the same configuration as at the end of the first part.

The third and last section of the choreography then presents a blended medley of modern, jazz and hip hop dance vocabulary as competitive performance contest between the three dancers. As Thomas F. DeFrantz has pointed out on behalf of the cultural significance of hip hop dance forms, they are – apart from exhibiting "bold assertions of expertise, of resilient virtuosity," and "the power of the body" – primarily important, because they present "a mode of cultural identification and recognition that links African Americans in corporeal orature" (in: Lepecki 2004: 64; 76). DeFrantz defines corporeal orature on the basis of hip hop's claim to citationality, which transcends the merely visual impact of the dances' reception process. Hip hop and other related social dance forms, he argues, are therefore performed not only to be visually consumed, but to call for action. Regarded as "forms of orality and affective physicality," hip hop ultimately then presents a "form of battle." (2004: 67; 72).

Apparently, this notion of agitating empowerment and pan-Africanist solidarity is also shared by *Epilogo's* final sequence. Since Andrade's choreography assembles different gestures, dance moves and vocabularies from an Africanist dance vernacular, *Epilogo's* danced message reaches from the Caribbean, to Africa and the Americas. Remembering Malcolm X through dance, thus becomes an articulate strategy of announcing that political message through a shared aesthetics of the 'cool' and 'spiritual,' as conveyed by the communicative call-and-response performance of the three dancers on stage. Accompanying the last choreography, furthermore, by the song lyrics of "Revolution," performed by the renowned U.S. Rap/Hip Hop formation *Arrested Development*, certainly adds to the performative subtext of this work, which even as a dance theatre stage performance owes most of its communicative powers to the street idiom's recalcitrance.

---

97 Compare video-tape version of Epilogo, NDTC 41st dance season 2003.

So when Andrade's choreography actually chooses more from a North American Modern/Hip Hop dance idiom than a Caribbean folk traditional one, then this work ultimately defies national boundaries. By linking the Africanist aesthetic heritage to Malcolm X's pan-African liberation struggle, *Epilogo* pays tribute to 'Brother Malcolm' as the Caribbean's adopted son of liberating promise. And finally, one may notice that whereas Andrade's use of dance vocabulary may vary, the revolting message/call to the ancestral heritage – already introduced by Andrade's African Cuban *Congo Layé* – remains insistently the same.

Marlon Simms: *Millennial Beings*, *'100 Park Lanes' Redemption*

An alumnus of the UWI Dance Society, NDTC dancer Marlon Simms is not only an outstanding performer, but has also appeared as a promising young choreographer in two recent works. *Millennial Beings* (2001), Simms' choreographic debut with the NDTC, as well as *'100 and Park Lanes' Redemption* are both expressive of a modern rather than folk dance sensibility and yet they, too, speak of Jamaican issues. Thus, *Millennial Beings* which has been hailed as an "exercise in form" chooses modern dance as Simms' mode of self-expression, i.e. the dance vocabulary he can most identify with (Batson-Savage 2003: E1-2). A duet for two male dancers, Simms choreographed *Millennial Beings* for himself and company member Mark Phinn as a composition which bespeaks a rather personal approach to his work. As Simms has described his dance motivation in the same *Gleaner* Interview, "Each time I danced, I just felt better about myself." While this commitment to the art form clearly communicates in his elegant dance style, it also subtly informs his choreography, which even in a high degree of abstraction conveys much of the choreographer's unassuming intellect. *Millennial Beings* thus explores the notion of instability and change at the turn of the century in a densely choreographed sequence of bodily movement metaphors, of which evidently no one interpretation will suffice. Yet, starting my analysis from the relationship between the two dancers, this assessment will focus primarily on the dancers' parallel interaction to certain sound cues and voice-over inserts as they allow for a preliminary reading on the now following terms.

When the stage-curtain goes up on the blue lit stage, only the dark shadow silhouettes of the dancers' bodies are revealed. Standing still in second position right behind each other, they form a single resting unit as the music sets in. The chosen sound-track from *The Art of Noise* can be considered programmatic, for what follows is indeed a sampled mix of composed noise, cut-in voice trailers and suggestive sound-scapes. Right at the beginning, a voice-over sequence is tuned into, which – reminiscent of political news propaganda – announces the following bits: "[...] to maintain law, stability in our country"/"given instructions [...] for appropriate steps to be taken to maintain law and order."[98] Accompanied by the sound of increasing rumble, the front dancer makes the first move by lifting his left arm to rest in an angle from shoulder high onto his head. This move is instantly responded to by the back dancer, who as the 'inverse mirror' lifts his right arm in the same angular manner. This pattern is repeated for several beats during which the posture – of what the audience perceives as a single moving unit – changes through different arm positions, leg extension and stretch, head turns, balance, plié, etc. Either in responding alternation or exact simultaneity, both dancers thus establish their interdependency during this very first sequence. Wearing the same costume, which consist mainly of body and face covering white strings on top of a leotard, they resemble archaic warriors through that particular body and face decor. Their very slow and controlled execution of movement, furthermore, evokes a statuesque impression of body outline, which – in response to the sound – invites the image of a functionally disciplined body-machine.

After approximately one minute, the sequence changes with the separation of the unit, as one dancer steps to the sight into a semi-head/shoulder stand, while the other changes into an arabesque with the face/torso oriented down to the floor. As the sound switches into a slowing down motor/propeller noise, both dancers get down to the floor, where they propel forward by center oriented bottom turns. Reaching the center, they get up again. Standing upright, one lifts his partner hip height and thus carrying him, he swings around in a carousel movement reminiscent of children simulating flight. While the decreasing propeller sound culminates in a detonation and the voice-insert: "Well that wasn't much of noise...," the lifted dancer is slowly levered down. As if responding to that explosion and the cynical comment, the dancers next continue to carry out individualistic walks at an increased speed of mechanized small steps with hunched over contract

---

98 Compare video-taped performance NDTC Concert in Honor of the Delegates of to the 14th International Meeting of University Administrators, 8 Jan. 2003, Little Theatre, Kingston.

torso and arms. Again, one dancer is lifted by lying onto the other's bent over back, facing the ceiling as if on a stretcher. Maybe wounded or as likely a corpse, who is then lifted again hip height and apparently lifeless. From that position the supporting dancer lowers his partner down to his hips and then turns around, thus presenting him to the audience in an almost accusing manner that possibly suggests 'why did this one have to die?'

Yet, the sequence presumes without much of a pause, as the dancers are already aggressively kicking forward again or fall to the ground in a 'beat down' fashion. The scene now reminds one increasingly of militaristic drill: sit-ups alternate with splits and push ups as well as the mutual weight lifts and testing counter-balances of the two dance partners. Momentarily defying gravity, they are yet conquered by it. Another voice insert comments: "Your agony must endure forever..." Primarily evoked by the violent aggressiveness of the sound, the two dancers convey an increasingly autistic image. Their disoriented movement sequences tread awkwardly on the same spot, to which they repeatedly return as they finally crawl onto the floor from stage right to off left, just like two soldiers in the rainy mud or jungle thickets. *Millennial Beings* ends to the sound of blowing winds and softening piano keys. 'After the storm' so to speak with the lights going down, both dancers return to the resting postures of the beginning, again controlled, settled and finally lying down onto the floor, opposite each other with facing feet and heads turned to the stage wings.

Marlon Simms and Mark Phinn in Marlon Simms' Millennial Beings, ca. 2001 (rpt. in: NDTC 40th Anniversary Programme).

Certainly, an abstract choreography like *Millennial Beings* lends itself to various interpretations, for example, in terms of the terror and wars, which have marked the turn of the century. Yet, Jamaica with one of the highest murder rates in the world, obviously has its own tragic history of ongoing violence to lament. The two defiant warrior protagonists of Simms' choreography may therefore also metaphorically represent the country's ongoing gunmen enmity, from which Jamaica's future generation harshly suffers. *Millennial Beings* thus tells yet another story of survival in a hostile environment and also of the 'agony' related to that. Especially, if one regards this work in relation to Simms' *'100 and Park Lanes' Redemption* – which he choreographed in dedication to the seven innocent victims, who died as a consequence of gunmen invading that Jamaican community – then, I am suggesting that Simms' choreography may even be read in yet another vein, i.e. as danced testimony. Thus, *'100 and Park Lanes' Redemption* performs the reconciliation with Jamaica's violence trauma in the sense that the seven women and the one male dancer on stage move through a sequence of gestured mourning.[99] Embodying commemoration, Simms' modern dance interpretation of the incident purports a quiet activism against deadening silence. As was commented by the *Gleaner* on March 1st 2005 on behalf of the '100 and Park Lanes' shooting, these crimes give "an index of the times that murder on this scale may never find eye witness to tell the tale in a court of law." Yet, if that is the case, then dance theatre may present the appropriate site to address these socio-political issues and to dance against the violence trauma of a society, where in fact almost every Jamaican will likely know if not the victims personally then almost certainly someone related to them.[100] The impact of modern dance in Simm's choreography therefore lies in its universal adaptability of vocabulary, since its free form allows the dancer to speak from his or her own socio-political perspective.

Christopher Walker – *Fragile*

NDTC dancer and choreographer Christopher Walker studied dance at the Jamaica School of Dance and the State University of New York Brockport in the U.S. and is currently teaching at Hobart and William Smith Colleges. As a choreographer he brings profound knowledge and understanding of Jamaican folk, African contemporary and U.S. modern dance idioms to the dance theatre stage, all of which he blends into a very engaging dance expression. Walker's original approach to

---

99 This observation is based on the performance given 'In Tuition' at the Little Theatre 2003.
100 Compare interview with Clive Thompson 21 Aug. 2003.

Caribbean dance theatre is demonstrated in his recent choreography *Fragile*, which he choreographed for the NDTC's 41st dance season in 2003. The dance begins to a cow horn signal and drums, as the curtain rises on a tableau of a single dancer leaping her way through couples and individual dancers in freeze positions. Dressed in richly coloured traditional African cloth and head wrap, the dancers' scenic arrangement suggests an African village. Yet, one dancer appears to be slightly 'out of frame,' since he is positioned on the apron of the stage and assumes more of an onlooker's perspective. Stepping out of the freeze, the couples embrace, while a woman soloist, who is tellingly dressed in the symbolic white robe of a spiritual leader, bends down under the imitative ripples of spirit possession.

The tableaux sequence invites the audience to invent their own memory images, evoked by the suggestive movements and relationships between the dancers on stage. Choreographed as a "dance for the griots, a dance for the storytellers," this scene points to the source of Walker's Caribbean dance theatre imagination.[101] While I have elsewhere interpreted this scene in the context of the loss of the Middle Passage, one can also regard the same image in terms of a trace, i.e. the maintained link to African culture and performance modes (Sörgel 2004: 93-99). For example, Walker composed the dance choreography in terms of the particular emotional fragility evoked rather than as historical evidence. In that sense, the topos of the Middle Passage has become distilled by the choreographer's imagination to an extent that certain movements and pictorial keys will instantaneously speak to the African diaspora's collective unconscious. To recall Ricoeur at this point, fragility of memory and identity are curiously intertwined, especially in the danced act of communal remembrance.

As the next scene opens to the song lyrics of "No More Auction Block," such image-memory is taken yet one step further, when the dancers run in from the stage wings as if they were throwing themselves against an imaginary center wall. Defeated they fall down to the floor, from where they build another wall of upright trembling bodies. The dancers cross their arms against their chests in a protective gesture, make a lunge to the left and wheel their arms on the right in a powerful pull. Being pressed down, these bodies collapse onto the floor to yet pull up again, before they disperse into smaller group units on stage. Up-stage, for example, a couple looks as if to attempt recovery from the

---

101 Interview with Christopher Walker 11 Aug. 2003.

floods, while in front another one is going through a series of progressing lifts in search for rescue. Movements and configurations overlap and alternate simultaneously so that the audience needs to choose focus. For example, one dancer pulls her knees close to her upper body, autistically rocking back and forth on her bottom. Literally stripped from the costume, the dancers portray human existence as reduced to movement and spirit, the very essentials of the dance. Symbolized in the rem(a)inder of the head wrap, the link to Africa prevails strong and while the same dancer crosses the stage in a last walk of this sequence, her head is held high and as Jamaicans say: "she walks good," even though her arms might dangle as if of a lifeless marionette.

Dancing the song of freedom, movement has the power to redeem – in "Redemption Song," the next section of the dance; we encounter the group of dancers as they are suspended from the chain. Entering in file from up-stage right, the dancers carry out individualized movements as soon as they reach center stage. And it is in these that one will find the traces of Jamaican folk forms most evident: a powerful half-circle jump up in the air which is a characteristic feature of the Pitchy Patchy in Jamaican Jonkonnu, the crooked posture of Dinki Mini, the backwards tilt and grounded shuffle of the Kumina. These African derived retentions again testify to survival in their use of social comment and satire: once directed against the planter oppressor, they have now become a powerful symbol of cultural resistance and spiritual strength. They are part of the African continuum in the New World and present on the theatre stage as much as in the popular culture on the Jamaican streets.

The last section then starts with a brief prelude, when two dancers present a solo in silence. After that all the dancers step in chatting to each other and smiling, before they finally join in a colorful finale to the backdrop of the rising sun. Wearing red, yellow and green half skirts to reveal bikini-pants of the same color and with a pearl string that is supposed to symbolize the umbilical cord as a link back to the mother(land), the costume expresses part of what has become known as the Caribbean carnival aesthetic: for on top of certainly celebrating the pelvis as the center of life and African Caribbean dance, this repeated display of carnival spirit testifies one more time to Jonkonnu's fierce final laughs, where appearances point one way, yet message turns around the other. "Fragile," indeed, these young dancers and choreographers have thus tuned their bodies into a powerful instrument of self-assertion. Whether it be to the music of British pop culture icon Sting, U.S. rap formation Arrested Development, the postmodern Art of Noise, or that continuously driven force of the ancestral drums, "authenticity" lies lastly within themselves and their danced out inner knowledge of who they are and what they want to be. Watching the NDTC perform, the company's artistic freedom of expression and joy makes every audience member realize what it may take to come to one's own terms at last.

Interlude V: Dance Beyond the Color Line

Over the past forty years embodied freedom and self-discovery have been the continuous force driving Jamaica's National Dance Theatre Company. Dance as the living epic of the Jamaican people has created imaginative and insightful dance theatre that will not only speak to the people at home, but also to those abroad in a distinctly Jamaican art form. As this final analysis of recent NDTC works has shown, folk-based choreography continues to inform even the company's more experimental or abstract modern works. Whether in message or theme, subtle pelvic moves or shoulder ripples, Jamaica's kinaesthetic body memory forms the backbone of the NDTC's distinct dance style. Jamaican dance theatre, furthermore, not only reflects the country's African heritage, but also manages to display it on a nationally significant level.

At the same time though, Jamaican dance theatre's postcolonial nationalism has from the very beginning been conceived of as part of Pan-Caribbean solidarity and the shared experience of black Atlantic diaspora. Spirit and epic memory in the Caribbean context thus do not only testify to the survival of the African aesthetic in the New World, but outline a performative paradigm that keeps kinaesthetic memory alive and points the body towards a self-assertive expression of cultural heritage and future. In *Against Race*, Paul Gilroy has described the recent transformation of the political implications of diaspora in terms of a "strategic universalism," which in its postanthropological outlook opts for a "cosmopolitan utopia" of diasporic interculture (2000: 326-336). In this respect, diaspora experience as expressed in contemporary Jamaican dance theatre interconnects cultural diversity with a decidedly anti-racist, postcolonial agenda. As Gilroy explains:

Diaspora allows for a complex conception of sameness and for versions of solidarity that do not need to repress the differences within a dispersed group in order to maximize the differences between one "essential" community and others. Diaspora's discomfort with carelessly overintegrated notions of culture and its rather fissured sense of particularity can also be made to fit with the best moods of politicized postmodernism. Identity conceived diasporically resists reification in petrified forms even if they are indubitably authentic. The tensions around origin and essence that the diaspora brings into view allow us to perceive that identity should not be fossilized in keeping with the holy spirit of ethnic absolutism. Identity, too, becomes a noun of process. Its openness provides a timely alternative to the clockwork solidarity based on outmoded notions of "race" and disputed ideas of national belonging (2000: 252).

Modern dance's malleability to culturally encoded variations thus proves as a particularly powerful mode of expressing precisely such articulations of sameness in full acknowledgement of co-existing differences. Through the dancing body's iconic signature, diaspora identity may thus operate transgressively even from within stereotypical notions. Jamaican dance theatre thereby transcends the binary opposition in a dance idiom and vocabulary that is simultaneously strangely anew and awkwardly familiar. In this respect, Jamaican dance theatre in fact emerges as the prime example of transnational as well as translational vernacular, which in Gilroy's terms may envision precisely the new millennium's utopia of a "planetary humanism" beyond the color line (2000: 333).

Natalie Chung in Christopher Walker's Fragile, 2003. Video Still.

Coda: After the Journey –
The Remains of the Dance ...

St. Thomas, 19th July 2003

Kumina in the field. I have no spirit, I'm not connecting. There's not even much of an atmosphere with all of us crowding in a half circle surrounding the booth stand in the Kumina yard. There's a post in the middle, surrounded by the drummers, the scraper and the shakas. White, black, green, yellow and red cloth hanging from it. They start beating the drum, the playing cast and kbandu. I recognize most of it from my reading and probably because I already have a preconception of what to expect, I'm not as stunned as I could be. The Kumina Queen's presence is of course captivating. She's huge, rolling her big belly, shaking her buttocks and heaving her heavy breasts – fertility is not just a concept, it comes to life. Her festival fashion dress distinguishes her from the other crowd, who are all dressed in street wear, baseball-cap and sneakers for the men, while the women though seem to make an effort for dress and head-tie. So I wonder, is the festival dress a costume for our "show" as well as the preaching? For I honestly didn't think they "preach" as much in Kumina. I really find the "Jesus"-talk surprising as there are a lot of things coming together here, making it a bit of Jamaican redemption scramble. A lickle bit of this a lickle bit of that. I'm not the only one to demonstrate fatigue. Wasn't Kumina supposed to be "scary"? Mystical? I do not feel the spirit here, but a heavy cloud of ganja lingers in the air and empty bottles of white rum appear as "new" instruments among the musicians. Yet, the "signs" are all there. The songs and the lit candle on top of the Kumina Queen's head and eventually one woman even gets "possessed" and someone with a video-camera follows her down the hill towards the ancestor's (dead)yard, careful not to miss a single thing. I realize how detached I am from what is actually going on. "One blood" for sure, but still very different people! And while the Queen, - I wish I knew her name - is pulling me up from the ground and "inviting" me in the circle ["one people"!] I don't feel "right" there. I can't roll the pelvis, not even shuffle the feet correctly and it don't seem like you should make the "effort" either, because as soon as you show the "effort" in your face, the spirit's gone, cause you don't connect to what you're doing. My body doesn't respond, for it doesn't know the language. De girl cyan't dance. It's a gift to be passed on. It's something that you grow into as you are born and raised. It cyan't be learnt. And I'm very much in doubt of it being made into a "technique" – because the moment you make it "technique" it's secularized, separated, void of spiritual meaning. While there might remain traces or probably, when something else is added as creative imagination the movement brings about something new that again bears spirit, but of a different kind. Well, Jamaicans own a gift that I obviously don't know how to talk about. Shuffling careful not to step on the candle between my feet on the ground, I feel fairly uneasy. Not joining or joining the circle doesn't make much of a difference for me. It's the same being in Kumina or anywhere else in this country [...] [1]

Enthusiasm notwithstanding, half-way through the field trip, I had obviously come to realize that I did not exactly connect to the ritual experience of Kumina nor particularly excel in performing Jamaican dances. I had become the Other. And yet, after coming back to this entry several times, I now enjoy the NDTC's dance theatre performances actually the more because of it. In fact, watching *Kumina* from my cushion seat in the audience, I do not have to feel as an intruder into somebody's sacred space, nor do I have any disturbing feelings about satisfying some sort of sensationalist desire for the supernatural or esoteric. This is not meant to criticize field work, yet I believe that a responsible ethnographer will need more experience than I had at that point. While I could not fully engage with the Kumina ritual as well as Jamaican Revival practice, dance theatre, however, allows for an easier access and understanding of these forms. Abstracted through the NDTC's modern dance lens, African Caribbean religions and aesthetics become more palpable for the foreigner, if he/she is willing to let these dances speak of their cultural heritage and postcolonial (hi)story. The NDTC's modern dance imprint thus serves their dance repertoire in that NDTC choreography does not exhibit the ultimate 'Other,' while at the same time

---

1 Entry from my personal research journal.

it carefully refrains from being the exact 'Self-Same.' Operating from in-between that binary, Jamaican dance theatre thus presents the epitome of postcolonial hybridity, which as an unfixed negotiation of alterity and sameness is as fragile as the NDTC's dance works. Only in an instant can such fluidity of transformative identity be achieved and yet it offers much more than mere possibility as dance theatre has become the legitimate site of Jamaica's national self-definition.

As concerns the research process and methodology: dislocating the scholarly self, in-between the tourist-I, the dance critic's point of view and what I actually like to conceive of as simply being "me," the journey to Jamaica's dance has actually taught me much more than just a couple of difficult dance steps. And lastly, I believe that this surplus information lies at the very heart of the NDTC's dance theatre works. Jamaican dance theatre is no dance for dance's sake, since there is a distinct story for each of the many folk movements to be told. Of course, this book can only provide a glimpse into the depth of Jamaica's dance heritage and political struggle, however, so it is hoped, such a glimpse might have otherwise been too easily overlooked. What hence poses as Jamaican dance theatre's "colonial mimicry" presents in fact a highly innovative dance style, which in its "syncretic theatre" blend of Caribbean folk and modern dance expression creates a nationally significant performance of postcolonial politics.

Bibliography

Books and Journals

Adamczyk, Alice J. (1989): *Black Dance: An Annotated Bibliography*, New York: Garland Publishing.
Adshead, Janet/Layson, June (1994): *Dance History: An Introduction*, London: Routledge.
____ (1988): *Dance Analysis*, London: Dance Books.
Ahye, Molly (1983): *Cradle of Caribbean Dance: Beryl McBurnie and the Little Carib Theatr,*. Trinidad and Tobago: Heritage Cultures.
____ (1978): *Golden Heritage: The Dance in Trinidad and Tobago*, Petit Valley: Heritage Cultures.
Albright, Ann Cooper (1997): *Choreographing Difference: The Body and Identity in Contemporary Dance*, Hanover & London: Wesleyan UP.
Allen, Carolyn (2002): "Creole the Problem of Definition". In: Verene A. Shepherd/Glen L. Richards (Ed.), *Questioning Creole. Creolisation Discourses in Caribbean Culture*, Kingston: Ian Randle, S. 47-63.
Allen, Zita (1988): "What is Black Dance?". In: Gerald E. Myers (Ed.), *The Black Tradition in American Modern Dance*, Durham, North Carolina: American Dance Festival, S. 22-23.
Alleyne, Mervyn (2002): *The Construction and Representation of Race and Ethnicity in the Caribbean and the World*, Kingston: University of the West Indies Press.
____ (1988): *Roots of Jamaican Culture*, London: Pluto Press.
Amkpa, Awam (2004): *Theatre and Postcolonial Desires*, London: Routledge.

Anderson, Benedict (1983): *Imagined Communities. Reflections on the Origin and Spread of Nationalism*, London: Verso.
Balme, Christopher (1999): *Decolonizing the Stage: Theatrical Syncretism and Post-Colonial Drama*, Oxford: Oxford UP.
____ (1995): *Theatre im postkolonialen Zeitalter: Studien zum Theatresynkretismus im englischsprachigen Raum*. Tübingen: Niemeyer.
Barclay, Alexander (1828): *A Practical View of the Present State of Slavery in The West Indies*, London: Smith, Elder & Co.
Barnett, Sheila (1989): "Jonkonnu – Jamaican Masquerade as Creolising Process (1690-1865)". In: Lisbet Torp (Ed.), *The Dance Event: A Complex Cultural Phenomenon*, Copenhagen: ICTM Study Group on Ethnochoreology, S. 62-70.
____ (1982): "Notes on Contemporary Dance-Theatre in Jamaica 1930-1982". *Jamaica Journal* 46, S. 80-87.
____ (1979): "Pitchy Patchy". *Jamaica Journal* 43.3, S. 19-32.
Baron, Robert (2003): "Amalgams and Mosaics, Syncretisms and Reinterpretations: Reading Herskovits and Contemporary Creolists for Metaphors of Creolization". *Journal of American Folklore* 116, S. 88-115.
Bastide, Roger (1971): *African Civilizations in the New World*, London: C. Hurst & Company.
Baxter, Ivy (1970): *The Arts of an Island*, Metuchen, N.J.: Scarecrow Press.
Bernabé, Jean/Chamoiseau, Patrick /Confiant, Raphaël (1989): *Éloge de la Créolité*, Paris: Gallimard.
Bettelheim, Judith (1988): "Jonkonnu and Other Christmas Masquerades". In: John W. Nunley/Judith Bettelheim (Ed.), *Caribbean Festival Arts. Each and Every Bit of Difference*, Seattle & London: The Saint Louis Art Museum in association with the U of Washington P, S. 39-83.
Bhabha, Homi K. (1994): *The Location of Culture*. London & New York: Routledge.
____ (1986): "Foreword". In: Frantz Fanon, *Black Skin, White Masks*, London: Pluto Press, S. vii-xiii.
Bharucha, Rustom (2000): *The Politics of Cultural Practice. Thinking Through Theatre in an Age of Globalization*, Hanover: Wesleyan UP.
Bilby, Kenneth/Leib, Elliott (1986): "Kumina, the Howellite Church and the Emergence of Rastafarian Traditional Music in Jamaica". *Jamaica Journal* 19.3, S. 22-28.

Birbalsingh, Frank (1996): *Frontiers of Caribbean Literature in English*, London and Basingstoke: Macmillan.

Bogle, Donald (1997): *Toms, Coons, Mulattoes, Mammies and Bucks. An Interpretive History of Blacks in Films*, New York: Continuum.

Bolaffi, Guido/Bracalenti, Raffaele/Braham, Peter/Gindro, Sandro (2003): *Dictionary of Race, Ethnicity and Culture*, London, Thousand Oaks and New Delhi: SAGE Publications.

Bolland, Nigel O (2002): "Creolisation and Creole Societies. A Cultural Nationalist View of Caribbean Social History". In: Verene A. Shepherd/Glen L. Richards (Ed.), *Questioning Creole. Creolisation Discourses in Caribbean Culture*, Kingston: Ian Randle, S. 15-46.

Boswell, David/Evans, Jessica (1999): *Representing the Nation: A Reader. Histories, Heritage and Museums*, London & New York: Routledge.

Bowen, Patricia (1980): *Joyce Campbell*, Kingston: Jamaica School of Dance.

Brah, Avtar/Coombes, Annie E. (2000): *Hybridity and Its Discontents. Politics, Science, Culture*, London: Routledge.

Brathwaite, Edward Kamau (1993): *Roots*, Ann Arbor: U of Michigan P.

____ (1985): "Chronicles of Unchaos". *Jamaica Journal* 18.4, S. 46-51.

____ (1978): "Kumina – The Spirit of African Survival in Jamaica". *Jamaica Journal* 42, S. 45-63.

____ (1974): *Contradictory Omens: Cultural Diversity and Integration in the Caribbean*, Mona: Savacou Publications.

____(1971): *The Development of Creole Society in Jamaica 1770-1820*, Oxford: Clarendon Press.

Buckland, Theresa J. (1999): *Dance in the field. Theory, Methods and Issues in Dance Ethnography*, London: Macmillan.

Buckner, Don (1993): "Jonkonnu in focus as JBC celebrates 30 years". *Dancescape* 1.2/3, S. 1;8.

Burroughs, Joan H. (1995): *Haitian Ceremonial Dance on the Concert Stage*, Ann Arbor: UMI.

Burt, Ramsay (1995): *The Male Dancer. Bodies, Spectacle, Sexualities*, London and New York: Routledge.

Campbell, Joyce (1976): "Jamaican Folk and Traditional Dances". *Jamaica Journal* 10.1, S. 8-9.

Carty, Hilary S. (1988): *Folk Dances of Jamaica: An Insight*, London: Dance Books.

Clifford, James (1997): *Routes. Travel and Translation in the late Twentieth Century*, Cambridge, Massachusetts: Harvard UP.

_____ (1988): *The Predicament of Culture. Twentieth-Century Ethnography, Literature, and Art.* Cambridge, Massachusetts: Harvard UP.

Cohen Bull/Jean, Cynthia (1997): "Sense, Meaning, and Perception in Three Dance Cultures". In: Jane C. Desmond (Ed.), *Meaning in Motion. New Cultural Studies of Dance.* Durham: Duke UP, S. 269-287.

Coombs, Orde (1974): *Is Massa Day Dead? Black Moods in the Caribbean,* Garden City, NY: Anchor Books.

Cooper, Carolyn (2004): *Sound Clash. Jamaican Dancehall Culture at Large,* New York: Palgrave Macmillan.

_____ (1993): *Noises in the Blood. Orality, Gender and the 'Vulgar' Body of Jamaican Popular Culture,* London & Basingstoke: Macmillan Caribbean.

Crahan, Margaret E./Knight, Franklin W. (1979): *Africa and the Caribbean: The Legacies of a Link,* Baltimore & London: John Hopkins UP.

Creque-Harris, Leah (1991): *The Representation of African Dance on the Concert Stage,* Ann Arbor: UMI Dissertation Services.

Csordas, Thomas J. (1994): *Embodiment and Experience. The Existential Ground of Culture and Self,* Cambridge: Cambridge UP.

Cumberbatch-Lynch, Carson (2001): *An Analysis of the Rivero Modern Dance Technique,* New York: State University of New York, Brockport College.

_____ (1986): *The Suitability of the Rivero/Cuban Modern Dance Technique for Application to the National Dance Theatre Company of Jamaica,* Kingston: Jamaica School of Dance.

Dagel Caponi, Gen (1999): *Signifyin(g), Sanctifyin', & Slam Dunking. A Reader in African American Expressive Culture,* Amherst: University of Massachusetts Press.

Dawes, Neville (1975): "The Jamaican Cultural Identity". *Jamaica Journal* 9.1, S. 34-37.

DeFrantz, Thomas F. (2004): *Dancing Revelations. Alvin Ailey's Embodiment of African American Culture,* Oxford: Oxford UP.

_____ (2004): "The Black Beat Made Visible. Hip Hop Dance and Body Power". In: André Lepecki (Ed.), *Of the Presence of the Body. Essays on Dance and Performance Theory,* Middletown, CT: Wesleyan UP, S. 64-80.

Desmond, Jane C. (1997): *Meaning in Motion. New Cultural Studies of Dance,* Durham & London: Duke UP.

Dils, Ann/Cooper Albright, Ann (2001): *Moving History/Dancing Cultures. A Dance History Reader,* Middletown, Connecticut: Wesleyan UP.

Dixon Gottschild, Brenda (2003): *The Black Dancing Body. A Geography from Coon to Cool*, New York: Palgrave.
____ (1998): *Digging the Africanist Presence in American Performance: Dance and Other Contexts*, Westport, CT: Greenwood.
DuBois, W.E.B. (1997): *The Souls of Black Folk*, Boston: Bedford Books.
Dunning, Jennifer (2001): *Geoffrey Holder. A Life in Theatre, Dance, and Art*, New York.
Emery, Lynne Fauley (1988): *Black Dance: From 1619 to Today*, London: Dance Books.
Fanon, Frantz (1986): *Black Skin, White Masks*, London: Pluto Press.
____ (1990): *The Wretched of the Earth*, London: Penguin.
Fernández Olmos, Margarite/Paravisini-Gebert, Lizabeth (2003): *Creole Religions of the Caribbean. An Introduction from Vodou and Santería to Obeah and Esperitismo*, New York and London: New York UP.
Fischer-Hornung, Dorothea/Goeller, Alison D. (2001): *EmBodying Liberation*. Hamburg: LIT.
Foster, Susan Leigh (1997): "Dancing Bodies". In: Jane C. Desmond (Ed.), *Meaning in Motion*, Durham: Duke UP, S. 235-257.
____ (1995): *Choreographing History*, Indianapolis and Bloomington: Indiana UP.
____ (1986): *Reading Dancing. Bodies and Subjects in Contemporary American Dance*, Berkeley: U of California P.
Foulkes, Julia L. (2002): *Modern Bodies. Dance and American Modernism from Martha Graham to Alvin Ailey*, Chapel Hill: University of North Carolina Press.
Fraleigh, Sondra Horton (1987): *Dance and the Lived Body. A Descriptive Analysis*, Pittsburgh: Pittsburgh UP.
____ (1999): *Researching Dance*, Pittsburg, Pa: U of Pittsburgh P.
Frank, Henry (2002): "Haitian Vodou Ritual Dance and Its Secularization" In: Susanna Sloat (Ed.), *Caribbean Dance from Abakuá to Zouk*, Gainesville: U of Florida P, S. 109-123.
Froude, James Anthony (1969): *The English in the West Indies, Or, The Bow of Ulysses*, New York: Negro UP.
Geertz, Clifford (1994): "Primordial and Civic Ties". In: John Hutchinson/Anthony D. Smith (Ed.), *Nationalism*, Oxford: Oxford UP, S. 29-34.
Gellner, Ernest (1983): *Nations and Nationalism*, Oxford: Basil Blackwell.
Gilbert, Helen/Tompkins, Joanne (1996): *Post-Colonial Drama: Theory, Practice, Politics*, London: Routledge.

Gilroy, Paul (2000): *Against Race. Imagining Political Culture beyond the Color Line*, Cambridge, Massachusetts: The Belknap Press of Harvard UP.
____ (1993): *The Black Atlantic. Modernity and Double Consciousness*, Cambridge, Massachusetts: Harvard UP, 1993.
Girvan, Norman (2001): "Reinterpreting the Caribbean". In: Brian Meeks/Folke Lindahl (Ed.), *New Caribbean Thought. A Reader*, Kingston: U of West Indies P, S. 3-23.
Glissant, Edouard (1989): *Caribbean Discourse. Selected Essays*, Charlottesville: UP of Virginia.
Gloudon, Barbara (1982): "Twenty Years of Theatre". *Jamaica Journal* 46, S. 63-69.
Goldberg, David Theo (1996): "In/Visibility and Super/Vision. Fanon on Race, Veils, and Discourses of Resistance". In: Lewis R. Gordon et al. (Ed.), *Fanon: A Critical Reader*, Oxford: Blackwell, S. 179-200.
Gordon, Lewis R./Charpley-Whiting, Denean T./White, Renée T. (1996): *Fanon: A Critical Reader*. Oxford: Blackwell.
Green, Doris (1996): "Traditional Dance in Africa". In: Kariamu Welsh Asante (Ed.), *African Dance: An Artistic, Historical and Philosophical Inquiry*, Trenton, New Jersey: Africa World Press, S. 13-28.
Guérivière, Jean de la (2004): *Die Entdeckung Afrikas. Erforschung und Eroberung des schwarzen Kontinents*, München: Knesebeck.
Guerra, Ramiro (1989): *Teatralización del folklore y otros ensayos*. La Habana: Editorial Letras Cubanas.
Gunn, Giles/Joseph, May/Fink, Jennifer (1999): *Performing Hybridity*. Minneapolis: U of Minnesota P.
Hall, Stuart (2001): "Negotiating Caribbean Identities". In: Brian Meeks/Folke Lindahl (Ed.), *New Caribbean Thought. A Reader*, Kingston: U of the West Indies P, S. 24-39.
____ (1997): "What is this 'Black' in Black Popular Culture?". In: Valerie Smith (Ed.), *Representing Blackness. Issues in Film and Video*, New Brunswick: Rutgers UP, S. 123-133.
____ (1996): "New Ethnicities". In: David Morley/Kuan-Hsing Chen (Ed.), *Stuart Hall: Critical Dialogues*, London: Routledge.
Hanna, Judith Lynne (1987): *To Dance is Human: A Theory of Nonverbal Communication*, Chicago: Chicago UP.
Harris, Wilson (1967): *Tradition, the Writer and Society. Critical Essays*, London: New Beacon Books.
Hegel, Georg Wilhelm Friedrich (1999): *Phänomenologie des Geistes*, Stuttgart: Reclam.

Helpern, Alice (1994): *The Technique of Martha Graham*, Dobbs Ferry, NY: Morgan Press.
Henry, Paget (1996): "Fanon, African and Afro-Caribbean Philosophy". In: Lewis R. Gordon/T. Denean Charpley-Whiting/Renée T. White (Ed.), *Fanon: A Critical Reader*, Oxford: Blackwell, S. 220-243.
Hill, Errol (1992): *The Jamaican Stage 1655-1900. Profile of a Colonial Theatre*, Amherst: University of Massachusetts Press.
___ (1972): *The Trinidad Carnival. Mandate for a National Theatre*, Austin: University of Texas Press.
___ (n.d.): *The Artist in West Indian Society*. Kingston: U.W.I., Department of Extra-Mural Studies.
Hillsman Barber, Beverly Anne (1984): *Pearl Primus, In Search of her Roots: 1943-1970*, Ann Arbor: UMI, 1984.
Hobsbawm, Eric, and T.O. Ranger (1983): *The Invention of Tradition*, Cambridge: Cambridge UP.
Hoetink, Harry (1979): "The Cultural Link". In: Margaret E. Crahan/Franklin W. Knight (Ed.), *Africa and the Caribbean: The Legacies of a Link*, London: John Hopkins UP, S. 20-40.
Horst, Louis/Russell, Carrol (1977): *Modern Dance Forms in Relation to the Other Modern Arts*, New York: Dance Horizons.
Hutchinson, John/Smith, Anthony D. (1994): *Nationalism*, Oxford: Oxford UP.
James, C.L.R. (2001): *The Black Jacobins*, London: Penguin.
Johnson Jones, E. Jean (1999): "The Choreographic Notebook: a Dynamic Documentation of the Choreographic Process of Kokuma Dance Theatre, an African-Caribbean Dance Company". In: Theresa J. Buckland (Ed.), *Dance in the Field. Theory, Methods and Issues in Dance Ethnography*, London: Macmillan, S. 100-110.
Johnstone, Albert A. (1984): "Languages and Non-Languages of Dance". In: Maxine Sheets-Johnstone (Ed.), *Illuminating Dance: Philosophical Explorations*, London: Associated UP, S. 167-187.
King, Llyod (1996): "The Space between this Anger". *Trinidad and Tobago Review* 18. 7-9, S. 11-15.
Kruger, Loren (1999): *The Drama of South Africa: Plays, Pageants and Publics since 1910*, London & New York: Routledge.
___ (1992): *The National Stage. Theatre and Cultural Legitimation in England, France, and America*, Chicago: University of Chicago Press.
Laclau, Ernesto (1995): "Universalism, Particularism and the Question of Identity". In: John Rajchman (Ed.), *The Identity in Question*, London: Routledge, S. 93-108.

Leaf, Earl (1948): *Isles of Rhythm*, New York: Barnes.
Leder, Drew (1990): *The Absent Body*, Chicago: U of Chicago P.
Lekis, Lisa (1960): *Dancing Gods*, New York: Scarcrow Press.
Lepecki, André (2004): *Of the Presence of the Body. Essays on Dance and Performance Theory*, Middletown, CT: Wesleyan UP.
Lewin, Olive (2000): *"Rock it Come Over" The Folk Music of Jamaica*, Kingston: U of the West Indies P.
Lewis, Daniel (1984): *The Illustrated Dance Technique of José Limón*, New York: Harper & Row.
Lewis, J. Lowell (1995): "Genre and Embodiment: From Brazilian Capoeira to the Ethnology of Human Movement". *Cultural Anthropology* 10.2, S. 221-243.
Lewis, Matthew (1999): *Journal of a West India Proprietor. Kept during a Residence in the Island of Jamaica 1834*, Oxford: Oxford UP.
Lo, Jacqueline/Gilbert, Helen (2002): "Toward a Topography of Cross-Cultural Theatre Praxis". *The Drama Review* 46.3, S. 31-53.
Long, Edward (1972): *The History of Jamaica. Three Volumes. 1774*, New York: Arno Press.
Lovejoy, Paul E./Trotman, David V. (2002): "Enslaved Africans and their Expectations of Slave Live in the Americas. Towards a Reconsideration of Models of 'Creolisation'". In: Verene A. Shepherd/Glen L. Richards (Ed.), *Questioning Creole. Creolisation Discourses in Caribbean Culture*, Kingston: Ian Randle, S. 67-91.
Mason, Peter (1998): *Bacchanal! The Carnival Culture of Trinidad*, Philadelphia: Temple UP.
May, Herbert G./Metzger, Bruce M. (1973): *The New Oxford Annotated Bible. The Holy Bible. Revised Standard Version. Containing the Old and New Testaments*, New York: Oxford UP.
McBurnie, Beryl (n.d.): "West Indian Dance". In: Errol Hill (Ed.), *The Artist in West Indian Society*, Kingston: University of the West Indies, S. 51-54.
McLeod, John (2000): *Beginning Postcolonialism*, Manchester: Manchester UP.
McQuillan, Martin (2000): *Deconstruction a Reader*, Edinburgh: Edinburgh UP.
Meeks, Brian/Lindahl, Folke (2001): *New Caribbean Thought. A Reader*, Kingston: U of the West Indies P.
Mills, Charles W. (1998): *Blackness Visible. Essays on Philosophy and Race*, Ithaca: Cornell UP.

Mintz, Sidney W./Price, Richard (1992): *The Birth of African-American Culture: An Anthropological Perspective*, Boston: Beacon Press.
____ (1974): *Caribbean Transformations*, Chicago: Aldine.
Mitchell, Jack (1993): *Alvin Ailey American Dance Theatre: Jack Mitchell Photographs*, Kansas City: Andrews and McMeel.
Mock Yen, Alma (2001): "Remembering Ivy Baxter: Her Life and Her Legacy". *Caribbean Quarterly* 47.1, S. 7-29.
Morley, David/Chen, Kuan-Hsing (1996): *Stuart Hall: Critical Dialogues*, London: Routledge.
Mousouris, Melinda (2002): "The Dance World of Ramiro Guerra. Solemnity, Voluptuousness, Humor, and Chance". In: Susanna Sloat (Ed.), *Caribbean Dance from Abakuá to Zouk*, Gainesville, Florida: U of Florida P, S. 56-72.
Murphy, Joseph M. (1994): *Working the Spirit. Ceremonies of the African Diaspora*. Boston: Beacon Press.
Müller, Grete (2001): *Sigurd Leeder. Tänzer, Pädagoge und Choreograf. Leben und Werk*, Herisau: Appenzeller Medienhaus.
Myers, Gerald E. (1988): *The Black Tradition in American Modern Dance*, Durham, NC: American Dance Festival.
Naipaul, V.S. (1967): *The Mimic Men*, London: Andre Deutsch.
Nair, Supriya (2000): "Creolization, Orality, and Nation Language in the Caribbean". In: Henry Schwarz/Sangeeta Ray (Ed.), *Postcolonial Companion*, Oxford: Blackwell, S. 236-251.
Nettleford, Rex (2003): *Caribbean Cultural Identity. The Case of Jamaica. An Essay in Cultural Dynamics*, Kingston: Ian Randle.
____ (2002): "Jamaican Dance Theatre. Celebrating the Caribbean Heritage". In: Susanna Sloat (Ed.), *Caribbean Dance from Abakuá to Zouk. How Movement Shapes Identity*, Gainesville, Florida: U of Florida P, S. 81-94.
____ (2001): *Mirror Mirror. Identity, Race and Protest in Jamaica*, Kingston: LMH Publishing.
____ (1996): "Foreword". In: Kariamu Welsh Asante (Ed.), *African Dance. An Artistic, Historical and Philosophical Inquiry*, Trenton, New Jersey: Africa World Press, S. xii-xviii.
____ (1995): *Inward Stretch Outward Reach: A Voice from the Caribbean*, London: Macmillan.
____ (1985): *Dance Jamaica. Cultural Definition and Artistic Discovery, The National Dance Theatre Company of Jamaica 1962-1983*, New York: Grove Press.

____ (1971): *Norman Washington Manley and the New Jamaica. Selected Speeches and Writings 1938-68*, London: Longman Caribbean.
____ (1969): *Roots and Rhythms. Jamaica's National Dance Theatre*. London: Andre Deutsch.
____ (1969): "Pocomania in Dance-Theatre". *Jamaica Journal* 3.2, S. 21-24.
____ (1968): "The Dance as an Art Form – Its Place in the West Indies". *Caribbean Quarterly* 14.1/2, S. 127-135.
Novack, Cynthia J. (1995): "The Body's Endeavors as Cultural Practices". In: Susan Leigh Foster (Ed.), *Choreographing History*, Bloomington and Indianapolis: Indiana Univ. Press, S. 177-184.
Nunley, John W./Bettelheim, Judith (1988): *Caribbean Festival Arts. Each and Every Bit of Difference*, Seattle & London: The Saint Louis Art Museum in association with U of Washington P.
Ortiz, Fernando (1965): *Africanía de la música folklórica de Cuba*, La Habana: Editora Universitaria.
Patterson, Orlando (1967): *The Sociology of Slavery*, London: McGibbon.
Perpener, John O. (1992): *The Seminal Years of Black Concert Dance*, Ann Arbor: UMI, 1992.
Phelan, Peggy (1995): "Thirteen Ways of Looking at Choreographing Writing". In: Susan Leigh Foster (Ed.), *Choreographing History*, Bloomington and Indianapolis: Indiana UP, S. 200-210.
Pickering, Michael (2001): *Stereotyping. The Politics of Representation*, Basingstoke: Palgrave.
Pigou, Elizabeth (1987): "A Note on Afro-Jamaican Beliefs and Rituals". *Jamaica Journal* 20.2, S. 23-26.
Puri, Shalini (2004): *The Caribbean Postcolonial. Social Equality, Post-Nationalism and Cultural Hybridity*, New York: Palgrave Macmillan.
Rajchman, John (1995): *The Identity in Question*, London: Routledge.
Reckord, Michael. "Dance as the Critic Sees It." *Dancescape* 1.2/3 (1993): 2; 11.
Regitz, Hartmut/Regner, Otto Friedrich/Schneiders, Heinz-Ludwig (1996): *Reclams Ballettführer*, Stuttgart: Reclam.
Ricoeur, Paul (2004): *Memory, History, Forgetting*, Chicago and London: The U of Chicago P.
Roach, Joseph (1996): *Cities of the Dead. Circum-Atlantic Performance*, New York: Columbus UP.
Robbins, Bruce (2000): "Race, Gender, Class, Postcolonialism: Toward a New Humanistic Paradigm". In: Henry Schwarz/Sangeeta Ray (Ed.), *A Companion to Postcolonial Studies*, Oxford: Blackwell, S. 556-573.

Ryman, Cheryl (1984): "Jonkonnu – A Neo-African Form. Part 1". *Jamaica Journal* 17.1, S. 13-23.

―― (1984): "Jonkonnu – A Neo-African Form. Part 2". *Jamaica Journal* 17.2, S. 50-61.

―― (1984): "African Retentions in Jamaican Traditional Dance". *Inside Jamaica* 3.1, S. 18-21.

―― (1980): "The Jamaican Heritage in Dance: Developing a traditional typology". *Jamaica Journal* 44, S. 2-14.

Said, Edward W. (1994): *Culture and Imperialism*, London: Vintage.

Sankeralli, Burton (2002): *From Attempted Theory to Failed Praxis. A Look at Creolist Ideology*, Mona: University of the West Indies.

Sartre, Jean-Paul (1995): *Anti-Semite and Jew*, New York: Schocken Books.

Savigliano, Marta E. (1995): *Tango and the Political Economy of Passion*, San Francisco: Westview Books.

Schechner, Richard (2002): *Performance Studies. An Introduction*, London: Routledge.

――/Appel, Willa (1990): *By Means of Performance: Intercultural Studies of Theatre and Ritual*, Cambridge: Cambridge UP.

Schuler, Monica (1979): "Myalism and the African Religious Tradition in Jamaica". In: Margaret E. Crahan/Franklin W. Knight (Ed.), *Africa and the Caribbean: The Legacies of a Link*, Baltimore: John Hopkins UP, S. 65-79.

Schwarz, Henry/Ray, Sangeeta (2000): *A Companion to Postcolonial Studies*, Oxford: Blackwell Publishers.

Seaga, Edward (1969): "Revival Cults in Jamaica: Notes towards a Sociology of Religion". *Jamaica Journal* 3.2, S. 3-24.

Sheets-Johnstone, Maxine (1984): *Illuminating Dance: Philosophical Explorations*, London: Associated UP.

―― (1980): *The Phenomenology of Dance*, New York: Books for Libraries.

Sherlock, Philip/Bennett, Hazel (1998): *The Story of the Jamaican People*, Kingston: Ian Randle.

―― (1967): "Pocomania". In: O. R. Dathorne (Ed.), *Caribbean Verse. An Anthology*, London: Heinemann.

Shepherd, Verene A./Richards, Glen L. (2002): *Questioning Creole. Creolisation Discourses in Caribbean Culture*, Kingston: Ian Randle Publishers.

Sklar, Deidre (2001): "Five Premises for a Culturally Sensitive Approach to Dance". In: Ann Dills/Ann Cooper Albright (Ed.), *Moving History/Dancing Cultures*, Middletown, CT: Wesleyan UP, S. 30-43.

Sloane, Hans (1707): *A Voyage to the Islands, Mardera, Barbados, Nieves, S. Christophers and Jamaica, with the Natural History of the Herbs and Trees ...Volume I*, London: Printed by B.M. for the Author.

Sloat, Susanna (2002): *Caribbean Dance from Abakuá to Zouk. How Movement Shapes Identity*, Gainesville, FL: University of Florida Press.

Smith, Anthony D (1999): "History and Modernity. Reflections on the Theory of Nationalism". In: David Boswell/Jessica Evans (Ed.), *Representing the Nation: A Reader. Histories, Heritage and Museums*, London: Routledge, S. 47-60.

Smith, M.G. (1965): *The Plural Society in the British West Indies*, Berkeley: U of California P.

Smith, Paulette (1981): *Pukkumina in Modern Dances*, Kingston: School of Dance.

Sörgel, Sabine (2004): "Spirituality and Epic Memory in Christopher Walker's Fragile, NDTC 41st Dance Season 2003". In: Christopher Balme/Meike Wagner (Ed.), *Beyond Aesthetics. Performance, Media, and Cultural Studies*, Trier: Wissenschaftlicher Verlag, S. 93-99.

Soyinka, Wole (1999): *The Burden of Memory, the Muse of Forgiveness*, Oxford: Oxford UP.

⎯⎯⎯ (1976): *Myth, Literature and the African World*, Cambridge: Cambridge UP.

States, Bert O. (1985): *Great Reckonings in Little Rooms. On the Phenomenology of Theatre*, Los Angeles: U of California P.

Stern, Robert (2002): *Hegel and the Phenomenology of Spirit*, London: Routledge.

Stuckey, Sterling P. (1995): "Christian Conversion and the Challenge of Dance". In: Susan Leigh Foster (Ed.), *Choreographing History*, Bloomington and Indianapolis: Indian UP, S. 54-66.

Tanna, Laura (1987): "Dinki Mini". *Jamaica Journal* 20.2, S. 27-31.

Thomas, Helen (1995): *Dance, Modernity and Culture: Explorations in the Sociology of Dance*, London: Routledge.

Thompson, Robert Farris (1974): *African Art in Motion. Icon and Act*, Los Angeles: U of California P.

Todorov, Tzvetan (1984): *The Conquest of America: The Question of the Other*, New York: Harper Collins.

Torp, Lisbet (1989): *The Dance Event: A Complex Cultural Phenomenon*, Copenhagen: ICTM Study Group on Ethnochoreology.

Turner, Victor (1992): *The Anthropology of Performance*, New York: PAJ Publications.

____ (1990): "Are there Universals of Performance in Myth, Ritual, and Drama?". In: Richard Schechner/Willa Appel (Ed.), *By Means of Performance*, Cambridge: Cambridge UP, S. 8-18.
Vogel, Susan Mullin (1986): *Aesthetics of African Art. The Carlo Monzino Collection*, New York: Center for African Art.
Walcott, Derek (1974): "The Muse of History: An Essay". In: Orde Coombs (Ed.), *Is Massa Day Dead? Black Moods in the Caribbean*, Garden City; NY: Anchor Books, S. 1-27.
____ (1996): "The Sea is History". In: Frank Birbalsingh (Ed.), *Frontiers of Caribbean Literatures in English*, London and Basingstoke: Macmillan, S. 22-28.
Walvin, James (2001): *Black Ivory. Slavery in the British Empire*, Oxford: Blackwell.
Warner-Lewis, Maureen (20003): *Central Africa in the Caribbean. Transcending Time, Transforming Cultures*, Kingston: U of the West Indies P.
Welsh Asante, Kariamu (2001): "Commonalties in African Dance: An Aesthetic Foundation". In: Ann Dills/Ann Cooper Albright (Ed.), *Moving History/Dancing Cultures*, Middletown, Connecticut: Wesleyan UP, S. 144-151.
____ (1996): *African Dance. An Artistic, Historical and Philosophical Inquiry*, Trenton, N.J.: Africa World Press.
Williams, Cynric R. (1826): *A Tour Through Jamaica, from the Western to the Eastern End, in the year 1823*. London: Hunt and Clarke.
Williams, Eric (1964): *Capitalism and Slavery*, London: Andre Deutsch.
Wood, Peter H. (1988): "'Gimme de Kneebone Bent': African Body Language and the Evolution of American Dance Forms". In: Gerald E. Myers (Ed.), *The Black Tradition in American Modern Dance*, Durham, NC: American Dance Festival, S. 7-8.
Wynter, Sylvia (1970): "Jonkonnu in Jamaica. Towards the Interpretation of Folk Dance as a Cultural Process". *Jamaica Journal* 4.2, S. 34-48.

Periodicals

Allen, Desmond (1982): "Midnight Rendezvous at Barking Lodge". *Sunrays Sunday Sun Magazine* 31 Oct., S. 11-12.
Anderson, Jack (1980): "Jamaican Troupe Dances in Brooklyn". *New York Times* Nov.

Anthony, Michael (2000): "Beryl McBurnie (1913-2000). The Belle of the Dance". *Trinidad Express* 12 April, S. 20-21.

Archibald, Charles (1951): "A West Indian Triumph". *The Daily Gleaner* 19 March 1951.

Batson-Savage, Tanya (2003): "Art Lends Helping Hand". *Jamaica Gleaner* 13 July, S. E 1-2.

Brown, Suzanne Francis (1995): "Roots and Rhythm". *Skywritings 100* Aug./Sept., S. 42-46.

"Costumes Colour the NDTC's New Season". *Jamaica Gleaner* 30 July, S. C4.

Crawford, Lenore (1958): "Dancer's Rhythm Storm Stirs Stratford Audience". *London Free Press* 17 July.

Graham, Molly (1958): "Audience Is Delighted Here at Debut of Carib Dancers". *Beacon Herald* 18 July.

Heap, Brian (1998): "Healing the crippled Spirit". *Sunday Gleaner* 9 Aug., S. 5c.

"Jamaica. Interview with Rex Nettleford" (1965): *Dance and Dancers* Nov., S. 20-23.

"Keeping 'Caribbeanness' Alive in Dance" (2002): *Caribbean Beat* Nov./Dec., S. 48-52.

"McBurnie: A Great Life" (2000): *Trinidad Guardian* 31 March, S. 1.

Mclain Stoop, Norma (1978): "All the World's a Stage for Clive Thompson of the Alvin Ailey American Dance Theatre". *Dance Magazine* Oct. S. 78-85.

Philp, Richard (1978): "Twenty Years Later: The Alvin Ailey American Dance Theatre". *Dance Magazine* Oct., S. 62-77.

____ (1976): "Carifesta '76: Caribbean Quest". *Dance Magazine* Nov., S. 67.

"Spirit of the past with Art of Modern Theatre" (1955): *Daily Gleaner* 14 Aug.

Tobias, Tobi (1983): "The Latest Imports". *New York Magazine* 10 Oct., S. 71-72.

Walcott, Derek (1960): "Bacoulou Dancers Typically Antillean". *Sunday Guardian* 28 Feb., S. 10.

____ (1964): "A Summing Up". *Sunday Guardian* 2 Aug., S. 4.

____ (1965): "A Sense of Joy". *Sunday Guardian Magazine* 7 Feb., S. 4.

____ (1966): "Patterns to Forget". *Trinidad Guardian* 22 June, S. 5.

Whyle, Justin (1995): "Kumina Causes a Stir as the Curtain Comes Down on NDTC's Season of Dance". *The Daily Gleaner* 23 Aug., S. 9A.

"W.I. Dancer Takes London By Storm". *Public Opinion* 17 March.
Williams, Peter (1972): "Caribbean Return: The National Dance Theatre of Jamaica's Second London Season". *Dance and Dancers* Nov., S. 39-42.

Lectures and Audio Sources

Coester, Marcus (2004): "Yankipong, Pakit, Zaambi Mpunga, Nkuyu und Jangkunnu – Afrikanisch-Jamaikanische Religion, ihre Götter und andere Formen spiritueller Macht oder Aspekte afrikanisch-jamaikanischer Religiosität im besonderen Hinblick auf historische und gegenwärtige Manifestationen von Myal". Lecture presented at the Annual Conference of the German-Jamaican Society, Königswinter.
Lawrence, Monica (2003): "Kumina from Field to Stage". Lecture presented at Cultural Studies' Seminar, Kingston: U.W.I., Mona Campus.
Marley, Bob (2001): *Legend. The Best of Bob Marley and the Wailers*, New York: Sterling Sound.
Nettleford, Rex (2003): "Jamaican Dance Theatre – Celebrating the Caribbean Heritage". Lecture presented at Jamaica School of Dance. Summer Workshop, Kingston: Edna Manley College.
Rowe, Maureen: "Roots and Branches – The Precursors." Tape-recorded Lecture Demonstration, Kingston: U.W.I. Mona Campus, Library of the Spoken Word.
Stewart, Kingsley (2003): "Dancehall". Lecture presented at Jamaica School of Dance, Summer Workshop. Kingston: Edna Manley College.
Whylie, Marjorie (2003): "Traditional Music and Its Relationship to the Dance". Lecture presented at Edna Manley College, School of Dance, Summer Workshop 2003, Kingston: Edna Manley College.
____ *Heritage*, Kingston: Jamaica School of Music.

CD-ROM and Videography

All rehearsal and archival performance videotapes are housed in the archives of the National Dance Theatre Company of Jamaica, or at the CARIMAC Centre of the University of the West Indies, Mona in Kingston. The following CD-Rom and videotaped performances of NDTC choreography were professionally produced and are available commercially.

National Dance Theatre Company of Jamaica. 40 Years 1962-2002. CD-Rom. Produced by Patsy Ricketts Productions in association with The National Dance Theatre Company of Jamaica, 2002.
The National Dance Theatre Company of Jamaica. Video. Produced by CPTC/Creative Production and Training Center, Kingston. Includes Kumina, The NDTC Singers, and Gerrehbenta.

Miscellany

All miscellany may be found at the West Indies Collection of the University of the West Indies, Mona Campus, Kingston, the NDTC Archive, Edna Manley College of the Performing Arts, or Jamaica's National Library in Kingston, Jamaica.

Barnett, Sheila (1987): "The Dance – Its Development Over 25 Years". Unpublished Typescript, 1987.
———. "Notes on Contemporary Dance-Theatre in Jamaica 1930-1979." Unpublished Typescript.
"Bruckins Party." Booklet. African Caribbean Institute, n.d.
"Formal Opening of the 'Little Carib' Thursday November 25, 1948 at 9 p.m." Souvenir Programme 1948/1988.
Fuller, Maud (1982): "Seen Twice – Notes from the North". *NDTC Newsletter* Feb.
"In Celebration of Diversity. The National Dance Theatre Company of Jamaica UK Tour 2001". NDTC Tour Program.
"Our Heritage in Dance. An Exhibition held at the National Library of Jamaica October-November 1982". Exhibition Program.
McBurnie, Beryl: "Dance Trinidad Dance". Booklet, n.d.
NDTC 40th Anniversary Program 2002.
NDTC 30th Anniversary Program 1992.

NDTC Stratford Festival Programme 1963.
NDTC Newsletter July 1983.
NDTC Newsletter Feb. 1982.
Nettleford, Rex (2002): "Scenario Cave's End". NDTC Fortieth Anniversary Season. Unpublished Script.
Ryman, Cheryl: "Kumina – Stability and Change (1974-1984)." pp. 81-128. Unpublished Research Article. Kingston: African Caribbean Institute.
___: "Core Vocabulary Structures and Form of Jamaican Dance Theatre. With particular reference to NDTC of Jamaica (1982)." Unpublished Booklet. Kingston: National Library of Jamaica.
___ (1978). "A-B-C of African Retentions in Jamaica: Dance." Unpublished Typescript. Kingston: African Caribbean Institute.
"Sun Over the West Indies by the Jamaica Company of Dancers and Singers. Dir. by Noel Vaz and Rex Nettleford". Howard University Intercultural Exchange Program 1961.

Interviews

Interview with Joyce Campbell 15 Aug. 2003, Kingston.
Interview with Rex Nettleford 7 Aug. 2003, Kingston.
Interview with Rex Nettleford 22 Aug. 2003, Kingston
Interview with Arlene Richards 23 Aug. 2003, Kingston.
Interview with Eduardo Rivero 13 Aug. 2003, Kingston.
Interview with Clive Thompson 21 Aug. 2003, Kingston.
Interview with Christopher Walker 11 Aug. 2003, Kingston.

TanzScripte

Gabriele Brandstetter,
Gabriele Klein (Hg.)
**Methoden der
Tanzwissenschaft**
Modellanalysen zu Pina
Bauschs »Sacre du Printemps«
April 2007, ca. 350 Seiten,
kart., zahlr. z.T. farb. Abb.,
ca. 28,80 €,
ISBN: 978-3-89942-558-1

Sabine Sörgel
Dancing Postcolonialism
The National Dance Theatre
Company of Jamaica
März 2007, 238 Seiten,
kart., 27,80 €,
ISBN: 978-3-89942-642-7

Christiane Berger
Körper denken in Bewegung
Zur Wahrnehmung
tänzerischen Sinns bei
William Forsythe und
Saburo Teshigawara
2006, 180 Seiten,
kart., 20,80 €,
ISBN: 978-3-89942-554-3

Susanne Foellmer
Valeska Gert
Fragmente einer Avantgardistin
in Tanz und Schauspiel der
1920er Jahre
2006, 302 Seiten,
kart., zahlr. Abb., 28,80 €,
ISBN: 978-3-89942-362-4

Gerald Siegmund
Abwesenheit
Eine performative Ästhetik
des Tanzes.
William Forsythe, Jérôme Bel,
Xavier Le Roy, Meg Stuart
2006, 504 Seiten,
kart., 32,80 €,
ISBN: 978-3-89942-478-2

Gabriele Klein,
Wolfgang Sting (Hg.)
Performance
Positionen zur zeitgenössischen
szenischen Kunst
2005, 226 Seiten,
kart., zahlr. Abb., 25,80 €,
ISBN: 978-3-89942-379-2

Susanne Vincenz (Hg.)
Letters from Tentland
Zelte im Blick: Helena
Waldmanns Performance in
Iran / Looking at Tents:
Helena Waldmanns Performance
in Iran
2005, 122 Seiten,
kart., zahlr. z.T. farb. Abb., 14,80 €,
ISBN: 978-3-89942-405-8

Leseproben und weitere Informationen finden Sie unter:
www.transcript-verlag.de